A
More Goodly
COUNTRY

other books by John Sanford

The Water Wheel
The Old Man's Place
Seventy Times Seven
The People From Heaven
A Man Without Shoes
The Land That Touches Mine
Every Island Fled Away
The $300 Man

A
More Goodly
COUNTRY

A personal history of America

John Sanford

HORIZON PRESS   NEW YORK

Library of Congress Cataloging in Publication Data

Sanford, John B.   1904—
    A more goodly country.

    1.   United States—History—Fiction. I. Title.
PZ3.S2245 Mo [PS3537.A694]   813'.5'2   74-28317
ISBN 0-8180-0814-8

Manufactured in the United States of America

to
William Carlos Williams
1883-1963

in bronze above a doorway

CONTENTS

NORTH AMERICA　　　　　　　　　　　　　　*A.D. 1000*

A PLACE CALLED HERE

We found sweet water in Vinlandiam, or Vinland, which we named it for its grapes, and voluntary wheat grew thick there, as if sown, and fruits that were new to us tinselled the trees. Day lasted longer than day at home, nor did the grass so soon wither, and for that savory smoke came down the wind, the air seemed brewed of spice and herb. A fair land to fall with, agreed we all, and we wintered well upon its shore. We slew some few inferior people before we left. Skraelings, they were. . . .

If you'd been the first blue-eyed blond to make that landfall, you'd've been Leif, Vicar of Christ to the West, or, dressed in a skin shirt and skin buskins, you'd've been some thrall at the oars and blown your nose in your hair—and, known or nameless, you'd be a pinch of carbon now, a tooth turned to stone. If you'd seen the world as the world was then, you'd be a thousand years dead, but even so, even so. . . !

LEIF ERICSON

VICAR OF CHRIST

*Leif was a large man and strong, of noble aspect, prudent and
moderate in all things.*
                              —Rafn: *Antiquitates Americanae*

His father was Eirikr, Eirikr hinn raudi, from which in Icelandic Eric
the Red, after the color of his hair, it's said, or the blood he shed on
much of Norway. A belly-god, he was, eating his meat while there
was still some run in it, and well he served his other needs too. Mars
and Venus ruled him, and ever at the ready he wore their weapons,
wore them at dawn and noon and through all four phases of the
moon—wore them, alas, for the passage at Jaederen.

There, over nothing now known (a she, it might've been, or
kindred game), he clave some swain a new fontanelle, gave him two
half-heads each with an eye to observe the other. A bruit was raised,
and the plea of chance-medley failed to down it: the braining was
murder, and Eric was done with Norway. Westward a thousand miles
Iceland lay, an easy pull for thirty oars if all the thirty lasted. Some
died, though, and some played out (both kinds went over the side),
but Odin so willed, and the rest of them made it.

At Drangar, downwind came a muliebrian smell that slued Eric's
head, and upwind he pursued it to where it arose, seeding there for
Thorstein and springing there for Leif—after which more murder.
Eyiolf the Foul, a clown, a *klunni* with a craze for the chase, had
bagged a brace of Eric's oarsmen, not on the wing, the sporting thing
to do, but stock-still and staring. Eric rived his skull from pole to
pole, and the *klunni* fell with harelips, a left and right nose, and an
ear on either shoulder, like a pair of epaulettes. Then, curious af-
tercrop of the affray (had the man interfered? had he merely passed
by?), Eric did the same for a certain Duelling-Hrafn.

Undone now in Iceland too, still Eric stayed to pick a last bone.
One Thorgest had possession of divers timbers, some hewn from the
rowan tree and some gotten from the birch. To all these, an equal
claim was laid by Eric, and had he been a leek-eater, a turner of the
second cheek, strife might've stopped at words. But in his view, wood
was *ferae naturae*, which is to say, of a wild nature, like the bear, the

fox, the whistling swan, like all that was found in the forest, nor did it ever lose that nature, and there could be no property in it that Thorgest might acquire by seizing it. Taken by force, it must be held by force: it was still a wild thing.

Thorgest was more than willing, and he said so over flagons—an ale-house cock, they called him, and they thought he'd prove a capon in the field. They were deceived. Waiting not to be sought by Eric, he ran the man down on his own terrain, Drangar, and there a clash of arms occurred, and much hot blood became cold. Thorgest lost two sons in the action, as the story-tellers have told, *and certain other men besides*, but no mention is made of the rowan-tree wood or the wood that was wrung from the birch. Only this is known now, that Eric fled further west.

He reached in the end a country that he gave this name to, Greenland, as though fruit all year and berries grew there, as though meadows flowed in streams of air and the leaves of trees outlived the seasons, like the trees themselves. Greenland, he called that bourne, a wile of his to beguile the mind from thoughts of ice, for it was ice all. Men might be persuaded thither, he said, if the land were known by a vernal name.

Leif was a large man and strong, of noble aspect, etc.

It was white, Greenland, even on the maps, it had white isles along its shores and a white and unknown mass—ice all, it was, but Thorstein braved it to be at the side of his redhanded father. Not so Leif, a leaner beast with thinner skin and finer hair, not for him the cold and the meaner share of the feast, wherefore when on some emigrant air came word of the warmer east, he ran behind his running nose to the Hebrides.

There *a lady of fine family and rare intelligence* went to the grass with him on receipt of a ring, a mantle, and a belt or baldric of walrus tusk, and, with desire squandered, his gaze went beyond her, to where Norway was. *I am no longer a lone woman*, she said when she saw that he dwelt on the outgoing tide; *I am with child, and on thee I charge it. I shall bear thee a scion, and I shall rear him and send him to thee.* A wave fawned on his feet, but not Thorgunna: *It was promised me in a dream*, she said, *that thou wilt profit as much of your son as is thy due from this our ardent parting, and his name shall be Thorgils, and there shall be something about him not al-*

together natural before his time comes. She was still on the beach when his oars began to sweep.

In the Old Country, where now the Cross was come, they ordained him Herald of Jesus Christ to the New. The holy man said nothing, of course, of his lady of quality, nor of the price he paid for the ride he got. With the fire they gave him, he went to make it hot for Greenland, and he told them not of the one that would be unnatural, Thorgils, his natural son. He simply went, Vicar Leif, Leivi Vicarius, and he wound up a long way past Greenland. He reached a place called *here!*

Leif was a large man and strong, etc.

CHRISTOPHER COLUMBUS, I   *1492*

THE LOG OF THE *SANTA MARIA*

Friday, 3rd of August

We sailed from Palos at eight in the forenoon,
And heading southwest with a five-mile breeze,
We held our course till the sun had its day,
And Spain was lost in the larboard leadening:
We were on our way to the Canaries and Japan.

Saturday, 4th of August

We corrected southwest by a quarter south.

Sunday, 5th of August

The wind held good all day long and night,
And we reeled off a hundred and twenty miles.

Monday, 6th of August

Give or take, the day's run was ninety miles,
And we'd've doubled that, more than doubled,
If the *Pinta* hadn't balked in the afternoon.
She unshipped her rudder and went like a crab,
Walked sideways on the water, wasting wind,

Misspending a daylong fund of westbound wind,
While all-thumb hands fumbled with her bum.
Christ alone knows how it got out of whack—
Or does the Rascon bastard know, or Quintero?
They beshit themselves in dread of the voyage;
Can they now, instead, be shitting the ship?

Tuesday, 7th of August

Day and night, we made seventy-five miles.

Wednesday, 8th of August

And now the *Pinta's* taken to making water;
It must be a Spic that taught her the trick.

Sunday, 12th of August

Three floundering days—and it's Tenerife.

Wednesday, 5th of September

Big with brag, the crews sound newly brave.
Forgotten ashore their unfathomed future,
Drowned in wine, buried in work and women,
But we leave with the tide in the morning,
And the dead will rise to be downed again.

Thursday, 6th of September

The ebb drained us out of the Gomera roads
As if a bung had been started in the sea—
And between us and gold only an arc of water!
But the wind was merely an old man sighing,
And all day we heard laughter from the beach.

Friday, 7th of September

Boys swam to us today, and still laughing,
They showed their holes and blew our way,
And then they went, leaving a galling wake.
The crews were much amused by the horseplay.

Saturday, 8th of September

A northeaster caught hold after sundown,
Driving us twenty-seven miles by midnight.
We took a strangling sea across the bows.

Sunday, 9th of September

We made a hundred and forty-seven miles,
And during the run, the world went under.
The crews broke down when it foundered,
Wept in fear, and spoke of turning back.

Monday, 10th of September

The steering today disgraced the art:
Our course was west, but only in yawing
North and south did we touch the mark.
Still, we had a solid run, and I said so,
A hundred and eighty miles, I crowed—
But for some, we come hourly nearer the verge,
And men mumble in their sleep now, and turn,
And watches keep watch and yearn for Spain.

Tuesday, 11th of September

I gave the crews a bargain distance today.
We logged a hundred and twenty miles west,
But I cut off a dozen to sweeten the news.

Wednesday, 12th of September

Behind us today, a hundred miles more,
But it came to something less for the crews.

Thursday, 13th of September

A running stream, the wind, all day long,
All day long fulled sail pulled us west,
All day we flowed, four miles each hour,
But with day's end came an odd occasion:
The needle and north were separate ways.

Friday, 14th of September

We had a sign today—birds in the Flood!
The *Niña* saw a *rabo de junco*, the reedtail,
And later a *garjao*, the swallow of the sea,
And when I swore that where these were,
Land was, nor would we find it far away,
The crews quit puking and began to pray.
We ran sixty miles, fifty for my seasick gulls.

Saturday, 15th of September

A flame from Heaven plunged into the sea.
The run, just ninety miles, came out less.

Sunday, 16th of September

A few clouds this day and a small rain,
And we ran a hundred and seventeen miles,
But I shaved some to stave off the trots.
The crews spotted bright green tufts of grass,
And they rejoiced, supposing land was near,
Taprobane, maybe, or it might be Japan!
I let them dream: if there's more than water,
If there's land within a thousand miles,
May God stuff me with it, piece by piece!

Monday, 17th of September

Today grass again, and herbs from rocks,
And among the herbs a living thing, a crab.
Tunny-fish were seen, and a boatswain-bird,
And when the crews drew samples from the sea,
They said it seemed to be sweeter than before.
I tried it myself, and it'd pickle herring.
A hundred and fifty, was the run today,
Less ten to the men for good behavior.

Tuesday, 18th of September

The *Pinta*, Mr. Pinzon, spoke us at noon:
A flight of birds had overhauled the ship

And flown straight on west (toward home?),
And being the crack sailer of our fleet,
She was on tiptoe to follow their passage,
To be the first of us to make a landfall.
Go, I said, and she was away from the mark
As if she'd outrun the sun to the horizon.
We made good a hundred and sixty-five miles,
Stumbling on the *Pinta*, undaring after dark.

Wednesday, 19th of September

We had fine-grained rain and so little wind
That, flying all canvas and even our drawers,
We bagged enough for only seventy-five miles.
An *alcatraz*, the booby-bird, lighted on deck,
And the men had another sign, one from the sky:
They grieved when the sign got sick and spewed.

Thursday, 20th of September

This was a day on wings, a day of birds:
Two boobies found us out amongst the weed,
And a third, and then a bird we took by hand,
A swimmer, a riverbird with mittened feet,
And landbirds, two or three, came singing,
And last, at evening, a fourth *alcatraz*.
We plodded twenty miles through a swamp.

Friday, 21st of September

I didn't have to fake a shorter run today:
Forty was all we made, and I reported forty.
We had little wind, and there was much weed,
And the fleet sailed it like toys on a lawn.
A whale rose veiled with the deep-sea grass,
And the main breathed slowly in its sleep.

Saturday, 22nd of September

Some lead-swinger must've wet his finger today
And spread his education among the crews:

The men seem to know it's a one-way wind,
From Spain, never *toward* it, never homeward.
That gave them the flux for ninety miles
And made them miss an evil omen—the petrel.

Sunday, 23rd of September

They were goose-loose too for the Lord's Day,
And equally so from the mouth, babbling wind
I'd've given an arm to catch with canvas.
All we could make good was sixty-six miles.

Monday, 24th of September

A strong swimmer would've lost us this day:
We drifted a mile and a half to the hour
And got left by the squid, even by the weed,
We walked on water, or, worse, we crawled.

Tuesday, 25th of September

We walked today, but not on water—air!
Land was sighted when the sun went down,
Land, a long low wreck with its deck awash.
Mr. Pinzon, the *Pinta*, thanked God kneeling
And said the *Gloria* for his kneeling crew,
And on the *Niña*, they shinnied up the masts
For a heavenly view of an earthly Japan—
Land, a rip in the seam of the sea and sky!
On the flagship, we made it half and half:
We prayed a little and rubbered a little—
It might've been land, but it wasn't Japan.

Wednesday, 26th of September

There was land at dawn, but two miles down:
It'd been a cloud the men saw, now blown away
And no mar on the horizon—the tear was sewn.
Mute and mutinous, men stare at their knives.

Thursday, 27th of September

We made seventy miles, but I counted sixty,
And when the *dorados* came, the fish of gold,
The crews killed them quietly, practicing.

Friday, 28th of September

The Ark would've given us a brush today.
We had little weed, less wind, and no talk,
And running forty miles, I reported the same.

Saturday, 29th of September

Cargoed with food and sick of the world,
Today a booby came to roost in the shrouds,
A birdload of garbage, a booby-galleon,
A prize for the frigates, flying thieves
That ate its heaves while on the wing.
I eased seventy-two miles to sixty-three.

Sunday, 30th of September

I shortened our forty-two miles by nine,
A nine-mile lie is what I told today—
Not so tall a tale, none of the seven sins.

Monday, 1st of October

A fairish run under heavy showers of rain.
We put seventy-five miles behind our prats,
But the count stopped at sixty for the men.

Tuesday, 2nd of October

The weeds seem to strain from east to west,
Reeds in a river that trends toward Japan,
And we had a run today that won its name,
A downstream hundred and seventeen miles,
Which became, in the telling, some few less.

Wednesday, 3rd of October

The men ran me ragged today, tired me dead:
Steer by legs, they said, go zig-and-zagged,
Tack, they told me, and my back grew cold.
I needed another auspice, and if God knew,
It was He that sent one—fruit-bearing weed.
We had a run of a hundred and forty miles,
Twenty of which are missing from history,
As I'd be too without that floatsome fruit.

Thursday, 4th of October

A hundred and ninety miles, a high run
That I lied lower, to a hundred and forty.
A ship's boy struck a booby with a stone—
A hailstone? a gallstone? a stone from where?

Friday, 5th of October

Again the ships ran as if they'd taken fright,
A hundred and seventy-one miles they fled,
But, strange to say, we were three dozen shy
When the men came aft to learn our position.
Today's marvel—fish on wings, fish that fly!

Saturday, 6th of October

Mr. Pinzon put in his two centavos today.
Drop the Indies, he said, and head for Japan,
Take Japan, he said, and let the Indies go—
As though he knew what I don't and God forgot,
Where land is, Japan, the Indies, or home.
We were good for a hundred and twenty miles,
But I pruned twenty-one—I piss on Pinzon!

Sunday, 7th of October

Day and night the men seek for signs of land,
Peruse the flight of birds, the rain and wind,
Pore over my lies, study the hues of the sea,

Employ eyes and prayer and other witchery—
All this to tell the crews the Where of Land.
But I dream of it, rerun my first-time dream,
The one I had when I first beheld a ship,
First spun the hearsay globes of scholars,
And had again the first night out from Palos—
And I come awake with dust in my mouth,
Dust in my hair, and I can see it tumbling
In slants of sun, land, it's land on the air!
I add a little something to the Crown reward,
A silk doublet for the hand that raises Earth,
And suddenly all, even I, are in the rigging.
The run was short today, eighty-four miles,
But I made it shorter to keep us nearer Spain.

Monday, 8th of October

The sea today was like the river at Seville,
And down it we idled some thirty-six miles.

Tuesday, 9th of October

We made ninety miles, and I counted fifty.
All day long there were birds passing by.

Wednesday, 10th of October

When the day opened with water to the sky,
The sea a hollow circle, a circumference,
I wondered how much longer I had to live.
The men told me, and I took their word:
Three days, they gave me, three more days
To say my prayers for an earth to pray on,
And then, they said, if no terra was seen,
My kneeling-stool would be Neptune.
We made a hundred and seventy miles,
And I slashed the figure by thirty-five.
A fine day the Lord picked to give us wind!

Thursday, 11th of October

We ran a hundred and fifty miles today,
But I cut off nothing, confessed them all:
I sighted land at ten in the evening!
(Note: Don't forget to claim the reward.)

CHRISTOPHER COLUMBUS, II   *1492*

THE WAKE OF THE *SANTA MARIA*

All this did I behold with my bodily mortal eyes.
                              —Bartolomé de Las Casas

The crews scanned the skies for news of land, and in birds unknown
to Spain, in the trend of the wind and in rain on the run, there were
clues, they said, of India. The Admiral read the sea and knew better:
it was still too green to be near the main, still too free of the small
and several goods it should've borne, the fruit, the weeds and wood,
the leaves; the nearest earth was downward, a mile or more away,
but he'd die if he spoke his mind, and he'd be the first dead man to
find it. Instead, he wrote the truth in the log and lied to the men,
and thus he lived to take home his tithe of all trove, pearls, spinels,
plate, and to quarter the royal arms with his five anchors azure and
his five islands gold.

Thirty-two days out from the Grand Canaries, a light was seen at
evening—moving, it was said, as if someone ran with a torch—and
soon, in the middle watch, a long low mass appeared, lying black on
blue in the west. *Cipango!* cried the men, and they chanted hymns
and adored the Master's feet. *Cipango!* and beyond it the Great
Khan's *Kinsai* that Polo had told of, or *King-sze*, as some insisted, or
Quinsay, which was the Master's way to speak it—but however said,
however spelled, it held the pearls a tenth of which were his.

Morning came with naked hundreds, savages of cinnamon hue,
and thinking the voyagers to be above the law of nature, they bent
their backs in awe, but, no harm being offered them, they made bold
to lay on hands. Sundry wares were trafficked, as a mass of yarn for a
hawk's bell and a parakeet for the jingles of a tambourine, and then

it fell time for *The People From Heaven*, as the savages called them, to go ashore and claim, in the name of God, new worlds for Castile and Leon. Their convoy to the beach was the cinnamon host, singing most unsweetly as they swam.

There on land, the royal standard was displayed, together with two banners, each bearing a green cross whereon reposed a broidered *F* for Fernando and for his queen a broidered *Y*, and then the whole company—the Master, the men, the brothers Pinzon, even Luis de Torres, the converted Jew—knelt and offered up thanks to El Cristo Rey for a safe passage upon the waters to that place. Now ensued the act of taking possession, which with solemn words and ceremonials (*Domine aeterne et omnipotens*, etc.) was seemly done, the same being set forth fully in written testimonies there and then made. Guanahani, the island had been called, after a certain monster that lived in the legend of the savages, but it was Guanahani no more. It became, in honor of the Savior, San Salvador.

Seized of the island, the Christians now sought what they most desired it to contain, and by dumb show and depictions drawn in the sand, they strove to make known the aim of their quest. In the end, the brutes seemed to understand, for they pointed to the south and west distance, still more removed from Spain, and they spake of *nucay*, or, as some heard it, *nozay*, and of *guanin*, though this, a substance containing copper, was reputed to stink, and they spake, finally, of *caona*. . . .

. . . *whereupon we showed them certain objects, which in their gibber they pronounced to be* caona, *and on being asked where more such might be found, the stuff being gold, they levied a store of the same from their children, who were at play with it, and bestowed it upon us most freely. Nor were they ill content with what we gave them in return—buckles, barrel-hoops, and bits of shattered glass. These last ravished them, and they wore them in their ears.* . . .

To learn where it grew, the men now made them a miscellane of gifts: little red caps, latchet-points and coins, nail-heads, which were greatly coveted, and, past all price, mismated colored shoes. Always some realm beyond the sea was named, but once attained, it became no more than a place on the way to the one pursued. Many such were touched by the ships, and in each a few grains were found, at best a pinch, but the source, as before, remained out of reach.

The crews began to sense deceit (was the feast at an end? was Easter over and Christ returned to the tomb? was blood to be shed again, and by whom, and whose, and where, and when?). They had staled of being led from little to less, and from less to nil: if there was some, they said, there must be much. They believed in the fire betokened by smoke. . . .

. . . *as slaves, the savages required no gifts, nor got them. No more was it their parrots for our molasses: it was their travail for our mercy. We let them live if they worked themselves to death. They died in high numbers, some in streams whilst diving for the yellow stones we honed for, some as we bestrode them, armed and armored, like knights on knaves, and some simply where they stood or slept or sat, but they came cheap, and it did not pay to save them when they sickened. Often they misbehaved, and we were obliged to chasten them, as by hewing off their hands for theft, and the stake was their quittance for spitting on the Cross. At times, we suffered our dogs to course them, though rarely without reason, and as for their women, when we used them in common, it was never in the presence of their children. . . .*

And now there was gold in leather pouches, and there were spices, though not from Calicut and Seylan, and there were strange fruits in the seed and dried roots soon to be tried in Spain, and there was one other gift made in the New World and taken to the Old: the pox. The Indian women had been comely, and they were remembered by some who lay strapped down and dying of them. Hair like black wax, they may have thought, breasts a twain of hemispheres, two perfect halves of one, the belly a maelstrom, and the pudendum on the edge, like a leaf. . . .

Todo esto yo lo vide con mis ojos corporales mortales.

THE MISSISSIPPI   1519

RIVER OF THE HOLY SPIRIT

So the Spaniards called it, but to the Chippewas, it was simply a great water that welled up from another world. It began as a pool, they told the whites, a puddle, really, an *alberca* that would hardly hold the moon, a bath for birds, they said, but only if the birds were small. At first, it would move no more than dust—a pinch too much, and even dust would dam it—but soon it grew, and it would bear minor things, a leaf, a feather, spiders, clouds, and then major things, trees and the places where trees had stood. There it browned with the earth it had eaten, there it drowned deer and children caught too near its run, there serpents sunned on snags and kites fed on the fly, and at the last, where it joined the sea, it seemed to seethe, a stew of sticks, shells, sand, bones, and a day's journey out from land, its taste would still be sweet. There were Spaniards who, believing what they had heard of this wonder, went to seek it. Many, like its other odds and ends, became a part of it.

JUAN PONCE DE LEON   *1521*

A REMEDY FOR TIME

At the fote of this mountayne es a well, noble and faire, and the water theroff has a swete savour and reflaire, and wha so drinkes thryes of that well, evermore thai seme yung.
                                        —John Mandevill's Book

A well, it was called by some who claimed to have seen it, while others, no less certain, held it to be a font or fountain that gushed up from the ground, but all agreed it was only to be found upon a certain isle of the Indies—Taprobane—within the realm of the King of Candy. The site was said to be movable and wandering, as the seas were and the wind, and the flow might appear where fancy led it, here now and now there, but none disputed the spurgent work of its waters.

All manner of spicery they contained, and albeit one's ills and ails were many, each would they lave away. Calenture cooled at the quaffing of a drench, and the blood and pus of issue ceased. Aposteme shrank, and they that suffered trismus left off gnashing teeth. Taint, brash, and the festination, known to some as agitans, these were voided, and dartre, and icterus, and pamphilus with its blebs, and cynanche, the dog-collar disease, these too flowed from the body with the body's fluids, and the man became hale.

But there was more, it was warranted, and the more outweighed
the rest, for the waters, so that they were three times supped, would
replevin youthhood. Gums would grow teeth again, and hair, gray or
gone, would flourish as it did before, and the eye would clear and the
tongue taste, and breath would seem less air than silk, and, best, the
forgotten finger would remember how and where and when to point.

Many had sought that isle and the well or spring or fount in the
shade of a mountain named Polombe, and near as many had failed,
some, young when they sailed, sailing on till dead of age. But one
came who knew the way, or it may be it was writ for him to read in
spume and weed and the flight of birds, and he lived to kneel on the
transcendent strand. He called the place Pascua Florida in honor of
the day, and not, as error made it, for the flowers that began where
brine ended.

In truth, flowers were few there and the people hostile, and being
jealous of their heath, though little it seemed but tree and sand, they
greeted those come to claim it with bow and spear, a beggarly show
of arms. When the lombards spoke from the ships, they fled in fright,
leaving their dead on the shore as broken meat. These were the first
paschal lambs killed in Florida: Spain's gain was also God's.

The isle taken, it remained to find where the storied seep issued
from the terrain. But there was none now to say and none to make a
sign, for the mouths on the beach were filled with flies, and the
hands lay quite some way from where they'd grown. It was proposed
that lots be cast, as by a ring suspended or wax let fall in wine, but
the Adelantado was sixty-and-one, with little time left to turn time
back, and therefore, waiting not on divinations, he went at the head
of his men into the forest.

They were sore encumbered, what with petronel and caliver, with
pike and halberd and suits of steel, and from within as well they wore
themselves down, for they bore in their bowels the sanguinary flux.
Always in the daytime gloom, they sensed inimical eyes, ahead,
aside, and closing in behind, and at night arrows came to remind
them that the eyes would be there at dawn. And to these dolors the
dog-days added, and as the troop moved on, its grief could be heard
no small way off.

But worse than the woes of the forest were those impending in a
swamp so vast that it was not doubted to be the last stage of the
earth. No savin grew there, and no red bay and yew, only verdure

rooted in slime, all strange, as were the vines that wreathed its hair. No mountain was seen, though men were sent to the tops of trees, and when they told of more mire to where sight ended, it was known that never would they thrice drink of the magic waters, no, nor not even once. Many then, of hunger and of their wounds and maladies, lay them down to die or fell to the hydras that dwelt in the morass.

Now it was that the enemy chose to show more than eyes. Their bowmen filled the air with feathered rain, and Christian blood ran till it began to run cold. The Adelantado, Juan Ponce de Leon, took a shafted flint in the groin—the Fountain, once, of Youth—after which he lived not long.

FRANCISCO DE CORONADO   *1540*

DRAW ME NOT WITHOUT REASON

In the year of the incarnation of the Lord 1540, Francisco de Corona-do, with 300 horse, marched northward from Culiacan to seek the Seven Cities of Cibola that had been vouched for by Fray Marcos de Niza. There, the friar had affirmed, the houses were of hewn stone jointed with lime, the least of them two stages in height and some, as God was his witness, three, four, and even five, and the doorsills and lintels were a daze of turquoises, gems so like the tint of Heaven as to seem chips of fallen sky, and as in Heaven, the way was paved with blocks of gold. But Coronado did not find these cities, nor, in some ruin, some pale blue pile of residue, did he find where they had been. Two years he wandered, but he did not find them.

Long later, in the year of the incarnation 1886, at a place known to the Sioux as Kaw, or Kansa, which meant *people of the south wind*, there would be taken from the ground, where it lay deep in the buf-falo-grass, a Spanish sword. It would lack a hilt, and it would be so rusted over as to suggest of rusting through, still when polished with brick-dust, a fine-made blade would slowly appear. Transversely graved near the tongue would be the name *Gallego*, in token of Juan Gallego, Coronado's captain, and lengthwise of the fuller would be this inscription: *No me saques sin razon. No me embaines sin honor.*

It would speak. *Draw me not without reason*, it would say, and it would give the Sioux as a reason, and it would say *Sheathe me not without honor*, but honor must have been lost, for no scabbard would be found. It would be found in no nearby stream, no other stand of grass, no flat of sand—gone when honor went, it would never be found.

HERNANDO DE SOTO   *1542*

ADELANTADO OF FLORIDA

He was with Pizarro in Peru. Where else could a captain of horse, a spic *condottiere*, have put together as his share of the pickings two hundred thousand cruzados in gold, enough to buy him the groin of Doña Ysabel de Bobadilla, with coin to spare for an usher, an equerry, and a chamberlain, and pages and footmen and other servants requisite for the menage of a brand-new Marques—where but in Peru?

His portion for ending a civiliation, two hundred thousand likenesses of the crusader's cross—and he lavished them on the wines and whores of Estremadura. When, therefore, Cabeza de Vaca, that had sailed with Narvaez, returned with tales of a place where gold (let God judge him if he lied!) sprang from the earth, where it flashed in the waters and depended from the trees, who will wonder that Ysabel's minor lips were forgot, along with the major-domo?

Once only the Marques sent tidings to the Court. *Very noble gentlemen*, he wrote, and he told of a new land that was nothing if not a magazine of plenty, a depot that would subsist an army without its knowing a want, and he spoke of a town that was called Ocale, so large and so extolled that he scarcely dared repeat what the air was rife with—the multitudes of turkeys kept in pens, the herds of deer tended as kine were tended in Spain, the rumor of pearls. . . .

What more there was straggled in with the survivors. The figs as big as a fist; the anane, whereof the pulp was like a curd; the mamei, that recalled the peach; the guayaba, in form a sort of filbert; the humpbacked cows and the conies; the bagre, a third of which was head, and the barbel, and the pereo, and the peelfish, with a snout a cubit long; in short, the gold that grew, that swam, that flew and ran —no man had sought it, alas, no man born in Spain.

The treasure that had drawn them was the kind that would weigh in the purse and chime in the palm, it would shine when shone on and sometimes glow in the dark, it would buy the heart's desire and take the place of fire in a woman of stone.

Three years had they wandered, only to be stopped in the end by a flow of water so great that it tore loose the earth and bore it away, and it was there, by that spate, that the Marques had sickened and died, and his men, those that were left, wrapped his body in a blanket weighted not with gold but sand and sank it in the stream.

VIRGINIA DARE   *1587*

FIRST LADY

BORN: At Roanoke Island, North Carolina, 18 August 1587, to Eleanor, wife of Ananias Dare, Esq., a daughter, Virginia.

Nine days later, Governor John White, grandfather of the first English child delivered on American soil, sailed for home *for the present and speedy supply of certain known and apparent lacks and needs, most requisite and necessary.* It took him three years and three hundred and fifty-five days to return, and he found *the houses taken down and the place very strongly enclosed with a high palisade of trees, with curtains and flankers, very fortlike; and one of the chief trees or posts at the right side of the entrance had the bark taken off, and five feet from the ground, in fair capital letters were graven* CROTOAN, *without any sign or cross of distress.*

He searched for some time, that grandfather of Virginia Dare, but of the one hundred and sixteen souls he had left behind on the dunes, he found no wind-grayed bone, no salt-faded rag, no blurred or bottled word, no word at all save the word *CROTOAN*; he found no stiff scalp with stiffened hair, no coshed-in skull, no scaled pot, no rotten pone, no written word save the word *CROTOAN*; he found no telltale ash, no mildewed trash or unstrung beads, no wax tears from some sprung-for candle, no hound on a grave, no grave on stilts, nothing but the lone and graven word *CROTOAN*.

There were voices on the sand and in the air, but they spoke no tongue that White could understand. There were clouds of heron crying *as if an army of men had shouted together*; there were parrots, falcons, and merlinbaws; there were clam-birds, there were wrens in the cattail, there were plover and willet and clapper-rail—but their cries made no sense in English ears, and the search, begun at that right-hand gatepost, ended there. Gazing at the still strange word, White spelled it once aloud, as if charging it to make its own meaning known, but CROTOAN it was and only CROTOAN, and he reboarded ship and sailed away forever.

Had he stayed longer, would he have found the fact of the matter? Would he have found, in some Indian town, one hundred and sixteen mummied heads on poles? Would he have found their teeth slung on Indian necks, their skin drawn tight on drums? Would he have found the pots in use, the rusted wrecks of tools, the torn Bibles, the clothes again but wrongly worn. . . ?

DIED: On or near Roanoke Island, North Carolina, Virginia Dare, daughter of Ananias and Eleanor Dare, on an unknown day between 1587 and 1591.

JAMESTOWN   *1607*

THE PEOPLE FROM HEAVEN

. . . Bid Pokahontas bring two little Baskets,
And I will give her beads to make her a chaine.

> They gave us death for nothing, nothing else:
> Other bagatelles we paid for through the nose
> And all the new drains they made with shot.
> For the Coastal Plains, we got papers of pins,
> For the Bay of Chesapeack three-a-penny trash,
> Spit for the James we got, and such names as Dog.
> But when their meat ran out, their drink ran in,
> And then, O Great Hare, how they wept and died,
> How like women died the skinflints of Virginia!

> *CAPT. SMITH: God, being angrie with us,*
> *Plagued us with such famin and sicknes*
> *That living were scarce able to bury dead.*

Onely of Sturgion did wee have great store,
Whereon our men would so greedily surfet
As to bring on flux and cost many their lives;
The Sack, Aquavitie, and other preservatives
Being kept onely in Capt. Wingfield's hands
For his owne diet and his few associates.

A good sign, their coming from the sunrise sea,
Gods of the dawn, they were, as in the Promise,
Wherefore we chose to ignore such omissions
As the white robes they were supposed to wear
And the wizard-skiff that would bear them ashore.
Their ship was made of wood, not serpent-skin,
And what garb they wore was wrought of steel,
But for aught we knew, the styles had changed,
And thus deluded, we let the wrong gods land.

CAPT. WINGFIELD: Capt. Smith is a liar.
It is a lie that I did much banquit and ryot
Before the many hungry eies of the Collony,
And that I served Ratcliffe with foule Corne
And denyed his sonne a spoonefull of beare.
I did alwaies give every man his allowance
And onely when the quantity was much reduced
Did I seal up the rest against emergencie,
Yet, Lord, how they did long for to supp up
That little remnant left in the comon store,
For they had emptied all their owne bottles
And all other that they could smell out!

They began to die on the sixth day of August.

CAPT. SMITH: He has stuffed his relacyons
With many falsities and malycyous detractyons.

John Asbie went first, with a bleeding bowel,
And then of dropsy George Flowre drooped,
And next came a Gent., one William Bruster,
And now Jeremy Alicock turned up his toes,
Slender ones, like fingers, those of a Gent.,
And under the daisies that same summer day
Went a certain Midwinter, an off-season name.

CAPT. WINGFIELD: Twice a liar is Smith,
For it has been proved before his face
That when in Ireland he begged like a rogue
(Without a lycence), and to such as he is,
I would not that my name should be a companyon.

And now two more dead followed arm-in-arm,
One Gore (one Gower?) and one John Martine,
And then Pickhouse (some said Piggase) died,
And next a Power expired, a Cutter of Ice—
Gosnold, they called him, a man of mark,
Judging by the guns that boomed at his grave—
And then it was high time for low Will Rods
(Rods, Roods, Rodes, spell it as you like,
As long as it's clear he wasn't a Gent.),
And Cape Merchant Stoodie, and Throgmortine,
And Sergt. Jacob, and Mister Benj. Beast. . . .

We went among the maize, measuring our food,
Counting our hopes of lasting out the year,
And we found enough, but no ear to spare
For such unmanned and godless guests as they.
Still, we all had a say, and one of us spoke
And said, Let us feed these foolish children.

CAPT. SMITH: God pleased, in our extremity,
To move the Indians to bring us some Corne,
When we rather expected they would destroy us.

POKAHONTAS: And why did we *not* destroy them?
Why, being savages "inconstant in everie thing
"But what feare constraineth them to keepe,
"Being quick to anger, craftie, and quick to run,
"And being so enamoured of all Ornamentations
"That they sporte dead Rats tied by the tail
"And even greene and yellow colored snakes,
"Which crawl and lapp and often kiss their lips,"
And why, being savages "continually in warres
"And eateing their enemies when they kill them,
"Or any stranger if they make him their prisoner,"
Why, being savages "that lick up man's spittle

"In a barbarous fashion, like foule Dogges,
"Whensoever a settler spits in their mouthes,"
Why, being savages "that poyson their Arrowheads
"And worship Oke, the Sunne, and other Devvils,
"Acknowledging neither a God nor a Resurrection,"
Why, my people, why did we not destroy them?

HENRY HUDSON   *1609*

THE MEN IN THE MOON

From the Navesink highland, an Indian watched a white bird swim toward him over the edge of the world. It was soon seen from other places—the tops of trees, the sloughs where berry-vines grew, the waterway that was called *River of the Steep Hills*—and to all, though they knew not its import, it was a sign sent by Manitou. A Neponset saw it from a dune on Paumonok, a Raritan from the hook of sand at land's end, a Ramapo from a crabbing-shoal—and to none was the bird a ship and the ship a Hollander of 80 tons, the *Half Moon*.

. . . At three of the clock in the afternoone we anchored (and) sent in our boate to sound and they found no lesse than foure, five, six, and seven fathoms, oozie ground, and saw many salmons. . . .

There were men in the bird's plumage, or things like men, but these were known to be harmless if gifts were made that pleased. The canoas were therefore heaped with such offerings as green tabacoos and a choice of dried meats, and then around the bird, as around a fire, a circle was made, drawn on the water, the people singing as they drew it.

Some with their offerings upheld to view, they were about to go nearer when something gross was said or something grossly done—none knew what, it would seem—and suddenly arrows flew, and it fell that one of these forced the mouth of a man on the bird's wing, and Death went in, and the man or thing died. The bird thereupon swam away, and the people took their oblations back to shore. A few, before quitting the stream, noted a red froth on its ripples, as though a red wind blew.

At the last, only one was left on the strand, and while the rest were in their towns atoning, he read of times to come in the onward river. Not trees did he see but trees of stone, not vines but fruitless wires, and there would be rubber tires and rubber fish, and tin, and ash, and token suns in broken glass, and in grease and trash all grass would die, and there would be wheels (what were wheels? he wondered) and sticks that spoke and spirits that walked on the sky, and it would avail not to stroke snakes and take in smoke for luck, and no rattle shaken, no beaten drum, would void or ease the omen: the times to come were on the way.

POKAHONTAS   *1617*

LADY REBEKAH

It came to pass that in the fifteenth year of her age, Pokahontas, the well-loved daughter of the werowance Powhatan, was promised to a certain lesser chieftain known as Kocoum or, as some heard it said, Cocowam, but that one, however went his name, did not in the end enjoy the felicity of getting the maid to wife.

> . . . *The women are tall and comely made, and they do walk straight and with no common grace. They are very strong of body, full of agility and hardihood, and so inured to extreme that they may couch unsheltered in the rime and rain of winter. . . .*

Pokahontas was lost to her Indian in this fashion. Soon before the ceremonies, she was seen in the company of the Potomacks by the young captain Samuel Argall, and so paradised was he by her lineaments that he connived at her abduction. With the bribe of a copper kettle, he obtained possession of her person, and, confining her on board of his ship, he removed her to James Towne.

> . . . *For raiment, since the women seem not to weave, they use the skins of wild beasts, or, failing these, they make resort to grasses and leaves. But ever are they clad about their middles, for they are shamefast to be seen bare. . . .*

There dwelt in that settlement an English gentleman, John Rolfe by name, that lately had come away to the Colonies with his wife. The latter had borne him at Bermuda a girl-child (which was so appelled in honor of the place), but it betided that the woman died upon reaching Virginia. It was after the said calamity that Master Rolfe took his first sight of Pokahontas, and at once he knew for her an ardent desire.

. . . Some have their breasts artfully wrought with sundry patterns painted under the flesh. . . .

A desire that was coupled, however, with a higher intention, for Rolfe purposed to wed her. Argall's mind in the matter is unrevealed, but he parted with his prize for the asking, it seems, or at best for a copper kettle. Owning the maid, if maid she still was, Rolfe conceived it his duty at this juncture to imbue her with a soul and thus save her from Satan.

. . . For all that they are so easily delivered of child, they do cherish their young most dearly. . . .

She requiting his passion, Pokahontas readily gave her consent to being baptized a Christian and named Rebekah, whereupon there was much rejoicing, as ever there is for a brand snatched from the burning, and no great while ensued before plans for espousal were laid.

. . . A maid may be known from a married woman in this: the maid will shave the fore part of the head close and plait the rest; the other, cutting no part, will plait all. . . .

The marriage was solemnized in the church at James Towne. A goodly number of the Colony were present at the peculiar but proper union, as were a deputation of Algonkwin savages from Werowocomoco. These last in general comported themselves well, though some were seen to relieve their stresses, as children do, in that place where they sat or stood.

. . . For a visitor of note, the naturals provide a woman as bedfellow, she first being reddened with the powder of a dried root that they call pocone. *. . .*

From England now, advices to Master Rolfe aquaint him that various enterprises were in need of his vigilance, from which it followed that he took passage in a ship early departing the settlement. With him went his wife Rebekah, and after the perils of voyaging, they made safe arrival oversea. There Master Rolfe shewed his strange companion to the Court, which most graciously did receive her, and then how the people did run in her train through the halls and streets of London!

. . . The women, though burdened with all manner of drudgery, the while their men pleasure in wars and hunting, yet do they bear their years well. . . .

In that city was domiciled captain John Smith, the same that Pokahontas once had saved the beating out of his brains by her father's braves, and that ever since she had so scarce seen as to suppose him no longer living. He, learning of her proximity, came now into her presence, making a leg, as to royalty, and calling her Lady Rebekah.

. . . These women in their troths will seek a great distance of blood from that of their husbands, close consanguinity being repugnant to custom. . . .

Thus addressed by him, she turned away her face, it may be for hurt at no warmer welcome from one so cherished that she had claimed his life. And thereafter a sickness became seated in her, and she wasted sorely till in the *George*, the ship that was to take her back to Virginia, she died. None had told her, for none knew or remembered, that in Hebrew, whence the name, the meaning of Rebekah was *the noose*.

. . . A chief ruler or king of those people has as many women as he will for his needs. . . .

Bereft by this latest frown of fortune, Master Rolfe went himself in the *George* to James Towne, and there he met and wedded with the woman Jane Peirce. He did not live out five more years. The naturals killed him in a massacre.

SLAVERY IN VIRGINIA

WHERE ALL THE BLUES BEGAN

There came, about the last day of August,
A Dutch man-o'-war that sold us 20 Negars.

You're near Virginia now, you Niger-babies,
And when you land, let the sleeping past lie,
You understand? let its dogs doze on or die,
Look green about the weaklings lost at sea
And say the grub was simple, yea, but savory,
And tick it off as a Prince of Liars dart
That we picked a new she each day and night
And queued up tight for a crack at her cart,
And re the welts on your back and the galls,
Stay dumb if you're smart, or you go to starboard
And your balls go to port, and, best for last,
Nobody ast you to come along—you stowed away
While some of us was running off at the mouth
                                    about Virginia.
Wood, you say, is there wood in the place?
There's enough to shoe every Hollandaise foot
Or, if such be gone, to crutch a race of crips,
There's wood for windmills, ten-pins, canes,
Wood to make coffins with, wood for whistles,
Wood for pencil, pipe, and bench in the park,
Wood for spoke and shield, for yoke and cross,
For a horse like the wheeled one lost at Troy
And a stake for the back of a new Joan of Arc,
Aye, wood to seat every knickerbockered ass—
If it's wood you need, there's wood to burn,
More, indeed, than you can shake a stick at!
                                    In Virginia,

They thirst for the Putchamin, a kind of plum
That's green at first and in the long run red,
And when red ripe, ripe as a come-fresh tit,
Tho some lean to the *cerise*, which is fed them
By the breeze while they drowse supine below,

And for drink, they grow the Messamine grape
And, better than the Malaga, the scuppernong,
And *fraises* are there, and the Raspise fruit,
A little nothing-at-all that goes to the brain
Like Brandywine, and you'll find there yarrow,
Which we know and use as Pellitory of Spain,
And the tuckahoe root, and the Musquaspenne,
And sasafrage, and chinquapin, and tobacco.

In Virginia,

They've got a critter they call the Aroughcun,
A tree-climbing beggar, a second-story beast,
And the aerobatic Assapanick, a bird in fur,
And the Opassum (cat, rat, and swine in one)
That plays dead while they club it to death,
And the Water Mussascus, poison on the plate
But, ounce by ounce, money under the floor
Because its smell is stronger than that of
The whore who wears it, and the Beares,
It is said, are kin to those of Muscovia,
And there are Deare too, and hares and Conies,
And Otters, martins, Powlecats, and Weessels,
And Minkes as well, and the silver-side Foxx,
And here only lives the Beever, a river-dog
With a tail for a rudder as bare as a racket:
All these, also the Vetchunquoye, all these

in Virginia.

Common the blackbird with red epaulettes,
And the fisherman Osperaye, and the Goshawke,
Iron hooks on iron wings, and it has your kill
Before the smoke from your gun whiles away,
And the trees are leaved with wilde Turkies,
And, walking, you seem to flush the very earth
As covert Partriches start from the grass,
And Crayne come over in squalls, like rain,
And if a square mile of the Chesapeake's gone,
Seek it under an equal square of sitting teal,
And where water is, the baldhead Wigeon too,
And the Herron, called by some the Shitepoke.

In Virginia,

You'll find a St. George's dragon sort of fish,
And one, kind of like a Tode, that feeds on air
And the which a pin-prick would explode,
And pan-handled Stingrayes, and Congerees,
And white Salmonds, and Pearch, and Drummes,
And Plaice, and soles, and the spectrum Trowt—
Don't slaver, nigger: you'll eat if you slave

in Virginia.

PLIMMOTH PLANTATION, I   *1628*

A MAN OF PRETIE PARTS

*This year Mr. Allerton brought over a yonge man for a minister
to the people. His name was Mr. Rogers, but they perceived,
upon some triall, that he was crased in his braine, so they were
faine to send him back againe.*
    —Bradford: HISTORY OF PLIMMOTH PLANTATION

Perceived? With what sense did they perceive?
Was he crased to the touch, did he *feel* far gone,
Or did they tongue him for a tang of the moon?
Or being downwind of the pulpit, and too near,
Did they smell out the storme in his braine?
Did he shew his phrenzy to the casual eye
By britches unbuttoned, say, or worn ass-front,
By right shoe on left foot, or by shoon forgot?
Or, lastly, did he *sound* unsound, was he daft
By reason of some unreason he put in the ear?

Did he hold with mixt and promiscuous dauncing
(Viz. lascivious saltation to wanton ditties),
Wherein a man and a woman conjoin and posture
In the maner of man and wife, tho not undrest?
Did he speak openly for play in the streete,
For pitching the bar or skirmish with a ball?
Or did he say he saw no ill in Sabbath sleepe,
Whether in the strait pew or the straiter bed?

Did he lower his head when a whore passed by,
Or did he say he would lie with squaw or white?

Did he spit twice when speaking of the Jews,
And did he damn the Pope and similar Okies,
Or did he refuse, saying he could not say
Who was to be sent to hell and who saved?
Did he hold with high wines and strong waters,
Did he make up rimes and, smirking, read them,
Did he defend that peeces, powder, and shotte
Should be sold to the Indeans and they shewn
What charge to use for foule, what for deare,
And what for the pale-faced psalming robbers?
Did he inveigh against the keeping of slaves,
Did he urge wigs for men and waves for women,
Contrary to usage and the Canon of Modestie,
Did he sware idly, did he prophane the air. . . ?

Crased? In what way was he crased?

PLIMMOTH PLANTATION, II   *1632*

NOR HIS ASS

*This year, one Sir Christopher Gardener came into these parts.
He brought over with him a servante or 2 and a comly yonge
woman, whom he caled his cousin, but it was suspected she
(after the Italian maner) was his concubine.*
    —Bradford: HISTORY OF PLIMMOTH PLANTATION

From their pews they watched her, and through screened eyes when
she passed them in the road, and in their dreams at night and noon,
she performed on her back in bed and fully dressed abroad. She per-
formed for most of the smiths and all the wrights, for a cordwainer, a
cooper, and a chapman, for scrivener, soldier, leech, and even (the
whore!) for one who wore Geneva bands. They all knew her, after
mankind's maner—deep in fallen leaves they knew her, and cheap
between two rows of maize, and she was theirs in novel ways and

secret places, in their privies, wives, and minds, and all thought such sinning went unseen.

The Narragansetts, though they might eat of white meat, would not lie with it, wherefore they were free to stand and gaze at the long-prays while they split fancied thighs in fancied ditches. The savages were too civil to laugh with their faces; they laughed instead by signs of the hand.

THE JESUITS   *1632-49*

THE FIRST KNEE ON CANADA

We caught fireflies in the darkening meadows,
And threading them into on-and-off festoons,
We hung them up before the altar and the Host,
And they made light for God, Ghost, and Jesus
While we, adoring, put the first knee on Canada.
  Who's that nailed to the cross, Blackrobes?
  If he's an enemy, let your chief eat his heart,
  But if he's an Oke, you've killed yourselves
  Unless you burn tobacco and invite him down.
  Take our advice about such things, Blackrobes;
  Listen to us, for we know the ways of the land,
  And you, on your knees like women making food,
  Have already offended us with your ignorance.
  Fireflies must not bow down to graven images!
We said, "Unhappy infidels (meaning Dogges),
You that live in smoke only to die in flames,
Repent you and choose between Heaven and Hell!"
  We said, "The sky is the palace of thunder,"
  But it was clear that they did not understand.
  "The sky," we said, "the blue wigwam overhead,
  The sky is the home of thunder, comprenez?,
  And thunder is a turkey-cock, a cock but a man,
  Yet in one thing he is neither man nor bird,
  In one thing strange to all that walk or fly:
  He comes forth only when the wigwam is gray.

Grumbling, he flies to earth to gather snakes,
Snakes and other objects that we call Okies,
And if you see flashes of fire as he descends,
That fire attends the beating of his wings,
And if the grumbling now and then is violent,
Be sure his children have been brought along.
"Which do you choose?" we said. "Heaven or hell?"
We said, "Heaven is a good place for Frenchmen."
"Which do you choose?" we said. "Heaven or hell?"
We said, "The French will not feed us in Heaven."
"Which do you choose?" we said. "Heaven or hell?"
We said, "Do they hunt in Heaven? do they dance?
Do they make war or hold festivals in Heaven?
If not, we will not go, for idleness is evil."
"Which do you choose?" we said. "Heaven or hell?"
We said, "If our dead are in hell, as you say,
If for want of a few sprinkled drops of water,
Our babies live in hell, we would go there too."
We wrote, "We find that pictures are invaluable
In bringing about conversions among the Hurons;
We have learned that these holy representations
Are half the battle to be fought against them.
We desire some more showing souls in perdition,
And if you sent a few drawn on paper or canvas,
With three, four, or even five tormenting devils
Visiting different punishments on the damned,
One with pincers, another applying fire, etc.,
They would have a lasting effect on the savages,
Especially if the drawings were made distinct,
If they revealed misery and rage and despair
Written on the (red) faces of the condemned."
We said, "We see plainly that your God is angry
Because we will neither believe nor obey him.
Ihonatiria, where first you taught his word,
Is ruined, and then you came here to Ossossané,
And here too we were skeptical of your God,
And now the wolves pick Ossossané's bones,
And then you went up and down our country,
And from rising to setting sun you found none

To do the bidding of your God and bow down,
And therefore the pestilence is everywhere."
We said, "Do you believe, then? Do you repent?"
We said, "We know a better cure, a medicine
That will work more wonders than wafer or wine:
We will shut you out now from all our houses
And stop our ears when your God gives tongue,
And then, neither hearing him nor seeing you,
We will be innocent again, as before you came,
And avoid the penalty for refusing to be saved."
Our mission suffered from no lack of visitors,
For the Hurons flocked there to see the marvels
That we had wisely brought with us from France,
And in expectant silence, from dawn to evening,
They squatted on the ground before the door,
Waiting for a performance of the repeating-lens,
Which showed them the same object eleven times,
And the magnifying-glass, wherein a simple flea
Became so monstrous as to overwhelm the eyes,
And the mill, which they never tired of turning,
And lastly, the miracle of miracles, a clock
That struck the hours from one to twenty-four:
They thought it was alive and asked what it ate,
And when at the final stroke we cried "Stop!"
And it stopped, their admiration was boundless.
The incomprehensible mysteries of our Faith,
The clock, the glass, the lens, and the mill—
All this served to win the Indians' affection.
    They proposed that a number of young Frenchmen
    Should be invited to settle amongst our people
    And wed our daughters in solemn and holy form,
    But we said, "Of what use is so much ceremony?
    If these young Frenchmen desire our daughters,
    They will come and take them when they please;
    They will do again what they have done before."
They led Brébeuf out and bound him to a stake,
But if they hoped he would plead for his life,
For what God gave and only God could take away,
The red wretches were doomed to disappointment,

Even as they were doomed to everlasting flames.
The priest addressed the converts he had made,
Promising Heaven if they retained their faith,
Thus angering the Iroquois, and to silence him
They scorched him with coals from head to foot,
And when, as if they were bound and he free,
He spoke further, they cut away his lower lip,
And they thrust a red-hot iron down his throat.
His mouth made no words now nor uttered pain,
And they tried a subtler means to overcome him,
For they took it to be an augury of disaster
If torture failed: they brought forth Lalemant,
That Brébeuf might see his agony and cry aloud
For his brother in Christ if not for himself.
Naked under his cassock of pitch-soaked bark,
Lalemant fell to his knees, saying these words
After the sainted Paul: "We are made a spectacle
Unto the world, and to angels, and to men!"
Whereupon the red devils put fire to the bark,
And Lalemant blazed up like a canoe on a beach,
But the only sound from Brébeuf was an "*Ave.*"
Frenzied, they made him a collar of hatchets
Heated till they smoked like stones from hell
And hung it around his neck to smoke out fear,
But he was grateful, as if they had healed him,
As if it were proud flesh they had burned away,
And he gave them a prayer in payment for pain.
Then they poured boiling water over his head,
Saying that the Iroquois too knew how to pay,
That their hot water was for the Jesuit cold:
"Now *we* baptize *you*, Blackrobe," they cried,
"That you may be happy in your white Heaven!"
And they tore strips from his limbs and body
And devoured this unholy food before his eyes,
Saying, "The more a man suffers on the earth,
So you say, the happier he will be in Heaven,
And desiring to make you the happiest of all,
We torment you badly because we love you well"
But he sanctified their feast with a blessing,

And they scalped him and laid open his breast,
And they came in a crowd to drink his blood,
Thinking thus to imbibe some part of his valor,
But he was dead, and his valor was in Paradise.
   We do not pretend, like the people from Heaven,
   That each of us is a manitou in his own right,
   We do not pretend that we are more than men,
   And being men, we endure the disasters of men,
   Among which are those that come with friends
   That are not friends, and you that speak of God
   And teach the Word, the word being "Mine! Mine!"
   You are no man's friend, you traders from Heaven
   That offer a word and would take our world away!
"Which do you choose?" we said. "Heaven or hell?"
   We choose Heaven, but not for us—for Brébeuf.
   He was brave, like an Indian, and in admiration
   We give you this gift as a shroud for his body
   When the time comes to send him on his journey:
   It is a coat of bear-skin that our women made,
   And in your cold Heaven it will keep him warm.

ANNE HUTCHINSON   *1638*

THOSE TOTAL DEPRAVITIE BLUES

I doe cast you out and deliver you up to Sathan.
                              —Rev. John Wilson

Anne Hutchinson, being called before the Great and Generall Court
of Masachuset and there charged with having comported herself in a
sedityous maner, which is to say a maner tending to promoat hatred,
stryfe, and discontent, and having sware to the truth of the Testimo-
ny she was about to give, did depose and say, not without con-
tumacie, that she denyed the allegation and defyed the allegator.

    The learned and reverend Court poynted out that in mayntayning
a Covenant of Grace to be superiour to a Covenant of Workes, the
accused had flowne in the face of the establisht Creede, whereupon
she avouched that the Lord Jesus Christ had revealed Himself to her

and ingendered her belief, this to the horrour of the Assemblage, for to Sedityon must now be added the graver charge of Anabaptysme, a cult accurst since John of Leyden's daie.

In despite of the comon dismaie, still did the accused persist in her antinomian wordes and waies, saying that the Saviour had not stopt speaking to the world in 22d Revelation. Contrarywise, she said, He was speaking at that very moment, nor was the last worde even yet spoken. Moreover, she saw fitt to add, He dwelt in her Boddie, a bright and morning Starre, and He litt the dark, wherefor she needed not to go with eies upon the ground in shayme of Adam's sinne. Nay, she said, she was saved by the saving grace of Jesus Christ within.

This avowance did produce among the convocation a most violent Appall, as tho the Fiend himself had been heard. When shocke abated, it was observd that what the woman had said was the rankest of Heresys, in that she claymed a mirracle in a time when mirracles were past, thereby setting the Booke at naught. She was not by this dire dictum silenced. Rather did she seeme to become the more frowarde, for she repeated that Christ was insyde her and stirring, infusing her spirrit wondrouslie.

It was now clear to the Court that if these Hereticall teachings were not supprest, the rule of the Cloth was at an end in Masachuset. Should it be suffered that the people believe each of them contayned a moietie of the Holy Ghoast, or conscience, as the woman called it, then all would sitt in judgement of their owne Actes, and being God and man in one, none would condemn himself for sinne and none be damned, not though he be so deprayved as she.

Upon due deliberation, it was found that the woman Hutchinson had become informd by a divelish Dellusion, rendering her unfitt for the society of that place, and the sentence of the Court was that for having troubled the Church with Lyes and Errour, she be declared a Leper and constrayned to withdrawe from the Congregation and the Collony.

It remaynes but to discrive her departure, and that brieflie. Suffice it that in her pryde, she went with necke unbent, back strait, and steppe firm, abating not a jot her demeanour before the Court. Certain clods and clapperclawes made it their busines to tell her that she had got her comings, and they made shift to spitte upon her garments and in her road, but she scorned them, saying *Better to be cast from the Church than to denye Christ*, and she was gonne.

Postscriptum

Shortlie after her excommunication, it was reported to the Clergie and Magistrates of Masachuset that the Exile had been deliverd of a monstrous Birth. This she would fain have lett on to be an hydatidiforme Mole were it not for a Mr. Clarke, physition, who accuratlie defined the material exprest by her Privities. It was a membrayne, he said, stuft with jags and dollops of flesh, 26 in number, some contayning winde and some water, and some were hard-composed, like the lobe of a Livver, but all were possest of a most melancholie stinke. There was no secundine, he averred, and this alone would have served to nominate the true father of the ejectamenta—not man, God forfend, but Diabolus!

ANNOTATIONS   *1606-46*

WINTHROP'S *JOURNAL*

being a selection from marginalia found in a copy of the work

iv: A servant of one of our company had bargained with a child to sell him a box worth 3d. for three biscuits a day all the voyage, and had received about forty. . . .

What good to tie his hands to a bar on the deck of the *Arbella* and hang a basket of stones from his neck? what good to make him stand there, stooped over, whilst two hours passed? They got a look at the shape of his fud, but they saw nary a one of those forty biscuits.

ix: At the last court, a young fellow was whipped for soliciting an Indian squaw to incontinency. . . .

Was it worth what he paid for it, a dozen of the best and well laid on? did she bite him and buck, make him fight for his life, or did she lie like a wife, her thighs quite still? did she delight him with cries, did she clamp and claw him and upsidedown her eyes? did she draw, when they kissed, a blister of blood, or did she come coldly while he hotly went?—oh, and was she built plumb with the world or level, like a Chink?

xii: At Watertown there was a great combat between a mouse and a snake; and, after a long fight, the mouse prevailed and killed the snake. Mr. Wilson, a very sincere, holy man, gave this interpretation: That the snake was the devil; the mouse was a poor contemptible people. . . .

Ah, it was there, then, that the Darkness Prince was shown the Light, there that Evil ended. Watertown, you say? W-a-t-e-r. . . ?

xx: The scarcity of workmen had caused them to raise their wages. Many spent much time idly, because they could get as much in four days as would keep them a week. . . .

Solution: Double their hours or halve their pay, and if that doesn't do it, shoot them.

xxi: Robert Cole, having been oft punished for drunkenness, was now ordered to wear a red D about his neck for a year. . . .

Did the *D* in its rounds ever meet an *A*? That would've been a red-letter day.

xxv: A wicked fellow, given up to bestiality, fled to Long Island, and there was drowned. He had confessed to some, that he never saw any beast go before him but he lusted after it. . . .

Drowned, the poor bugger? Well, he was bound to come to a bad end.

lxi: One Hugh Bewett was banished for holding publicly that he was free from original sin and from actual also. . . .

A second Christ, and banished only! Where was the faith of old in the power of pain? He should've been rushed through all fourteen stations of another Passion!

lxv: A godly maid of the church of Linne, going in a deep snow from Meadford homeward, was lost, and some of her clothes found after among the rocks. . . .

To other godly maids of Linne, if you have to sinne, don't bare your asse—it gets ungodly cold in Meadford, Mass.

lxx: Mr. Hopkins came to Boston and brought his wife with him, who was fallen into a sad infirmity, the loss of her understanding and reason by giving herself wholly to reading and writing, and had written many books. . . .

The word'll do that, all right. It'll wrack the world, wring it, wry it, turn it inside-out and outside-in. It'll speed it, slow it, set it aspin, it'll thin the air and thicken water, darken day and gay the night. It'll craze you, the word will, and long before you die, it'll kill you.

lxxv: Billington was executed at Plymouth for killing one. . . .

One what? One servant, or, if servant himself, one master? One wife, one Indian, one Saltonstall, one holier-than-thou, some clerical son-of-a-bitch? Or was it one boy who might snitch about their sport in the woods?

xc: At Ipswich there was a calf brought forth with one head, and three mouths, three noses, and six eyes. What these prodigies portended the Lord only knows. . . .

The cow knew too. They portended a cockeyed run on her tits.

JOHN COTTON   *1652*

DEATH OF A CLERGYMAN

Sister, doe not shut your Eyes agaynst the Truth. The soule is
Immortall.   —Rev. John Cotton to Anne Hutchinson

He was old now, and death was near: the wind was on the way. He
could hear it among the trees, and it made the grass seem to flow,
and it put a fleeting mar on the finish of a stream. It was on the way,
the wind, and when it came and blew on him, he would die and start
to live. He was close now, he knew, to the door that opens once.

The trope pleased him, and he spoke it—*the door that opens once*,
he said—and the reason for his pleasure was this, that he had so lived
as to know what lay beyond the door, a place of boundless light,
where error was not and all was grace. Death's door, it was called,
but so far from leaving the world, he felt sure that he was about to
enter it. To such as he had been for eight-and-sixty years, death was
only life's beginning. He dwelt on his fasts and vigils, on his lustra-
tions and prayers, on alms quietly given, on the nails he had driven
through his palms—yes, he knew what was on the other side of the
door, the evergreen and everlasting world, the one for which this was
but the waiting room.

And now the wind came and tried the door, and the door opened,
and as he died, there was one last knowing instant when his face
grew a vast appall: he stood on the threshold of nothing; death was a
hole in the wall.

THE QUAKERS   *1660*

PASS NOT OVER THE BROOK

In the name of the Lord Jesus Christ, I do declare thee, Anne
Hutchinson, to be cast out from this church, a heathen and a
publican from this day forth, and I do deliver thee unto Satan
for the destruction of thy flesh.   —Rev. John Wilson

As Anne, damned, went toward the door, there was one that rose and
went with her and took her by the hand. Her name was Mary Dyer,
and against her too now time began to run.

They say of her that she was a person of no mean extract, of piercing knowledge in many things, grave and comely and wondrous fit for great affairs, but they say this as well, that she contained a proud spirit and was much addicted to revelations. She held the Gospel to be evergreen and growing, a never-blowing bloom, a tale always in the telling, now and on the morrow as once in Palestine. The Book signified nothing to her: if it embraced the Word, it was the Word lifeless, movable type that moved no more. The living Word was the Light within, and each man glowed with it, lit his own way—each was a lamp from which Jesus shone out on the world.

Odd to the mind of the ministry, some few of her kind were even odder to the eye. There were those who went about with pans of burning brimstone on their heads, and others blacked their faces or, in token of an empty sermon, broke an empty bottle in the pews, and two zealous goodies publicized their privates in the road. But the durable sin of the Ranters was their ranting, which to many of the people was something more than senseless sound: a sweet belief, they found it, that each should be father, each son, each the paraclete.

A sweet belief, but it got them bark in the pulpit and bite in the street, it got them spittle and avoidance, and when, as often, the pure felt the itch, they were frisked for a hellish signature, the triple tits of a witch. It got them knotted cords on the bare back, fines and close confinement, a hot spike through the tongue, and an amulet to wear, a pair of their ears. Their Inner Light got them outer darkness—exile —and the penalty for coming home, for crossing the vale below the Mount of Olives. . . .

On the day that thou passeth over the brook Kidron, thou shalt surely die.

And yet four crossed over and were cast in jail, and Mary, ravished by the love of the living God within her, followed in their trail. She lay there long with them, and then she was freed and sent away. But stay she could not, and upon her second return, she was tried and given death, and they stood her on the gallows, tied her skirts, covered her face with Mr. Wilson's kerchief—and reprieved her!

She still lived, but she would not accept her life from those that persecuted her. Expelled once more, she once more came back, and this time they kicked the ladder out from under her feet, and on the forbidden side of the brook, she was dead.

THE DEUCE IN MASSACHUSETTS

Brother Narragansetts and other russet Dogges,
Pequots, Patuxents, Tarrentines, and Pokanokets,
I bring you from Salem heap big English love,
(What's love, brother? Is it something to eat?)
I bring, after being spat upon only seven times,
I bring you fish-hooks and doctored fire-water,
I bring buckles, buttons, and bolts of shoddy,
I bring a Bible and two shoes for the left foot.
(What's love, brother? Is it good with meat?)

.oOo.

There shall be found out amongst us none, none
That causeth his son to pass through fire, none
That consulteth with the familiar Spirits, none
That employeth a Wizzard or a Divination—none,
For they are Witches that practice these things,
And (Ex.22.18) we shall not suffer them to live!

We accuse you of irregular Strength in Lifting
And such other and prodigious Pranks and Feats
As only a Diabolical Assistance would explain:

I seen him grab a gun with a six-foot bar'l—
I couldn't of budged it with block and fall—
And hold it at arm's-end like it was a pistol,
And once he taken that same fowling-piece—
It weighed ten stone if it weighed ten ounces—
And just by sticking his thumb in the muzzle,
He twirled it overhead like I'd do with a hat.
I ast him where a puny man got such strenkth,
And he said, "Brother, a Indian's helping me,"
But the only one in sight looked kind of limpsy
Because he was hanging by the neck from a tree.

We accuse you of preternatural use of the Eye,
And urging the signature of names upon a Book,
And, failing, of visitations in sundry Shapes
And being Cat, Cock, or Rodent, as you please:

He went by one day with a book under his arm,
And straight off my little boy fell in a fit
That pretty near to scared my front teeth out.
I worked over him till I was blue in the face,
But the bluer I got, all the blacker the fit,
And finally a neighbor had to give an advice:
"Hang the boy's blanket in the chimney-corner,
And come morning, if there's anything in it,
Chuck it in the fire and burn hell out of it."
Y'know what I found in that blanket next day?
A toad, b'Christ, and bigger than your head!
He stunk up the parlor like old Horny himself,
But I laid ahold of him with a pair of tongs
And give him some of his own in the fireplace,
And no sooner did he get a taste of them coals
Than he made a flash like a pan of gunpowder,
And he went up in smoke and clean got away.

We accuse you of torments with Invisible Hands,
Of biting, pinching, and vexatious Prickings,
Of producing Phlegm, Fever, and Running sores,
Blindness, Tumors, fits, and the Bloody Flux:

She didn't never have a sick day in her life
Up to the time he first laid eyes on her,
And now, b'God, she don't never have a well one!
She's gimpy on the on-side and then on the off,
And often as not she's plumb stiff all over,
And if she ain't on fire, she's froze up hard,
And when she ain't deaf, she's dumb and daft.
I'm talking about my daughter, not my horse,
But she's got the heaves, and she breaks wind
So's two men can't hold a carpet to a keyhole,
And all day long she hawks up clams of phligm
With nails and crooked pins and other hardware,

And when she tries to say *Heaven* or *Christ*,
Her tongue crawls down its hole like a snake,
But you give her *Hell* to chaw on, or *Devil*,
And b'Jesus, she'll talk a blue streak, saying,
"That bites, but it makes me speak right well!"

We accuse you of making a League with the Devil,
Giving you the power of Levitation and Estoppel:

I'm adriving my cart past his house one day—
Which if he built it any closer to the road,
He'd be living acrost the way from himself—
And my hub lays a scratch alongside his wall.
I gum up my wheel a lots more than his paint,
But he sasses me a good fifteen to the dozen
And swings threats around his head like a cat.
Now him being a kind of spleeny little sprat,
I don't let all that gas of his bother me any:
I just give him a regret and tend to my business.
But when I try going through some gate-posts,
Same as I done with that rig for years on end,
Damn if I don't get stuck betwixt and between
Even though there's nothing holding me back,
Only air, and I have to go fall them posts
Before I can stir a inch one way or the other!

We accuse you of Mischief on the heels of Cursing:

Him and me, we once got into a little dispute—
I disremember what about, the weather, maybe—
But if it rared up fast, it fizzed out faster,
And it was done before it was begun, or was it?
I say "was it" on account of two good reasons.
One: I took the nosebleed after that argument,
And there wouldn't nothing stop it but prayer.
And two: me that never had a louse in m'life,
All of a sudden I come up lousier'n a monkey;
I was crawling even when I was standing still;
I was et up setting, and I was et up on the hoof;
I tried soap, psalms, and other kinds of poison,

But finally I had to build me a nice bonfire
And get rid of every stitch outside of my pelt.

We accuse you of entering upon women Entranced:

a) He come one night when I was laying in bed,
And after throwing a spell into the old man,
He set down on top of me for two solid hours.
b) He pulled pretty near the same stunt on me,
And if he didn't stick out the full two hours,
At least he done a sight more than just squat.
c) For a wee man, he was quite a night-walker:
He come to me one time in the shape of a rabbit,
But he could of give a rabbit cards and spades.
d) You ask me, he could spare the Big Casino:
He swore he'd rip out my privities and bowels
If I so much as made a move or opened my face,
But I fooled him—I didn't put up any fight.
e) I wake up all at once in the dead of night,
And there he is, poking about the bed-clothes;
I'm scared pink, but anyhow I let out a holler,
Saying, "The whole armor of God be between us!"
And phutt! he's gone like a busted soap-bubble!
I'm scared so loose now I got to go make water,
And there I am, bareback on the chamber-pot,
When something picks me up, pot, water, and all,
And shakes me out like a apron full of crumbs!
Come daylight, I tell m'self it's only a dream,
But there's one fact teases me and always will:
Every time I use that pot it throws off sparks.

We accuse you of attending Hellish Randezvouzes
And practicing Magic with the Powers of the Air:

He hires me once to wreck a old cellar-wall—
It holds up the kitchen, but it's his house,
And so long as the place don't cave in on me,
I'm glad to get the work and take the wages.
Well, I'm slamming away with m'sledge down there,
And I finally hit a stone that don't ring true.

A couple of good shots, and she comes unstuck,
And out pours the damnedest assortment of junk
That ever a man seen the sunny side of hell:
Poppets made of hair, hog's bristle, and rags;
Pins without a head and heads without a pin;
A sackful of toe-nails and a black cat's ear;
A broken broom, a dead mouse, and a fake nose;
A witch-cake of pebbles, corn-meal, and blood;
A punkin and a hymn-book printed upside-down.
I ask him, "What for you saving all this crap?"
And he says, cool as a witch's tit, "What crap?"
And I'm stumped—because the crap ain't there!

We accuse you of having the Markings of a Witch—
Hidden Teats, sunken Flesh, and Webbed Feet—
And using them to reverse the course of Nature:

It was raining pitchforks with the tines down,
And it was no good walking except you had fins,
But that didn't stop him coming in dry as a bone
And slapping dust off himself fit to choke you.
I said, and there was others there to hear me,
I said, "Man, I couldn't keep that rain off me
Without I growed more feathers than a duck's ass,"
And all he said was, "I scorn to be drabbled!"

We accuse you of Rebellion against the Church:

a) He said death is sure, but tithes are surer.
b) He said he believed in gynecandrical dancing.
c) He said he favored gimp, ribbon, and galloon.
d) He said if some went hungry, all were damned.
e) He said Indians go to Heaven, and Negars too.
f) He said all he knew about Christ was hearsay.
g) He said if he was Satan, he'd want to be God.
h) He said if he was God, he'd want to be a man.
i) He said he *was* a man, so he'd smoke on Sunday.
j) He said there was no hell but here in Salem.

There shall be found out amongst us none, none
That causeth his son to pass through fire, none

That consulteth with the familiar Spirits, none
That employeth a Wizzard or a Divination—none,
For they are Rebels that practice these things,
And behold, Rebellion is as the sin of Witchcraft!
If you would answer this, brother, answer now. . . .

.oOo.

Brother Narragansetts and other russet Dogges,
He said, "The brother shall deliver up the brother,"
Pequots, Patuxents, Tarrentines, and Pokanokets,
He said, "Beware of men, for they will scourge you,"
And, angered, they tied a rope around his neck
And stood him on a branch in the two-legged tree,
And then once more they nagged him for speech,
But he had spoken, and he was done with words,
So they cut the branch, and the world fell away,
And soon, between Heaven and earth, he died.
(What's love, brother? Tell us more about love!)

WITCHCRAFT, II   *1691*

EVIL FROM US DELIVER

If thou wouldst spite the Devil, call him Black John.
—old saying

At Salem Village in New-England, there came before an assize of the
Court of Oyer and Terminer a person known to all as John Black, and
this Black, in the presence of many, did there and then pray that he
be made to stand his trial for the crimes of Conjuration and Nigro-
mancie. Now, at that very time, some ten or a dozen had been
hanged for the offenses aforesaid, and several score of others that had
been cried out against were in durance *ad referendum*. But despite
the diabolism widely at work in the country, the good name of John
Black had not been aspersed until the man undertook to asperse it
himself.

Being put upon his oath, Black deposed in manner following:
"What a mean company of familiars hath the colony thus far seen! A

rabble of wamble-wits—old men lacking teeth to stop their spittle drooling, balding crones with warts and wens and running sores, and all thy doltish and thy daft! These are thy unclean spirits, thy war-locks and figure-casters, but I tell thee this, that with suchlike louts and loons, the Prince of the Power of the Air would scorn to com-pound—and I know whereof I speak, for, lo, I am He!"

Persuaded by this screed that Black was demented, the Magistrate, Mr Wm Stoughton, was not slow to require his removal from the chamber, though with as little force as possible. A bailiff sought to comply (*molliter manus imposuit*, which is to say, gently he laid hands upon him), whereat, however, Black jibbed, saying he would not be grabbled.

In further defial of the droits of the Court, Master Black caused to be spread upon its record this avowal: "I am come now from a Sab-bath held where four roads meet, and if any would know the place, let him look where nothing grows, and he has found it. There, girt by my hags, I took the shape of a he-goat, with a face in front and a face behind, and one by one my furies bowed down and kissed me *in tergo*, meaning full upon my arse. Nextly did I rummage them up for their marks, and when they proved insensible to prickings two inches deep, I bade them sing, which same they did for upwards of an hour, so: *Alegremos, Alegremos! Que gente va tenemos!* Began then our banquet, a feast of snakes and rats and all their offal, and bats and the shite of bats, and worms and wormcast, and witch-cakes, and a cordial of blood and rheum, the whole of it taken from golden plates and crystal goblets. And at the last, they cast off clothes and gamboled naked, each with a cat for a collar and a second cat worn as a tail—and then the cock crew, and I was alone with naught but the fragrance of all things foul. *Alegremos, Alegremos!* thought I, and I made my way here."

Mr Stoughton then heard testimonies from certain witnesses of good report, and taking these together with his own views, he gave it as his opinion that Black's unhinging stemmed from a spell or weird wrought by a fiend or fiends as yet unknown. Some few there that knew him best were deputed to attend him home from Court, and on the way he spake thrice this gibberish: "Glory the and, power the and, kingdom the is thine for. Temptation into not us lead. Bread daily our day. Done be will thy. Name thy be hallowed. Heaven in art which."

None understood him, and at his door he laughed.

AD LIBS BY A FICTITIOUS CHARACTER

Child, what art thou?
Oh, I am your little Pearl!

As Mr. Hawthorne says, the first thing I saw was the scarlet A on the breast of my mother's gown. It was a nearby brightness in a gray-green world, and it drew me as any other would've done, a red flower, a red bird or berry, or fire as it played. It was there at the start, and it stayed, as much a part of Hester as her eyes. But Mr. Hawthorne seems to have been unaware of the second thing I saw, a strange lack since it was a second A, this one black.

I was three months old at the time and in my mother's arms on the pillory, pilloried too, the fruit of her sin and therefore no less vile than she. All Boston had come to view us, and faces paved the market place, paned the windows, grew on trees. There was an absence of color in the crowd—the uniform garb was black—but a certain conical hat seemed somehow blacker than the rest, and so too a certain cape that fell in folds and flared, and I stared at the shape my father thus made: a sable A on a sable field.

I seemed to know him at sight, though I've never known how. He stood among the crowd, concealed by it, as he thought, like a shadow lost in the shadow night, but there was my begetter, the black letter A. Dimmesdale! Mr. Hawthorne says I touched him once (it was at the Governor's, he claims, and I was going on three), but if so, I must've done it to test whether one who looked so dead was still alive. His eyes were deep in his head, bits of sky in a well, and his hair lay senseless, nonconductive, and his skin was dry, like slough. If, as said, I touched him once, let it be known that once was all, but quite enough.

My mother must've touched him too, and not his hand, as I did, nor merely with her cheek; it must've been some other member that she reached, sunless, sallow. Mr. Hawthorne describes the result of that collision—I, a wild and flighty elf named Pearl, an airy child, the friend of weeds, sticks, rags, and the *ferae* found in the forest. He dwells long, Mr. Hawthorne, on the wrong they worked on me, but mum's the word on why. How could she have borne him bare, how endured that prying candle, that tallow finger in her private hair? and where, in what field did she lie, what pine-bough bed, to what rocks was her fall revealed? and did she cry aloud when his small flame singed her, did she pray when he came or wait till he went? Ah, the reverend Arthur! Pale psalmer, scratcher of itches, charmer of skirts, snake in the pubic grass—what did she find in his leached-out phiz, what soul sat behind those rank clothes, what imbued his sour stuffing?

To my mind, she sinned only in sinning with him. It was her affair that she chose to be ridden, and I didn't care where the rider took her, on the run or standing still or during a swim in a stream—but to receive such a one and make him my father! to couple with that quick-spent dip, that one-cent wick! my God, to be lit but once and then so dimly! And thereafter, for seven years, she wore the badge where the world could see it, while he sequestered his in his room. It was not enough that he carved it with a whip, it didn't matter that it bled and festered and appeared to glow in the dark: he let my mother alone be stoned by eyes.

Mr. Hawthorne says that she took me overseas when he died and, after a span of years, returned without me, and rumor ran that writings reached her from time to time, some wearing seals of an unknown bearing, and that monies made her late days easy and paid for the slate over her bones and Arthur's. But with no blood of my own, is it likely that blood would wed me? With no name but Pearl, would I be apt to flash his ring and bring to bed some belted earl, would I become My Lady, would I be called My Lady Pearl? Or would I, so to say, lie below nobility and sell what Hester had given away?

LOVERS OF THE UPPERMOST SEATS

FEB. 29, 1703-4
THE UNFORTIFIED HOUSE OF BENONI STEBBINS
STANDING ON THIS LOT WAS HELD BY
7 MEN BESIDES WOMEN AND CHILDREN
FOR THREE HOURS
AGAINST THE ASSAULT OF 200 SOLDIERS
AND THE WILES OF 140 INDIANS
UNDER A FRENCH OFFICER OF THE LINE
STEBBINS WAS KILLED
MARY HOYT AND ONE MAN WOUNDED
WHEN FORCED TO DRAW OFF
THE FRENCH HAD LOST THEIR LIEUTENANT
AND THE INDIANS THEIR CHIEF

The march began in snow, on the south bank of the St. Lawrence, and it wrote itself in three hundred miles of forest along the Richelieu and the Winooski to a stand of pines at Petty's Plain, and there, at the door of Deerfield, in snow it ended. Night was coming on, but no fires were made, though out across the still unwritten fields, fires could be seen inside the palisade. The panes of candled windows shone, and they that lay in the lilac drifts (Abenakis, Caughnawagas, and the French) ate the blown smoke of spitted meat. Two hours before dawn, they defaced the last white mile with their pacs.

All in the village—that is to say, all but its three Negro slaves—had lately engaged in a dispute about who sat where in church. To one of low degree, it mattered little, for his ass partook of his class, and any seat or none would have served; but to the rectal Elect, with their highborn bums, it mattered much. Voices, therefore, rose, and glass houses fell before stones. In the end, it was decreed that seating was to be by age, estate, and station, and the Seaters (Capt Wells, Lieutt Hoyt, etc.) were bidden to follow the following rules:

> *the fore seat in the front Gallery shall be equall in dignity with the 2d seat in the Body of the meeting house*
> *the fore seats in the side Gallerys shall be equall in dignity with the 4th seats in the Body*

*the 2d seat in the front Galery shall equall in dignity the 5th
seat*
    the 2d seat in the side Galerys shall equall the 6th
    the hinde seat in the side Galerys shall. . . .

How sat they when the French and the Indians came? Were they shot in the proper order, were their scalps lifted with due regard for rank and riches, or did they die anywhichway, like ordinary sons-of-bitches? No one knows, but however they went, forty-nine were sent to hell that night, where too there were seats to fight for, nigh or far from the fire.

Marched back to Canada—or toward Canada, for not all lived— were some five score captives. One who made it was Eunice Williams, seven-year-old daughter of the Deerfield preacher. Himself taken, he was long later ransomed, but Eunice the Indians would never give up, and though offered as much as a hundred pieces of eight, they said *We would as soon part with our hearts.* Nor was she eager to quit them, and loving them all, she grew to love one, and she married him and lived and died a squaw. She had no use for seats.

COTTON MATHER   *1728*

BLUES FOR A CHRISTIAN

I have committed unto my Lord Jesus Christ, the care of providing an agreeable Consort. I know that some surprising Thing will be done for me.

                                      —Cotton Mather

He got his surprise, all right: in Lydia George, the Lord provided a pair of thighs that would've worn out the Sower of Tares himself. There wasn't gism enough in hell to put her fire out; there was no end to her desire. She was cock-struck, that Mistress George, and the more the Master spent, the more he was drawn on, and in the end the pastor's horn of plenty went dry, and crying a last word, *Fructuosus!* (meaning fruitful), he died at sixty-five.

                      o

Wax-faced and one-gutted, he was, the very candle of a lad, and well into young manhood, whenever he spoke, he spluttered. Harvard took him in at twelve and at fifteen let him go, gorged with Syriack, Logick, Chaldee, Tully, and the belief that every living son-of-a-bitch was a sink of sin, lewd, profane, and idle, a stink, a drain, a sump of incest, whoredom, witchcraft, and adultery, a bugger or, if not, a buggeree. At seventeen, he preached his maiden sermon—God had sent him to lay on hands, he said—and at eighteen, he was ordained in wig and Geneva bands.

Within him now the rebel—Lust!—the civil war, the carnal must, and no prayer quelled it, no fast or vigil, no walks in the open air, and masturbation made it worse: the cure, alas, lay in the curse. Hence wife One, Abigail, who bore him nine children, the first without an anus, before dying slowly of cancer of the breast. *My health would infallibly have been destroy'd*, he wrote, *if she had recovered so far that I should have run the venture of sleeping with her.*

He got hot even as she cooled—*I thought myself arrested with an high Feavour*, he wrote—and the heat was for a woman of wit, *very aiery*, flirtsome, a swayer of skirts, a most alluring witch. Aye, witch, and to break her spell, he fell to his knees for days of prayer, fast, and mortification in divers other ways, but when he rose, there she was, *very aiery*, a sweet fume, a swirl of heady underclothes. It was hard on him, that *distressing Affayr*, but it was equally hard on his church, and as he whored, it hemmed, and he was finally forced to lower his sword.

It didn't stay lowered long. Wife Two was a sailor's widow, Hubbard by name, *honourably descended*, word had it, *and very comely*, but having come, sad to say, the comer went, taking with her stillborn twins prematurely sent. Once more bereft, the old cunt-hunter buttoned up with his right hand and wrote with his left, saying *If an impure Thought start into my Mind, I must presently reject it. . . .*

°

Present became past when the month was out, and he unbuttoned again, this time for wife Three, she of those nutcracker thighs—and lo! he had his little surprise from the Lord. *Quam deceptus!* he wrote, which is to say, How I was deceived!—and he died.

GOD IN THE HANDS OF AN ANGRY SINNER

Their foot shall slide in due time.

—Jonathan Edwards

Starting with just what I had in my pockets—
A piece of twine, a cold deck, a front tooth,
Also a bullfrog and a lickrish jawbreaker—
I thrown the world together in six days flat,
After which, being winded, I took my ease,
Took it, let's see, for six thousand years,
And never once, till I read your silly Bible,
Did it dawn on me that all you wisenheimers
Had me down as a kind of owly-eyed old coot
With crumbs and Sweet Cap smoke on my beard.
I ain't played out yet, not by a tidy step:
I'm Me Almighty, and I want some respect!
 Set, mister, and rest your hands and face.
I'll speak my mind standing-up-and-dicular.
This game leg of mine's giving me the grief,
And if I ever cocked it top of a porch-rail,
I doubt I'd be able to uncock it for a week,
Enough time to make another and better world.
Now, what's this about you laughing out loud
Spang in the middle of Doc Edward's sermon?
 It's as true as gospel, mister, maybe truer.
All the while you was doubled twice in two,
He was trying for his main holt on your soul.
 He tried too hard. I'm a bit ticklish there.
Well, laugh if you like, laugh your ass off,
But along with all the rest of the vermin—
The slugs, the bugs in bed, and the beetles,
The snails, the dunghill flies, the ticks,
The gnats, the nits and lice, the roaches,
The crabs, the mice, the worms and weevils,
The bots and bats and midges and chiggers—
You're headed for hell on a greasy street!

Easy now, mister. It's a ruinating hot day.
I'm about froze, but if you're making sweat,
It's hell you feel, and don't think it ain't:
The fire's flicking at you over the edges,
With three shifts of imps to huff and puff it,
And Old Ned in person is dreening out spit.
And me, I'm holding a sword accrost your head
Keen enough to cut water without getting wet.
    Quite a tool, mister. Quite a cutting tool.
It's the cuttingest damn tool you never seen,
And a skull don't turn it no more than a pie.
I'm good and mad, but just get me *bad* and mad,
And you'll be two men with half-enough face!
    Not so loud, mister. You'll raise the dead.
I done that before, and I can do it again.
    Well, don't do it here. I just cleaned up.
It's been so long since you had any misery
That you've got too big for your flannels.
You're all swole up like dinner in a snake,
And that head of yours is aching for a rock.
    Ain't it about time you stated your business?
I'm fresh from stringing new wire around hell,
And I seen the sorriest parcel of beggars
That Mephisto ever put through the sprouts:
There they was, all the stripes of mortal man,
Black, white, red, yella, buff, and piebald,
The wicked, the worse, and the in-between,
The hard-knot, the pucker-mouth, and the mean,
The horny and pimpled, the pimp and the pure,
The master of whoors, the mistress of madams,
The waster, the saver, and all other fools,
There they was, a dozen deep in the dismals,
And the *Woes*! I heard, the *O mes* and the *O mys*!
As they died without dying, dead but alive
To thirst, hunger, hot and cold, and pain,
It would've wrang any but the heart of a God.
So if you got anything to say for yourself
Before you get deep-fried like a cruller,
If you reckon you can stave off damnation,

With alms, or prayers, or a choice of psalms,
If you calculate you can save your bacon
By shivering and shaking and sighing *Alas!*,
Kneel, you stiffneck, and try to persuade me.
  I'm a man, and while I can work my joints,
  I aim to stand straight smack up and down,
  Licking no dust like a serpent so venomous
  That if it bit the shadow of a flying bird,
  The bird would break to flitters on the wing.
  I'm a man, mister, and I want some respect!
You're made of meat, blood, and more meat,
And with you begging to get hung on a hook,
I'll wind up splashed like a butcher's apron.
  I had an old man used to handle his hands
  Like you, for picking his nose and battery,
  But there come a day, I must've been fifteen,
  When I snotted him back and dealt out the blows.
By horsing in church and whaling on your sire,
You've gummed up two of my best commandments:
I always been partial to the 4th and the 5th,
Being a family-man and strict about Sunday,
So when it comes to going to Heaven or hell,
There won't be no such a way for you as up.
  He never doubled his fist again but to point,
  And when he pointed, it was mainly at rock,
  Because that's about all we had under fence.
  Could we of sold it, we'd been jackass rich,
  Or could we of et it, we'd be fat like you,
  But it couldn't be et, and nobody'd buy it,
  So we stayed pore as runts trying to move it.
  We moved it, yes sirree, stone after stone,
  But where we dug one up, we grown two more,
  And finally the old man flang down his pick,
  Saying, "The farm's yours, son, kit and cargo.
  Work hard, and you'll strike dirt some day.
  It's too damn tough to plow; I'm off to pray."
Praying wouldn't be a bad idea for puny *you.*
  If ever I hit dirt in that quarter-section,
  It was what the wind blew in from Timbuktu.

I didn't own enough soil to soil my nails,
And crops got wore out crawling on gravel.
I got so I was light-fingered about arable,
And I'd pilfer it by the tweak, like snuff,
And when I stomped the road, I'd load my hat,
And once in a while, to stuff a special crack,
I'd rake it in at night from my neighbor.
Thanks to my labor, and more to my thievery,
I actually fitted a crust onto that quarry
That kept my seed from dribbling to hell.
What keeps you from there is my whimsy will:
You're rocking that rocker on nothing but air.
You don't turn a hair of my head, mister,
Account of after the kind of life I've led,
There ain't a thing in the world can feaze me,
Not you, Jesus, fe-fi-fo-fum, or the grave.
In my day, I bore up under enough sour swink
To of wore Job down to a stink and a wail.
I got up in the dark and in dark laid down,
And between both darks, I catered to stones,
But I fail to recall the right sort of rain.
There's a man is falling a tree up the pike,
And I have to fix it so's he cracks his back,
Also I got four-five strokes to sow around,
And I know a kid just right for the fits. . . .
The kind of God I had, it was all or none,
It was drought or drown-you-out, none or all,
It was the plain and fancy plagues of old,
The blood rivers, the boils and the blains,
The hail and the locusts, the firstborn dead,
Ants that'd put away a cartwheel overnight,
Rats that fattened on sublimate of mercury,
And along with all those three-ring trials,
What about the covets for ox, wife, and ass,
What about getting rubbed by stray cats,
What about a clap after chapters in the grass?
If you've run out of rant, let me tell you
I just honed such a blade onto this sword
That you won't know you been cut in twain

Till you leave and pass yourself coming back,
So you might as well let out a bellow or two,
Just to get the swing of things in hell,
And you. . . .Why you taking your shirt off?
　　Say mister *once, mister!*
And rolling the sleeves of your underwear. . . ,
　　Say mister *once, mister!*
And spitting on your calluses. . . .
　　Say mister, *mister!*
I'm your Maker, and I want some respect!
　　Give you to three, mister. One. . . .
You wouldn't beat on a sick All Holy, now.
　　Two. . . .
I got a God of my own, and He'd be sore.
　　Three!
Well, if it'll make you feel better—mister.
　　Watch out for the steps. Your foot might slide.

GEORGE WASHINGTON　　　　　　　　　　　　1745

KING GEORGE

1st. Every Action done in Company, ought to be with Some
Sign of Respect, to those that are Present.
　　　　　　　　　　—Washington's *Rules of Civility*

He set them down in his copybook when he was thirteen years old,
coining some on his own but cribbing for the most from the French.
They came to a hundred and ten in all, his rules, and they were
ungramatickal many and quite a few mispeled.

2d. When in Company, put not your Hands to any part of the
Body, not usually discovered.

Which is to say, no gent at table will evict his teeth, nay, nor bare his
feet and pick their candy.

3d. Show nothing to your Friend that may affright him.

Keep mum your dreams, your aims, your sums and calculations, hide them, wear your heart not on but in your sleeve, feign a mind cold to *decolleté* and little boys' behinds.

5th. If you Cough, Sneeze, Sigh, or Yawn, do it not Loud.

Thus, belch you softly, and soft the sound of your sparkling guts, nor hiccup hard or hack up aught but soft-shell clams.

13th. If you See any Filth or thick Spittle put your foot dexteriously upon it.

Or, if your foot be small, your tricorne hat, or, that failing, fall delftly down and lap it up.

15th. Keep your nails clean and short.

To this end, that if pretty shows, none will seek the hidden sore.

23d. When you see a Crime punished, you may be inwardly Pleased; but always shew Pity to the Suffering Offender.

Let him see wet tears or, where tears have dried, salt; hide your passion for his pain and let him go without knowing you came.

29th. When you meet with one of Greater Quality than Yourself, Stop and give way for him to Pass.

Uncover, bend your neck, and make you small, sirrah, stand aside and yield the wall. You'll know his excellence, since he, knowing your baseness, will do none of the things you do for him.

32d. To one that is your equal, you are to give the chief Place in your Lodging.

Give him your seat at the head of the board, give him your bed with your wife in it (the choice meat, the best wine), but if he be less than equal, make him more so, make him eat at the door and drink at the trough, make him sleep downwind and a long way off.

35th. Let your Discourse with Men of Business be Short and Comprehensive.

Of all the riff and all the raff, least is he that buys and sells, wherefore not for him the "fine flowerets" of *politesse*. Stay less than a pace apart, if you will, spray his face with plosive p's, and quill your teeth, if you so please. Save banter for his betters, speak in lower-case letters, few and to the point, jew the man down, wave him away.

51st. Wear not your Cloths foul, and take heed that you approach not to any Uncleaness.

Lie not nor dine with swine and try to consort with the rich that bathe, touch naught but with glove or whiplash, and among the lowly close your eyes and hold your nose.

71st. Gaze not at the marks or blemishes of Others and ask not how they came.

Seeing one with a lesion on the lip, the tip of the tongue, or the tip of anything else, the man of quality will not lean toward it, peering and pointing, nor will he pick it, lick it, or flick it with his stick, nor will he mock, sneer, or feel superior. "My dear," he will say quite simply, "I think you have the pox."

90th. Being Set at meat Scratch not neither Spit Cough or blow your Nose except there's a Necessity for it. . . .

&c, &c, &c.

GENERAL EDWARD BRADDOCK   1755

WHAT WILL THE DUKE SAY?

The General, having been inform'd that you exprest some desire to make the Campaigne, has order'd me to acquaint you that he will be very glad of your Company. . . .
                                      —Capt. Orme to Col. Washington

The Monongahela fell to low water at that time of year—July, it was —and Braddock's two-mile train took it on foot, getting wet in the crossing only as high as the knees. There were thirteen hundred men, give or take a dozen, about half of them Lobsters and half in Colonial fringe, and when their van of six Light Horse ran into Pontiac's Ottawas and a hundred-odd French under Beaujeu, their rear was still at the ford. There was no ambush: the British fired first.

An early volley laid Beaujeu dead, and some of his Indians took French leave. Those that stayed, though, had scalps to show for it, for the British had been found in column, the right way for a walk in the woods but the wrong way to fight there. The road that six hundred axes had made for them was only twelve feet wide, and in that aisle four hundred and fifty men died in two hours.

"Is it possible?" Braddock said through blood from his lung, where a bullet had struck it rich. "Is it possible?" he said from the arms of Orme. "Who would have thought it?" he said to no man named—to Orme, it may have been, or to himself, or to someone soon forgot, or even to the red and buckskin rout that fled over his feet and sash. Orme cried out for bearers, offering, when none would stop, sixty guineas per head—five years' pay! "We shall know better another time," Braddock said, but the time, if it came, was in another world.

He was buried in that twelve-foot road, and for fear the Indians would scalp his corpse, the broken army was marched over it, and it was lost for seventy years. When found, finally, it was bones wearing the insignia of a Major-General. The high-ranked relics were taken a little way off, and four hemlocks were planted to mark the grave.

The battlefield, the long gash in the woods, has been marked by other things: by coke-smoke, more ash than air, by black ballast, by a forest of ties under track, by oil-slicks flowing like spiral rainbows, by dead dogs in the mud of Turtle Creek, by the carcass of a car.

"What will the Duke say?" General Braddock said.

SOCIETY OF FRIENDS   *1759*

GADFLY

Ah, you pretend compassion for me. . . .
                                                    —Benjamin Lay

Something must've kicked his mother: he was born with a crimp in his chest and a quirk behind, and his head was overgreat, unchristianly so, a waterhead, it seemed to be, and his legs were little walking-sticks, hardly more than the bones of legs, and they rared him only four-foot-seven from the floor. To match his ill-made body, he had a bunched-up mind, the kind that went with sortilege, hidden tits, the laying on of eyes. Even among the Friends, his one true friend was Sarah, the hunchbacked Mrs. Lay.

Rum, he was, and from the word go—a peewee farmer first, a peewee glover next, and then a sailor he chose to be, and he barely level with the rail! But when he spoke, he spake, that one, and before he was through with the sea, the Mediterranean knew him from the Straits to Scanderoon. By then, he was a Quaker, all fifty-five inches of him and nary a one of them meek. If you kicked his little ass, he'd kick your big one back: he never turned the other cheek.

When he showed up in Barbados, he was a merchant, and though no one knows what he bought and sold, he stuck his beak in Barbadian business: he fed slaves on Sunday and harangued their masters the rest of the week. The blacks were amused by the minikin man, no few stooping to rub his buckled back and make a wish. The whites he quite stopped short of entertaining, and if they took thirteen years to tire of his tirades, they did so all at once, and he went.

He and his Sarah took ship for Philadelphia, where a cave became their home, and from that time forward, freedom for the slave was his life. *I have often felt a motion of love*, John Woolman would write one day, but the wrung little Lay felt it before Woolman was ever born—the dwarf glover, the old salt, the seller and buyer of wares, he felt a motion of love while Woolman was still scrivening bills of sale for Sambos, and he felt it until he died.

It troubled him that Quakers held with servitude, that the Children of Light should dwell in the dark. He didn't care a sprat for hat-honor and the God he was supposed to contain, he didn't care about *being* as superior to *doing*, about plain dress, convincements, and spewing fewer words into the overburdened air—but he cared much about black sweat in the bread he ate and black blood on his meat, and to end the evil, he fasted forty days, like Christ. He nearly ended himself, wherefore he tried on other ways.

He refused flesh now, because slaves dressed it, and he found his food on trees or growing in the ground, and he wore garments of tow (wool being animal), and he refrained from cutting his hair. At times, he went barefoot to Meeting, where, trying to give testimony against Quaker slavers, he'd be flung out into the road, and then he'd lie there, saying he wasn't free to rise, no freer than a slave. And once he came with a book and a sword, and stabbing the one with the other, he drew blood from a hidden bladder, crying, *In the sight of God, you are as guilty as if you stabbed your slaves!* And once he posed with a naked leg in the snow, and to those who passed, he said, *Ah, you pretend compassion for me, but you do not feel for the slaves.* The slaves, the slaves, with him it was always the slaves!

Sarah, pious and loyal gnome, didn't live to see the Quakers disown slavery, but her husband did, the queer little being, the troll, the crank, the soul that stood on stilts, and when he joined her at eighty-two, he may have told her the news. They lie in pint-sized graves, the Lays, side by twisted side.

GEORGE WASHINGTON   1774

FIRST GENT OF VIRGINIA

13th . . . . *Killd Hogs*
—Washington's diary

He was a landed man, a squire, ranking one step down from a knight and a full flight higher than a mister. He ordered his coach from overseas (*a light gilding round the panels, a lining of lively colored leather*), his special blend of snuff, his kegs of scented powder, and his playing-cards, a dozen dozen decks at a time. By sail as well came his Rhone and Rhenish wines, the almonds he loved so much, and certain bespoken busts to touch his house with art—a Charles XII of Sweden, a Prince Eugene, a marble King of Prussia.

He *drank no smoke*, in the going phrase, but of whatever else flowed, he took glass for glass, plus a pint of cream on the way to bed. He had a craze for chance-play, for the sock and buskin, and for the science, as he called it, of the dance. He was a cocking-main cove and a crack cavalier (*the best horseman of his age*, Jefferson said), and always owing, he was always being driven by the duns. He had cash but rarely; he was known as slow pay.

He rode to hounds that he bred himself—*the bitch Mopsey brought eight puppies and the bitch Musick five*, he wrote, *and Dutchess was lined by Drunkard twice.* He shot at all that flew or ran, mallard and bald-face, fox, raccoon, and deer, and, neck or noth-

ing, he pursued other game too, namely the flashtail, and many a
flipped skirt showed him the upright grin. Two sluts picked his pock-
et once—while he swam in the Rappahannock, he said, but the
britches could've been down without being off. He lied now and
then. After all, he never heard the cherry-tree story.

He sued only when it was hot, cold, or lukewarm, and he was sued
straight back—the Dinwiddie feud didn't die till Dinwiddie did. He
was plagued by neighbors, poached on and stolen from, and passed
over and stung, and, worst, the weather hated him more than most,
but being one that manners seemed made for, he let it all go with
Good Gods and God Damns. He stood six-three, but he grew a foot
when offended, wherefore few were free with his given name, two or
three at most, and of those no woman, not even his wife.

He was a plunger in land (*a tract to please me must be rich*), he
raffled for buckles, for necklaces, for a carriage, he dined out and
dined in, and for trading horses on a Sunday, he was cited and mildly
fined. He leaned to lewd ditties, he stood voters to drink in despite of
the law, and he lost more at loo than he made. He scrupled not to
deal in convict labor, and in the year before Lexington, he paid his
tax on 135 slaves. He was never well. Smallpox mooned his face, and
the quartan fever shook his bones; he had carbuncles, ulcers, the life-
time trots, and pain in passing piss; and, toothless early, at the last he
was deaf in part and partly blind. *I have never been a day well*, he
said, *nor a day without company.*

He married money (the widow Custis brought him fifteen thou-
sand acres, a hundred thousand dollars, and 150 slaves: *I had to have
a manager for my estate*, she said), but his best friend's wife was the
wife he loved till he died.

RUNAWAY SLAVE   1775

THE MAN IN THE BLACK COAT

How does he look? What's on his mind?

If he had a name, none remembers it, wherefore call him Cato,
after every second buck, or make it Mingo, or Puck, or Jubilee, if the
fancy favors rich, or Barzillai, which means *made of iron*, or Simple
Simon, or London, or leap time and try on Abe. And now that the
son-a-bitch is known, a monikered ape in britches, the name of his
owner may be thought into shape, Stribling, say, or Dabney, or

Slaughter, or Pepperrell (double-spell the p-r-l!), or Moncure, Ruffin Byrd, or—good God and God damn!—why not First Gent George? '

Has he got the shakes, the sweats?

This Cato, this Quico, Quaco, or Sidon, he was Old Dominion as much as any white, and yet he didn't even own his own pair of balls. He was a sack of black skin, and all within it—bones, liver, lights, eyes, blood and other sap, the crows he'd eaten, and God, in there too and holding his nose—all thirteen stone of such crap belonged to a man on a porch, several steps up from the world. One night, though, the nigger greased, and the man spoke down to hounds and string-tie trash, saying, "Fetch me the fellow."

Is he thirsty, lonely, afraid of the dark?

He heard the first tantara of pack and horn from the far side of the Chickahominy. Day was time under ban, and roads ran one way only —back. A print in the dust, and the jig was up, and up too if there was fire or the ash of fire, if rinds or cores or fins were found, if a sound was heard in a silence, if standing water stirred. But no count was kept of frogs or berries or slugs in the punk of fallen trees, and no nectaries would speak of stolen sweet and no grass of eaten grass, and none would know of frost drunk or of one egg lost from a nest among the reeds.

Does he dwell on home, kin, familiar things?

Each dawn, he went to earth, or, better, went to water, and all day he sat upper-lip-deep in cattail, where fish eyed him and spiders tied his ears. Birds at first were wary of the dead-still head, but they soon grew game, and some of them came to probe his hair. The York was passed, and the Rappahannock, and fork and fall that are nameless yet, all in the night and many in the rain, and then he was on the Chesapeake, a week away from the man on the porch.

Is he cold within, does a cold wind blow?

He made the Severn on black steam, eating oats out of droppings and lice from his rags, and he crossed the Gunpowder on bark and beetles and the Bush on air and last year's leaves, and when he swam the Susquehanna, he yearned like a swimming dog. Now stubble was his fare, seeds too, and tares, and once a dove that he took by hand, and now he came to a wide water, strongly salt, and on the sand he breathed allspice on a tide of wind from another world.

Does he hone for warmth, hunger for titsy?

It was Jersey, and there were cherries in the bogs, and he ate them, and in the Toms, he used his feet as bait for crabs, and he ate those and their shells as well, and he ate Manasquan clams, sea-pickled jet-

sam, kelp, stranded fish, and, from stagnant pools, pistache slime—
and he made, one night, the Hudson palisade.

How does he look? What's on his mind?

His flight now entered its final third, to the River Charles, but
shall more rain fall and be measured, more crawl on New England as
names, the Housatonic, the Thames, or shall it only be said there was
no mile where his skin could dry, his hair rewind? And shall his feed
be more vermin and we determine its breed and condition, or shall it
be left thus, that there was no meal when hunger, the lingering
illness, was stilled?

*Is he short of wind, does he sport a yellow streak, does he
whimper for his torn clothes, his corn-shuck bed, his life on his
knucks, like a chimp—or is he brave enough not to call it quits
for a pan of grits and gravy?*

Let him hear voices in an early-morning mist, and let them speak
of some unchristened black, an undipped coon who'd run away, and
let a wind blow and him see faces, those of friends. And let them be
armed, and let them have a gun to spare, and powder, and let them
share flints and lead, let them give him bread to eat, let them bind
his broken mungo feet, let them let him rest and, resting, tell his
story, and then let the wind show more, the Lobsters on their way
uphill, and after some say about the white of the eye, let him kill or
die there, on the top of that hill.

How does he look now? What's on his mind?

ONE OF THE DAUGHTERS   1775

D.A.R.

*On taking command of the army at Cambridge, Washington
found it necessary to remove certain officers as undesirable.
One such, a Captain, was drummed out of camp for wearing
the garb of a woman.*°

Was the frock unbecoming, was it a slack fit, or was it simply *passé*?
Was an armpit crocked or a fichu frayed, were there too many slashes
in the sleeves and waist? Was the cap soiled, were the skirts torn or

---

°cf *Triumph of Freedom* by John C. Miller, p. 68

the ribbons greasy, was more lace worn than the rank allowed? Was an arm discovered, or a nipple's field, did body-clothes show, did hose yield to skin at the knees?

Whence came the Captain, and what was his name? Did he hail from Salem, a cold-pissing gent, or was he a backwoods draper with a taste for his goods? What did him in? Was it some tiffany hood, some pall or pelerine, some new way of doing the hair? What made him try a bow once, or beads, or a paper flower, what was the power of gaud and galloon?

Where did he wear his sword, outside or out of sight, and how did he carry cash? Did he ride astride, did he squat or stand, did he shave or favor shag? What was his quirk, and with whom was he queer, the ranks or the braid? And one for the last: what happened to the bastard when the drums no longer rolled?

THE DECLARATION   *1776*

REBELLION OF THE WELL-FED

> . . . *our lives, our fortunes, and our sacred honor.*
> —Declaration of Independence

There were fifty-six signers, all of them Gents: fourteen lawyers (among them a part-time moneylender), thirteen jurists (one a musician, *a writer of airy and dainty songs*), eleven merchants (i.e. smugglers), eight farmers (two being Tidewater rubes by the name of Lee), four physicians, a pair of soldiers, an ironmonger, a publisher, a politician, and the President of Princeton.

The Mob did not sign. The sailmakers, the cartwrights and the glassblowers, the grooms, the tapsters, the drovers and draymen—none such signed. The barbers, the fiddlers, the Wandering Jews, the horse-copers, the hatters and glovers, and those that stomped the high road with or without their scarlet letters—none of these signed, none made a mark. Only Gents wrote their John Hancocks, not cheap Jacks, not swabs or sweeps or keepers of an ordinary, not joiners or tinkers or catchers of rats at a penny a pound. That kind had lives, of course, but no fortunes, and therefore no sacred honor. The nobodies thus were missing—the mercer, the chandler, the hanger-on, the muff. To the City of Brotherly Love, no rough fellow, no greenhorn went, none but the Gent.

GEORGE WASHINGTON   *1776*

THE BOYS IN BUFF AND BLUE

By Ribbon to distinguish myself . . . 3s.4d.
                            —Washington's Account Book

And what did the boys wear—cocked hats and silk rosettes? Did they sport crossed baldrics, regimental facings, and epaulettes? Were their sleeves flapped and their coats frogged, were they stocked and gaitered dandies? Did their buttons blaze, were their clayed cuffs ghastly, and by sprig or chevron was their grade made known at a glance. . . ?

Good God and God damn, he never saw two of them alike! Their butts were buff, maybe, and their balls blue, but there all sameness ended. They wore what they had, rags, or what they could steal, stolen rags, and some, the thinner-blooded thieves, stuffed the rents with straw. The Commander-in-Chief flashed an azure sash (3s.4d), and his staff flaunted pink, but the mob looked like scarecrows on the run.

They ran well that year. They ran from Long Island, leaving behind a thousand-odd Toms and Dicks and a mixed bag of cockaded swells, three of them generals. They ran from Kip's Bay and Throg's Neck, they ran from Pell's Point, Harlem Heights, and White Plains, and then, fleeing Fort Lee, where they saved two twelve-pounders and lost their train, they fled the width of Jersey. West of the Delaware, with nothing else to run from, they ran from themselves, and no pleas could stop them, nor could bounties, threats, the flat of a sword, or the lash. They ran: when lead flew, so did they.

We shall be obliged to detach one half the army to bring back the other, the C.-in-C. said.

It must've been the worse half that stayed. They were swiggers, mostly, swilling whatever was wet, and being far from home, a randy few would've screwed a snake. They were dicers and braggarts and ghouls as well, and none went to hell in a true pair of shoes. They were a froward set, these citizens, and lest they seem less than equal, they scorned to salute. They were slovens in the line and fickle on picket, many taking pay to work for hire. Where they passed, there no bird, no fish or game (and commonly not even vermin) would remain: they slew air, water, earth, and all that grew green. With cartridges scarce—at one count, they were down to nine rounds a man—the no-fight cocks shot at crows and rocks and frozen cattail, but let them sight the enemy, and either their powder got damp or their pants.

But if the rank and file came two for a cent, their officers were high at a continental. They plucked the men like picaroons, cribbing their pay and shorting their rations, and come a slack day, they'd skin civilians, an Ensign being caught sacking a house of beds, bread, linen, china, and children's boots. That kind too took its dram, and as often as not they took it in battle, to stiffen their backs, to block their bowels. They sold medicines out of army stores, they wrote sick-leave papers at sixpence each, and they turned other pennies with shears and razor and by squeezing boils and pulling teeth. The men held them cheap, and now and then a wagoner or a sergeant would knock one down, piss in his face, and call it macaroni. That would cost the soldier 300 lashes, *well washed with salt water after his last fifty*, but there was someone at the whipping-post every second day.

With such, poltroons all, the C.-in-C. had to cross McConkey's Ferry on Christmas night and try to bag Rall and his Hessians. Once over, they had nine white miles to Trenton, but the boozing snake-fucking bastards made it, and even as the legend goes, they left bloody tracks in the snow. They lost four men to wounds (none died), but of the fancy-Dan Dutchmen, some nine hundred never saw home. Among the dead was Colonel Rall (Washington spelled it *Rohl*), and though they buried him there at Trenton, his grave was never found.

Fifty thousand pounds should not induce me again to undergo what I have done, the C.-in-C. said.

BYSTANDER IN PHILADELPHIA

If the delegates had been polled on the matter, all fifty-five might've told of having crossed his path that summer, some possibly more than once. They'd come upon him at the *George* and the *Queen*, they'd say, and in the city streets, and out where the city ended and the pave gave way to trees. He'd been seen on the wharves and in rum company, Indians, ebons, Hollandaises, and some that were ferrying to Camden had spotted him ferrying back. He'd stepped aside for Mr. Franklin's portable chair, he'd stopped to stare at merchandise, faces, fashion, and perhaps Mr. Pinckney (the Cotesworth Pinckney, say) had noted this, that when he passed the gaol, the rogues inside forgot to beg. They'd spied him at book-stalls and fairs, on the stairs that led to Mr. Peale's museum, on his legs with a glass, and sitting down at meals. The wreaths they brought to the Forge withered in the heat with his, those that went to church found him a goer too, and when they fished for perch in the Schuylkill, he was on hand to land his share. He was chanced on everywhere, the man, and the delegates, each supposing him beknown to someone else, were civil enough to nod on occasion, to raise a hat and give him the wall, but all through those three summer months, no one broke bread with him, no one heard him speak or spoke, and no one knew his name.

Had an inquiry been made, it would've shown him to be nobody in particular, an ordinary fellow from a line of his like, the modest product of medium factors, with a present that was only mass and a past that was only time. He was a set of quantities assembled by pairs now dead and himself headed for death's dispersion. He'd come from nowhere, and he'd soon return, but for this one season, though hardly aware of it, he sauntered through history, brushing its sleeve, breathing its air.

I found the Convention at Philadelphia very busy and very secret, wrote Richard Henry Lee.

At the State House doors, sentries turned the world away. No difficulties were made for Mr. Washington, of course, or for Mr. Madison, or for any of the fifty-odd others sent there to frame a more perfect Union: they came and went at will. But no one else entered the Great Hall that summer unless to spruce it when a session rose—and by then the words of the day had settled, and they were lost in a dust of ash and snuff and drift from powdered hair.

Very secret wrote Mr. Lee of the work that went on, but more so the work that was done in the mind. There the caged birds were, the words that no one uttered, those that would've revealed an intent to win from the people what the people had just won with sanguinary edemas and gangrene, with an eye or two, ears that froze and fell off, new holes in the nose, and four squits an hour that were due to the flux. *Very secret*, the birds that flew in five-and-fifty heads, and in the end there *was* a more perfect Union—for the rich. The poor didn't even get to keep their cheapened continentals or their warrants for pay and land. *Very secret*, the way they lost Paradise to the gents in the very room where a paper had been signed saying *When in the Course of human Events.* . . .

What of that fellow who'd cropped up all summer long, the sightseer, the passerby, the Doe, the Roe, the nobody in particular—did he go back to where he came from, wherever that was, or was he still in Philadelphia, at the *Black Horse* or the *City Tavern*, consorting with Nigers and Delawares, or reading Seven Articles posted on a wall? The delegates never knew. He'd been observed once by most, twice by a few, and after a while his image seemed to run, to blend with its frame, and it became hard to tell him from the man on his left and the one on his right.

FEDERALISM   1787

THE PEOPLE: A GREAT BEAST

Our real disease . . . is democracy.
—Alexander Hamilton

He was a misbeget on the isle of Nevis, in the British West Indies. His mother, Rachel Fawcett, or, in the Huguenot style, Faucette, had been the wife for a while of John Lavien, a Dane and possibly (Lavine? Levine?) a Jew. But whatever his breed, she'd fled his bed to grow him horns with a slow-pay Scot from St. Kitts doing business under the name of James Hamilton. The more benign called him a merchant and the less so a monger, but all agreed on this, that he couldn't swap nor could he sell. He proved them right by going broke, and then he proved something else, God knows what, by going further, God knows where if not to hell. By then, it was said, he too wore horns (ah, that Rachel!), and some made the sign when they spoke of the man. The son never doubted his well-born sire, though, and his lifelong bent was toward that welching Scotchman, by some odd filial calculation a gent. *My blood*, he insisted, *is as good as that of those who plume themselves upon their ancestry.*

Scarcely ten when his mother died, he became a charge on her family, and by the time he reached fifteen, his mind had grown beyond his age. Thus, from a great gulfing storm that spun up out of the Caribbean, he drew a contumelious moral that he aired to one and all. In his noted Hurricane Letter, he wrote of rains that tasted of salt, of perpetual lightning and the whiff of gunpowder on the wind, of a world going to smash, cosmic didoes with which he taunted man the creeper, crying *Where now, oh! vile worm, is all thy boasted fortitude and resolution?* The epistolet made his fortune.

It was shown to a certain Hugh Knox—teacher, physician, apothecary, presbyter—and he rose to it, all four parts of him. A purse was gotten up, and the young quill was sent to the American colonies, where he went to King's College until the British got mauled on Bunker's Hill. He volunteered for the Rebel army, and on being commissioned captain of artillery, he raised a company of cannoneers that fought shy of the Lobsters from the East River all the way to the Schuylkill. There he was brought to the eye of the Commander-in-Chief, who invited him to serve as an aide-de-camp. A two-grade jump accompanied the job.

He stayed on the staff for four years, but he did not come to care for the Great Man, his hugger-mugger moniker for the general. Neither for delicacy nor good temper was Mr. W. renowned, he confided to Philip Schuyler, *wherefore I have felt no friendship for him and have professed none.* Schuyler, latest in a line of patroons and kinsman of the Van Cortlandts and the Rensselaers, was himself a ranking officer, in command of all northern New York. He commanded it in a deeper sense: he owned it. His fief of fifty thousand acres lay along the west bank of the Hudson, and his summer cottage sat on a two-mile lawn. Still, he was pleased for some reason, honored even, when the skipjack sought his daughter's hand. He may have read that letter disdaining man: *Where now, oh! vile worm. . . ?*

Upward he went, the son of the fourth son of the Laird of Cam-
buskeith, and the upper he rose, the downer he got on the demos—
ambitious, he called them, vindictive and rapacious all. They'd been
pert enough at their anvils, bladders of gall, and winning the war had
made them more so. Low-bloods, they were, and he felt a cold finger
in his navel when he remembered the lashings they'd gotten, their
rations of high horse and higher herring, the swamps of shit the
wounded had putrefied in—and now, oh God, the beggars were com-
ing to town, and the beggars were going to vote!

To him, they were more the foe than the British had been. He'd
had no bone to pick with the British: they were his own, with tier
upon tier of class and a Crown to frown on change. His very model,
was England, where one ended as one began, rider or ridden, but
here, in these thirteen villainous shires, with the Crown gone and the
tiers tumbling, the bottom would soon be the top. It became the
work of his life to buckle the saddle back on the Beast, and knowing
that force and faith would fail, he pushed for no fourth George, no
second Jesus. The trick, if possible at all, had to be done with words,
the old ones in a new arrangement, and they'd be written so: *We the
People.* . . .

He suffered, John Adams said, from a superabundance of secre-
tions which he could not find whores enough to draw off. There was
one secretion, though, that the whores never tapped—ink—and he
wrote with it in spates, falls, tides of persuasion, he wrote as Pacifi-
cus, Camillus, Catullus, as Publius, Caesar, Phocion, Scourge, and
being a far cry now from that bounty-fed bastard on a Leeward isle,
he wrote as the son-in-law of fifty thousand acres and a grange with a
two-mile lawn.

He wrote well, for more clearly than most he could penetrate time
and sense the coming event. He knew, therefore, that monad man
was about to end, to lose his soul and become a hand, one of many
and all the same, a pea from a world-wide pod, usable, dispensable,
disposable, replaceable. That day was on the way—he could feel it,
the horsepower in the still unprinted dollar, the still unissued share,
he could dwell on a Pittsburgh that was still Fort Pitt and smell the
smoke of fires not yet lit. *We the People*, the new creed would begin,
and he'd know the high pleasure of signing its Seven Articles only
seven names down from Mr. Washington.

He'd never see the real fire, though, never sniff the real smoke, for
not always would he be blessed with luck on the west bank of the

Hudson. Near the village of Weehawken, there was a bench, or step, in the almost straight-up face of the Palisade, and at that place early one morning in the year 1804, he'd be shot through the liver by the Vice President of the United States (elected under Article II of the new religion), and the wound would kill him on the following day.

RIP VAN WINKLE   *1788*

IN THE KAATSKILLS

Even to this day they never hear a thunder-storm of a summer afternoon, but they say Hendrick Hudson and his crew are at their game of nine-pins.

—Washington Irving

It would've been better not to wake. It would've been better to sleep on, dead, deep in that glen where the Kaaterskill rose, and the bitterns hid, and the watersnake sunned when the sun was overhead. It would've been better there, where none came but the queer conjured crew of the *Half Moon*, and they but for a day of nine-pin thunder every twenty years. It would've been better to stay, to lie forever between two wales of dust, one a bygone gun and one a keg of Hollands, without a dog, without a wife, himself dust and by all forgot.

He wasted time well once. He built fences for others and let his own stock stray. He fished in the rain and fowled in the shine, and though weeds grew and slates fell, time went by on a one-way tide. He flew kites for children and told them tales of witches, ghosts, and the Iroquois, and their lurchers knew him and suffered him to pass. He ran errands for the village wives, never wondering who odd-jobbed for him, and holding it better to starve on a penny than live on a pound, he laughed at those who wound their watches.

Now some new do-nothing flies the kites and spreads the fictions, and some new pack trails him on his back-door rounds. There are new wives and new errands now, and new hounds drowse while time ticks by. Even the old Rip is new. Gone the free favors and the love of child and beast, gone the squanderer, sowing the hours where they yield the least. He has learned to think, and to all who'll listen, he sells his story for a drink of gin. He kills no time now: he's like the many, and time is killing him.

BENJAMIN FRANKLIN

OLD MAN ON A $100 BILL

There is no little enemy.
—Poor Richard
Hunger never saw bad bread.
—Poor Richard
He that drinks fast pays slow.
—Poor Richard
A fat kitchen, a lean will.
—Poor Richard
A used key is always bright.
—Poor Richard
Men and melons are hard to know.
—Poor Richard

He was too long left in the oven, Ben was, and when he first saw dawn or dark between his mother's thighs that day or night in 1706, he was fat, scrofulous, well-hung, and wearing glasses—and he seemed much the same, they say, when he died at eighty-and-some of stone, though he used at the end two pair of specs at a time. The main change was the change of date: it was 1790.

Old at birth, he kept on aging, and therefore it was no hobblede-hoy that blew in off the Delaware for those three-penny rolls to eat on the go up Market and then south along Fourth. It was a riper sort, in a suit of say or serge and sporting a crabtree stick, and if he had a thick look in the middle, it wasn't the middle of his head. That short walk took in the century.

at Fourth and Chestnut

A kite flew a nil wind in his mind, and in flight too were plans for a lightning-rod, a new kind of stove, and a lens to serve both near and far. His wife-to-be sat in some window he passed, its sixteen panes rippling him, flowing him even then toward France. Heard within his head, a little lyric tinkled like chink—*nothing but money is sweeter than honey*—but he'd known it, in rhyme and rhymeless, before he was dry. (He never did toy with coin, not at any age, and never did he chance it, buff it, shy it across a creek, or stuff it between a cheek and a gum-boil. It was seed, he'd found, and sown to good soil, it was bound to grow.)

on the way to Walnut

He thought of a teaching to be taught a dozen years hence—*write with the learned, pronounce with the vulgar*—he devised a flexible catheter, and he was kissed by Voltaire.

going east on Walnut

He brushed the skirt he'd flip to beget his bastard, and he heard, from the fringe of hearing, his armonica being played by Antoinette.

and making for Third

He squidded the world with ink: screeds to homespun gash and upper-crust slash, songs to drink to, and pieces on perfumes, Indian corn, and the art of having pleasant dreams; journals, prefaces, speeches, elegies, and an epitaph (his own); reflections on courtship and marriage, advice on the choice of a mistress—*below the girdle, it is impossible of two women to know an old one from a young one*—and a note on the cure of smoky flues; remarks, homilies, queries and inquiries, and a treatise on how to get rich; a set of rules for a life of virtue and a disquisition on catching cold.

and nearing Second

His bastard had a bastard and the last a bastard too, he perfected an instrument for taking books from high shelves, and Mme. Brillon, who sat on his lap in public, let him return the favor in her bath.

at Front and Walnut

He attended the coronation of George III, Tom Paine sent him the first copy of *Common Sense*, and he fancied a shop for himself wherein, along with books, he sold soap, slates, pounce, sack, powdered mustard, quills, compasses and quadrants, mackerel, spermaceti, saffron, ballads, and slaves—*a likely wench*, he thought, *about fifteen.*

and reaching the Wharf

He lived it all, and living ended, and twenty thousand came to see him put under ground at Christ Church. The French decreed mourning for him. His own country did not.

GEORGE WASHINGTON   *1793*

A CONSTITUTIONAL IN PHILADELPHIA

*In speaking to men of Quality do not lean or Look them full in
the Face, Nor approach too near them.*
                                        Washington, *Rules of Civility*

To see him in those days, you didn't have to climb a tree or pry apart
a crowd; you'd simply laze around at Front and High, and come
noon (he was the punctual kind), he'd show up to regulate his watch
at Clark's standard, after which he'd nod, once up and once down,
and walk his presence away. He liked the sun, they say, and when
out for air, he'd keep to the warmer side of the road, making the pace
for that tag-along pair—a bodyguard, one was, and the other Mr.
Lear, an all-purpose sort, clerk, candleholder, sander of signatures,
purse-string, less than kin and more than minion.

They stayed a step or two behind their man, and they'd do nothing
if you overtook him or, having gone on by, stopped to scan his lines:
you were free to look, every day if you liked and twice on the 4th of
July. He'd raise his hat now and then, to a face he knew, to a cap or
ribbons in some upper window, and even, if you behaved, to you, but
try to shake his hand, and you'd be there yet, a block of ice some-
where on High: he could stare you stiff without opening his eyes.
The lurchers of this world—he knew how to deal with that stripe.
Martha called him *Pappa* (good God, what if someone heard!), but to
the populace he was *General*, and you bowed when occasion allowed
you the use of the word.

It wasn't the worst, it was two of the best that he couldn't curb—
the first was that West Indian bastard, that pack-saddle child, a hard-
headed little beggar, a flint, and the second, and direr, that turncoat
squire, a sage, an *illuminé*, a sniffer of books. They'd craze him with
that feud of theirs, they'd put him in his grave! He'd listen while
each attacked the other (how much could he bear!), and he'd read
the vile gazettes they backed (a scandal, those scurrile rags!), and late
or soon, in trying to divide his favor, he'd tear himself in half.

And so out along High he'd go, drawn by his mind toward the
Schuylkill and the Forge. It was fifteen years back, that bad winter,
but the cold was stunning still, the hunger untold, the chances of

winning nil. All the same, they *had* won, and now what! The gentle-
man crying up the myriads, and the upstart the few! A landed lord,
Jefferson, a phrasewright, a violinist, a skirtraiser debonair, a Mister,
he'd been born to be, and a Jacobin he ended, a votary of faction,
egalité, and the guillotine, an overturner, renegade and odious, an in-
cendiary puck. And against him the foreign-born Hamilton, bred in
any kind of bed, a clever one with a cool and ready tongue, more
genteel than gentle, an untarred Tory, kiss-ass of Kings and puller of
strings for the rich. They'd be his death, that yoke of opposites!

You didn't have to smell or spy him out. Almost on the dot of
twelve, he'd come along High, and at Clark's standard, he'd take out
his watch and wind it. He wasn't hard to find. You only had to
wait. . . .

BENITO CERENO   *1799*

A VISITOR FROM THE *BACHELOR'S DELIGHT*

*Captain Delano, now with the scales dropped from his eyes,
saw the negroes, not in misrule, not in tumult, not as if fran-
tically concerned for Don Benito, but with mask torn away,
flourishing hatchets and knives, in ferocious piratical revolt.*
—Herman Melville

When Delano climbed the gangway and boarded the *San Dominick*,
he stood on the deck of a blackbirder. He'd seen that kind before,
though, and therefore he didn't stare on finding slaves at sea: they
were merely goods being taken to market, like pekoe in the tea-trade.
Nor did it awaken wonder that Don Benito, a fine-spun sort, seemed
drawn a shade too spare, or that, while rich in dress and language, he
was less cordial than custom called for: he was Master there, and he
might wine a guest or hang him, as he chose. It was quite fitting also
that he should be attended by that half-naked little nigger of his,
rather like a struck dog in the way love and *please* ascended from his
face. Nor was it odd that his fellows went about free of chains: they
must've learned from Death that none could walk, none swim back to
Ashanti. On the *San Dominick*, all was in order—black at work and
white at ease.

The scales never did drop from Delano's eyes: he stayed in the dark the livelong day of his life. He saw nothing on the slaver to sigh for—a bit more bark in its Master, maybe, and maybe a bit more bite, but the list ended there. Nor did he note queerness in the queer farewell at the rail, nor while waving to his late host from the whale-boat, and to the little black dog at heel. He was still benighted when Don Benito jumped his own ship, when three white sailors followed suit, when the hatchets began to fly, and simians jigged on the cabin roof. He was dead to all but the blacks' revolt, which he read as wrong deposing right: there could be no such thing as a whitebirder.

His mind fumbled with the notion, though—downeasters might be had for ivory one day, and Quakers bought with spice. . . ! Beating off the three clinging sailors, Delano's oarsmen rowed him back to the *Bachelor's Delight*, and there he had the guns run out, and the jigs' jig was up. The black pirates, those that lived, were carried to Lima, altitude 512 ft., and hanged a few yards higher to give them a better view of Peru.

ABRAHAM LINCOLN   *1809*

THE KENTUCKY ABRAHAM

He was born on a farm near Nolin Creek, he said, a lay of land known as Sinking Spring, or Cave Spring, as some called it, after a flow that came from a limestone rift. It was there, he said, that on a certain day. . . . But nothing was certain, not the day, the place, or the name. The past was blank time as black as space, and for all he could surely say, there was no cold sink in the rocks, or none he ever drank from, no chinked cabin, no farm he knew by any designation. He knew, if it was knowing, only what the dead had told him, and gone with them was his beginning.

He must've wondered off and on whether he hadn't begun with himself. There was no long continuation that led to him, no tether paying him out of yesterday's night. He was loose here in a small locale of light, a luminescence, it was, an emission, and he'd glow for a while and go out, and at the end, it may have seemed to him more of the void, as before he came.

In his lifetime, he never went back to Hardin County, never re-viewed the road he'd come from Sinking Spring, or Cave Spring (or

Rock Spring, as some few had it), but if he ever rose again, if his bones ever walked, he'd've found a cabin there, the very one he'd been born in, or so it'd be sworn to, and the grain of the wood, the knots, the nicks, the tallow-stain, all would've invited the recall of a single room, smoked and cured and candle-lit and a hundred years gone.

It was well he stayed away, for he'd not have remembered. There were paved paths instead of trodden grass, there were gardens where the corn-stubble stood, and the cabin no longer wore in the open air, in snow and sun and rain. It was a relic in a shrine; it was sixty steps up from the earth, behind festoons of chain. He'd not have known where he was when he saw the temple—Greek, was it, with that pillared porch?—nor could he have made his way unaided to the spring (Sinking? Cave? Rock?), and when at its rim, he stepped in someone's stool, he'd've been saddened by the living hatred and glad he died when he did.

THOMAS PAINE   *1809*

THE BONES OF A PAMPHLETEER

inflated to the Eyes

His ship, the *London Packet*, was sixty-three days raising Cape May, but long before that he was down with the putrid fever, and he had to be carried ashore. He must've been scribbling as he went, though, because in no time at all, as Atlanticus, or Aesop, or Vox Populi, he was addling our wits with words. Why did we suffer his rant, and why, when we saw the side he took, did we fail to cook his goose? We were none of his greasy business.

He was English, not exactly a foreigner, like some God damn Swede or Turk, but foreign enough in the whiggery he managed to work with his reed. We'd done a bit of leveling on our own, of course, with token bones for bottom dogs, but nothing to take the top dogs off—and then along came this nobody that none had sent for. He'd been a staymaker, we were told, and he'd sailed with a certain Captain Mendez aboard a privateer, and as an exciseman for the Crown at fifty pounds a year, he'd gauged the weight and worth of merchandise and tallied pipes of wine. He was a nobody, from a long

line of less, the sort due to be buried in an only coat and short a pair
of pennies for his eyes; his grave would wear till it wore away, and,
dead, he'd be a button or two and a minim of something that once
would've bled.

We let him stay, and he wrote his head off—and it was touch and
go whether he'd do as much for ours. We managed to keep them, but
he cost us the Scepter, and now, for want of a king, we have to rule
by seeming to be ruled. But what will happen when we run out of
bones. . . ?

and big with a Litter of Revolution°

He was a drunkard, we claimed, and brandy his drink, and the
stink he gave off would empty a room. He had the Scotch fiddle, by
which we meant the itch, he was awkward, rude, slovenly, and slow-
come, a slob, in brief, yet oddly vain, and though his style was coarse
and his grammar bad, his pen was for sale, and well it sold. He was a
little mad, a fellow-lodger said, and the thief who stole his bones
called him base. He was blue-balled with a love-disease, but so far as
one wife knew, he did no more with his member than draw it when
he pissed.

They're dispersed over England now, those ghouled bones of his,
they're lost, those that weren't tossed to dogs, they're gone, the ones
that weren't gnawed, forgotten, or flung away: somewhere a skull's
aquill with matches, and somewhere else phalanges are strung to jig
in the wind, and ribs, like fallen vaulting, lie haphazard on some
floor, but they bear no name, the relic ruins, and none can say they
once were Paine.

JAMES MONROE   *1823*

A LICENSE TO STEAL

At year's end, Mr. Monroe went before the Congress and proclaimed
his doctrine, the short-and-sweet of which was this: that the two con-
tinents of the new world, having cast off their bondage to the old,
were now and would always be free. A salvo of words, it was, a dare

---

°Gouverneur Morris writing of Tom Paine.

composed of air, but in his fancy, he seemed to deliver it from the Beaks above a plain of togas with their twain of purple streaks, and to his mind, it was so much more than sound that he could almost see it wind among the colonnades and pound the horse of Constantine. *Nay!* cried he to princes of chancred empires (to rustic lawyers, really, to heelers, smell-feasts, tailors, even, and, as low as the least, scum skimmed up from trade). *Nay!*—and in the vale at the foot of the Palatine, he saw the thunder he'd made roll away.

A good Virginian, Mr. Monroe was merely showing public respect for the Washingtons of Latin-America—Bolivar, San Martin, Sucre, Bernardo O'Higgins, greasers whose deeds were such that, but for a touch of tar, they might've gone far in any county on the James. You simply couldn't come right out and call them niggers or fetch them with a bell. They had names, the spics did, and not much smell when they stood downwind.

We could not view any interposition for the purpose of oppressing them—words, thought Mr. Monroe, fat round words, and a mouthful turned to pebbles that he spat at columns and stone and evergreen leaves. His palms itched for Paraguay, he could clearly taste Peru. . . .

THOMAS JEFFERSON   *1826*

NOTES FOR A SPEECH ON THE 4th OF JULY

Is it the 4th?
                                                        —T. Jefferson, last words

Say this to start with, that you never knew what made him run, the kind of juice, if juice he ran on, the trend of heart, the dint that spun his mind. And then say this, that to the eye, he stood foursquare with the rest of his breed: he was a hole-hunter with the best of whoresmen, he was one of many as a Latinist, a squanderer, a wine-swiller, a slayer of meat, a slave-driver, a collector of *virtu*, and a weigher of meat and manure.

Say that his mother was a Randolph, with blood that began when the world did—*raffiné*, it was, pure, clear, blue, a fluid sapphire—

and say that his father's was a more indigent humor, red, crude, and new from Wales. Mention the classic rules that shaped his wits, sigh when you name his school (sweet William, say, and Mary), quote the palindromes he wrote in Greek, praise his tongue for French, and stand adaze at its knack with Saxon.

Refer to books as his daily bread, head the list with the Boling-brokes, the Cokes and Paines, cite Locke, Vattel, and Burlamaqui, and these as well if you can say them right, Tully, Rapin-Thoyras, and Gassendi. Propound his love for the gloom of Ossian and prove it by the place he ticked for a tomb: he spelled the oaks of a lonely vale where the moon felled from a temple a shadow like a ruin.

Commend him on his flair for music, Bach, Purcell, and Pergolesi, and tell of a fire for the violin that made him the biggest buyer of gut in Virginia. And say this, that he was well-domained, a palsgrave, a palatine with many vassals, two-hundred-and-some, a rough guess put it, of whom Jupiter was his favorite buck and Sally his *filly de chambre*.

A gent, call him, or, in view of his low-test father, a half-gent, but give him a whole alphabet of caprices:

a) He was ardent for mimes and masques, for freak shows, puppets, strolling players.

b) He collected moose, mammoth, and caribou bones.

c) He sought to know where an opossum's pouch went when the creature was barren.

d) He studied the natural history of Diptera, among these the wheat-midge.

e) He hacked a chip from Shakespeare's chair.

f) He was a student of sign-language.

g) He gave inoculations for smallpox.

h) He let his pet mockingbird fly free—Dick, its name was, and he fed it from his lips.

i) He bought a macaroni machine.

j) He bought other things, thermometers, protractors, perspective-glasses, a solar microscope, a botanical microscope, a telescope, an air-pump, a theodolite, a set of Piranesi's drawings of the Pantheon, a clock weighted with cannonballs, and, for only forty-five shillings, a panther-skin.

k) And he bought these too, a manual orrery, an equatorial, and a planetarium, he bought pictures by Drouais and Van der Werf, he bought busts in plaster and busts in marble, he bought lamps, books, maps, music, walking-sticks, spurs, whips, bell-pulls, seeds, a harp-sichord with a celestini apparatus, carriages, odometers, and forty-four chairs encrusted with gold leaf.

l) He devised a bed that was slung on pulleys, so that it could be hoisted out of sight by day and lowered at night.

m) He geared an outdoor weathervane to another inside the house.

n) As names for new states of the Union, he proposed Cher-sonesus, Assenisipia, Metropotamia, Polypotamia, and Pelisipia.

o) He was a dandy in public and a sloven at home.

p) He invented the swivel-chair (confirm).

q) Of the new phosphorus match, which would sear to the bone, he advised that piss alone could put it out.

r) He believed in abortion and the use of contraceptives.

s) He had a sweet tooth for other men's wives and a sweeter one for the one in the song: *Of all the damsels on the green/ On moun-tain, or in valley/ A lass so luscious ne'er was seen/ As Monticellian Sally.*

t) He established a nail-mill, where his slaves turned out a ton a day.

u) He once drew a sketch of an Archimedes screw (why?).

v) He installed a dumbwaiter in his *salle à manger.*

w) He loved, of all lines in nature, the serpentine.

x) He stocked his cellar with wines so fine—Meursault, Margaux, Montrachet—that even the Federalists came to drink them.

y) He designed the Capitol at Richmond, say, but forget that he pinched it from the Maison Carrée.

z) He was so beguiled by measurements—areas, distances, prices, speed, yields—that in the end they supplanted what they measured, and he was left with numerals that numbered nothing.

Cast him up thus far and say he's in the daily run, a wildwood squire, one who'd live and die leaping something, a hedge too high, a wench too wide, say he's a country swell, a local nibs, a buyer of slaves and a seller too, a maker of nails, a Thomas who doubted even the Doubting Thomas, a book-wise man, an inkhorn, a middling sort of fiddler, a bird for the triangular bush, a liar on occasion, and a debtor dunned by mortgagees.

Ask why, then, he stands in city halls and small-town squares, why his face is seen on classroom walls, and he's evergreen in the names of places. Ask why they trot him out in themes and sermons, why he stares from stamps, cash, coins, and colophons, why a phrase of his will outlive its frieze. Was there more to the man than gentry ease, and did it spoil the next spasm, the next cork, the next spell of frittered time, was there a *devoir* owed, a call he thought he heard, and if so, did he know his last fifty years would be rowed upstream?

Say what it was that ten thousand acres of Virginia failed to satisfy, and two hundred slaves among whom Sally, and his nailery, and the sinuations of Monticello, France and its fancy gash, terms in high office, power, honors, dry wine, the violin, the winning ways of books —or are you still in the dark, still benighted about the light that lit his mind? Can't you see it with your other senses, that sun inside him, can't you feel the illumination, can't you breathe it in with air, admit it through your skin, and if you still don't understand, can't you even guess at grandeur?

Try. Sum up again the things he did, the things he owned, call him philosophe, land-gambler, overspender, buyer of anything, sawgut, scribbler, maker of jigamarees, dabbler, stargazer, lawyer, nail-monger, statesman, saver of bones, black-slaver, screwer of blacks, pursuer of happiness with his neighbors' wives—and then try, try to guess why for all his *things*, *things* were never the end of all. Try, and remember he died on the day you were born: the 4th of July.

SLAVERY   *1830*

THE PECULIAR INSTITUTION

The whole place was strewed with mutilation.
                                            —Aunt Cheney Cross, a slave

When a nigger get whimful, Master give him a pass and send him out in the road for the patrollers to catch. Pass say, "Beat hell out of this nigger and obleege."

God is a nice God.

Overseer say, "My name Big Jack Bible, and I got a tongue is four foot long with a buckle on it. Work hard, or you hear the buckle-end."

God is a momentary God.

Ham with sweet cream gravy is what they has for breakfast, and poach eggs, and grits, and they has biscuits, and honey, and batter-cakes, and surrup. That what they has.

I believe in superstition.

We shine their shoes till it crack our eyes.

I stolen a peach, and Mistress give me a straight lick with a crooked stick.

I ain't never seen no good times.

They whip us for running away, and they whip us for coming back, and all the worst if they sent the dogs.

They whip us for lying.

They whip us for lazing when we suppose to be shooing flies.

They whip us for not dropping corn in the checks.

They whip us for their meanness.

We work from sunup to sundown, and when some ole man die out there in the hot, Master make us tie a rope on his feets and drag him off.

We work from see to can't see.

When we get sick, they medicine us with the blue mass pill and the bitter apple, and we outside all night long.

I ain't never seen no good times.

If Master hear us praying, he get raging mad and tear up truck. We got to put our heads in a pot to pray.

When we get married, they tell us to jump over a broom, and that make us married.

Summertime, my work is wash Mistress all over in cole water.

Master say we just mules, and if we good mules, we get along all right.

I never seen nothing but work.

Master say the only time we be free is when he put us free with his shotgun.

When a nigger die, Master don't give us time to bury him deep, so the air soon stink, and the buzzards come around.

Master say we get whipped if we do a bad thing, and when we go and do it, we get what we been hearing about.

It's all work and half-fed.

I ain't never seen no good times.

Mistress whip us till we blister, and then she whip to bust the blisters.

Horns for this and bells for that—we live and die by bells and horns.

When I pray, I pray for shoes that fit my feets.

The dogs pull a ole nigger-woman out of a tree and et her tits off. She ain't got a sign of tits no more.

They allowance out such stingy meat my bones creep like dry leaves.

I'm a ole woman, and enduring my life, I guess I got skunt out of everything.

I belong to a Baptist preacher what he live in a rottendy house, and he just as sonabitchen as any other man.

I ain't never seen no good times.

Master is my pappy, but that don't stop him switching my naked ass.

I pray special for fresh meat.

Master never allow a overseer to throw a nigger-gal down and hike up her skirt to whip her. He do it himself.

We get whipped bad if they catch us with a paper of writing in our hand.

Niggers that belong to the Creeks has a easier time than us.

Master like to ride down to the quarters and count up how many little niggers does he have.

I suck so many of his children it stunt my growth.

Fourth of July is nigger-day.

Master hang me by the hands from the limb of a tree, and he spraddle my legs around the trunk and tie my feets together, and then he whip me till I judge I'm dead. After that, I'm ruint for babies.

The patrollers come once to whip a nigger-gal, but she drown herself sooner.

Niggers live in a one-room cabin with a nice dirt floor. Everything happen in that cabin—born, eat, sick, marry, die.

I know about a man what he would sell a slave and then steal him back to sell again. When he done that a lot of times, he taken the slave out and shoot him. Dead nigger don't tell no tales, he say.

Master is so fetched ignomous mean even the white folks stay away.

Mistress whip me with a cat what she has a lead chunk tied on it.

Once a week, my mammy has to go and stay in Master's bed.

I fall asleep while I seamstering, and Mistress waken me up with my needle.

Us niggers is all colors of black on up to white.

Master make me wear a bell and clapper till I twenty-one years of old.

Mistress mean enough to throw you in the middle of a spell of sickness.

Whites been free all their lives.

They catch a kitchen-nigger with meat under her dress, so they give her a thimble and say she got to fill a water-barrel by cockcrow.

A stud-nigger runned away, and when they got him back, Master say he must have two hundred licks. After he swang a hundred, it look like there ain't no place left to hit, but he give the full count. Next day, man runned away again.

Master say we can buy ourself free for only twelve hundred dollar.

Mistress is the real nigger-killer.

Master even beaten her once, when he find she fiddling around.

There was a lots of runawayers.

Mistress is too mean to die. The Lord don't want her, and the Devil is ascared of her.

Master beat on a nigger once, and the nigger pray to God to stop it, but He didn't. Then the nigger pray to Master, and he stop. "You was praying to the wrong man," Master say.

When Mistress took to whipping, she didn't know what stop was.

I ain't never seen no good times.

Mistress taken me by the ears and butt my head against the wall.

I want to be free as a frog, account a frog has the freedom to jump off a log when it please.

Master peel me naked and whip me till the blood flew, and the flies come to blow me.

I seen a ghost one night, and the ghost say, "Revengeance!"

I ain't never seen no good times. (°)

°For the material used in this section, the author is indebted to *Lay My Burden Down* (B. A. Botkin, ed.), a folk history of slavery based on the Slave Narrative Collection of the Federal Writers' Project.

THE ALAMO   *1836*

GONE TO TEXAS

To colonists who would accept the wafer and swear allegiance
to Mexico, land was offered at 4¢ an acre. Gone to Texas, they
wrote in the snow, and they went. . . .

Santa Anna went too, with fifty-five hundred dragoons and foot,
eighteen hundred pack-mules, and a daylong supply-train of oxcarts,
barrows, drags, and wains. A second force followed, the monte-men
and the sutlers, and behind these a third, the *soldaderas*, who cooked
and whored for the rest. A fourth army—*zopilotes* with a wingspread
of sixty inches—dressed all in black, a fourth army flew.

They went all kinds. Lawyers, farmers, clerks, merchants, a
great b'ar hunter, a farrier, a house-painter, a man named for a
knife (or a knife for a man), a cobbler, a Baptist preacher, a sur-
geon, a hatter, a poet, a jockey—they scrawled G. T. T. on
doors and walls and went. . . .

There were thirty-three wagons in the column. One of them car-
ried Santa Anna's fighting cocks and his private cockmaster. Another
held his necessaries of the field: a tea service, a chest of mono-
grammed china, a silver chamberpot, a marquee fitted with a bed
and an escritoire, and a sword that cost seven thousand dollars. Still
another was laden with his medals and insignia, his braided fore-and-
afts, and his uniforms, their tunics bulletproofed by frogging and
their epaulettes so stiff with sterling that when melted down they
made sets of spoons.

Under its pile of prairie grass, Texas seemed to flow in the
wind, to fly, a carpet of earth that would grow all things. . . .

He was born in Jalapa, famous before for the horse-purge root, and
he made it even more so. Some say that he spent his youth studying
Caesar's *Commentaries*, but others name simpler subjects, among
them rape, seduction, and treason, and they cite this in proof, that
once he was sentenced to lose a hand for theft (the right hand, was it,
or the left?). It was disputed as well that as a Lieutenant in the Army
of Mexico, he forged his Commandant's signature (an X) to a draft
for three hundred pesos, and it's either fact or false that he served
both Government and rebellion on the same day and was raised a
grade by each.

*On the running streams of grass, there were dahlias, primroses,
and violets, flower rafts, and from brimful basswoods, honey
fell. . . .*

They tell of him that wooing while in wine, he won the wrong
sister, and they tell too that on his way to the altar, he said, "It's all
the same to me." And when one day his wife lay dying, he ordered a
procession of priests and friars, and they burned six thousand candles
past her bed in vain—and she was hardly hard before he was, for a
fifteen-year-old girl. He enjoyed women as he enjoyed blood: they
were "the gravy of society," he said. He acknowledged five bastards.

*There were yams as big as a suckling pig and cane so high it
delayed the sunrise. There were grapes the size of apples, and
half a dozen cherries made a twelve-inch pie. The word was
that deer grazed three deep in that paradise, that doves flew
into open stoves and fought each other to light the fire—ah,
God, what would not that place provide! G. T. T., the drifters
cried, and they went there. . . .*

Napoleonito, they called him, but there was nothing diminutive
about his funk under fire and his spunk when safe. A spaniel at lick-
ing spit, he became President of the Mexican Republic eleven times,
five of his terms lasting less than a month. The assassins' assassin, he
was, and the ranking liar in any congress of liars, and when the
French blew his leg off (the left, was it, or the right?), he had it
buried with ruffles and flourishes and a suitable number of guns.

*They forgot, when they got there, that they were now Mex-
icans, and they forgot their vow to believe that the body and
blood of Christ were in the transubstantial bread and wine.
Worse, they forgot to pay their taxes, and when reminded, they
declared Texas to be free, and they showed it was so by plant-
ing cotton and bringing in slaves. . . .*

Santa Anna took a long walk to show them otherwise. It was a
march of eight hundred miles from the City of Mexico to Bexar, but
(men, packs, game-cocks, communal women, vultures, silver cham-
berpot, and all) he made it in ninety days. He found the fire-eaters
within the walls of San Antonio de Valero, a mission long abandoned
and now a fort named, after the cottonwood tree, the *Alamo*. They
watched him come, a rash two hundred, give or take a few—a
rhymer, a shoer, a jock, a great b'ar hunter, they watched a pin-
cushion of steel coming, and they saw wings draw black rings on the

sky. He called on them to surrender, but knowing him, they knew better and stayed under cover. After that, he parleyed with his guns.

The cannonade stopped at sunset on the twelfth day, and for the first time since the siege began, Bexar was quiet, and so too the llanos *roundabout and all Texas. They remained quiet only until dawn, when massed trumpeters played the* Deguello, *the fire-and-death call. . . .*

Of the two hundred in the *Alamo*, all but fourteen were shot dead or died on the bayonet, and because it was said to be Texan, the Mexicans even shot a stray cat. For Napoleonito, the bugles never blew. He lived to be eighty before trysting with his missing leg.

A MEXICAN SHEPHERD   *1836*

UNDER A LONE STAR

In a hollow on the plain of St. Hyacinth, a shepherd knelt before a swamp-grass fire, and looking up at faces like paper lanterns against the evening sky, he said *Me no Alamo! Me no Alamo!*

All day he had heard the sound of guns. It had come up over the savanna with the dawn and with black smoke, and the sun had seemed to be going down in the morning, and all day the guns had spoken and darkened the prairie air. And then it was dusk, and still the shepherd could hear the carbines talking across the ravines and bayous of the San Jacinto, and a wind came with the smell of blood, and the ewes were restless, and to quiet them the shepherd ran the risk of a fire. A small one, it was, hardly more than a hat would span, and flaring up, it died quickly down, but it brought the faces, the paper lanterns, and they glowed.

One of them said *Remember the Alamo, you greaser son-of-a-bitch!* and the shepherd was afraid, and he said *Me no Alamo! Me no Alamo!* but they shot him.

SAMUEL COLT   *1836*

NEW AND USEFUL

To all whom it may concern: Be it known that I, SAMUEL
COLT, have invented a new and useful improvement in Fire-
Arms. . . .

—Letters Patent

And then came page after page of specifications involving ratchets,
wards, arbors, shackles, and there were sheets of drawings showing
the gun as a whole, the gun's components, and the pieces contained
in the parts, and while much was shown that wasn't new, the arm
would kill five times in twenty seconds, which, if you were after
blood, might well be called useful. In the score-and-some years be-
fore Sam himself fell (to gout, they say), he turned out many a Pater-
son along the Passaic, and, in Whitneyville, many a Walker and
Dragoon. They repose on velvet now, those that remain, some en-
chased, some with stocks from the Charter Oak, and some quite
plain. Is there one of these, you wonder as you stare, that no man
ever fired save at the moon, or a knot in a plank, or a coin as it spun
through the air, is there one, inlaid with ivory, overlaid with gold, or
simply bare blue iron, that was never fired at all?

ELIJAH P. LOVEJOY   *1837*

A ROUND TRIP TO ALTON

Nobody cared a pinch of water for the man, neither the Pukes of Mis-
souri nor the Suckers of Illinois. He was a Presbyterian minister, that
Elijah P. Lovejoy, and it was common opinion he should've kept his
bill in the Book. Instead, he stuck it into other people's business—
slavery, for instance—and that didn't go down in St. Louis, where
slavery was, or across the river in Alton, where it wasn't. Nobody
liked him on either side of the stream, and the abolition he put in
that paper of his, the *Observer*, was liked even less, and one fine day
a bunch of people tore his press out of the floor and distributed his
type in the Mississippi. He didn't learn a thing from that, so when he

set up a second press, the same or similar people pitched it off of a bluff and into the channel for him. It's a plain historical fact that the fool went and bought himself a third press, and, by God and Christ, that one got a drowning too. He must've been dense or else deef to reason, because when his fourth press came, the only switch he made was to ferry it over to the east bank, and there, from some warehouse in Alton, he kept right on with his abolitioning. The people, a great big bunch this time, well, they just naturally went a-ferrying too, and when they caught up with that crazy-ike preacher, you know what they done? They killed him.

MARGARET FULLER   *1845*

THE BLUESTOCKING

I understand more and more of the character of the tribes.
                                                    —Margaret Fuller

Rising six, she could render Latin at sight, the Gallic and Civil Wars, Virgil, Horace, the *Metamorphoses*, and in its cadences, in its power and precision, she'd hold forth on bread, God, and J. Q. Adams as though no one had told her the language was dead. And in damsel days, her fare was Cervantes for his pratfall chivalry and Molière for the pungent lunges of his wit, and the Bard, of course, she·had by heart before she knew the curse. At Mr. Perkins' school, she rose at five and studied Greek and when free composed epistles that disposed of Milton, Epictetus, and Racine. She paid for such attainments with dreams of spectres, great faces coming toward her, staring worlds, they seemed to be, and there were trees that bled and raring horses, and she'd scream herself awake, or, still enwound with sleep, she'd roam the halls and moan till someone found her.

All who knew her called her plain. She had light hair, they say, and much of it, and in that day of snags and disencumbered gums, her teeth were reckoned fine. Her prize feature was her eyes, bright, large, long-lashed, and often slitted, and they could almost be seen in the act of seeing, as if they almost flashed. Her talk was deemed the best of the age, far-faring, many-tongued, and spangled, but nothing —talk, teeth, or eyes—made the world unmindful: she was plain.

She had to settle for spiritual *deliciae*, and at thirty-five she was still kissing and coupling in the unsprung bed of the soul. What rare ones, though, she shared it with! Sages, some were, and scholars, and divines, and one who proved what not at Walden, and there were movers, shakers, cloud-compellers, and many who merely thought out loud. For thirty-five years, she was a fruitful brain unlearned in love, a fallow know-it-all (or all things but one), and then she flew too near the sun and burned.

He was a Jew, her sun, a blue-eyed German, fluent, shrewd, a commission merchant, a buyer of something in the morning and a seller of something in the afternoon, a man of common sense, he was, unmoved by her uncommon mind, a common man. Nathan was his name, and he came from Holstein. Whatever she may have bestowed on him, a few mittened fingers or the whole naked works, she kept little out of her letters to him, and she wrote in such close symbols as *the first painful turnings of the key.* She must've alarmed him, either with her words or her thirty-five unlocked years: he withdrew, her Jew, he set, her sun.

When asked to return the letters (fellow! knave! shitepoke!), he put a price on them, whereupon she whose door had turned *on its golden hinge* made a note on the character of the *tribes.* Forgotten the rhythms of Ovid, the simple sequences of Caesar, forgotten the high mind, the immaterial life, the littleness of things—and because a beggarly Jew had bargained for a beggarly few per cent, the twelve tribes of Israel stood, condemned. *I understand more and more*, she claimed, but for all her store of learning, there was no blue in her blood, only in her stockings and her nose.

ANDREW JACKSON   *1845*

OH, LORD! OLD MASSA'S DEAD!

In some states, there are remote precincts where people still vote for Andrew Jackson.

—popular belief

He was born, so the story goes, on a patent held by a George McKemey of the Waxhaws (or Warsaw) settlement near the boundary between the two Carolinas, but whether the house stood north or south of the line, no one seems to have known. Some surveyor might've found a ciphered stone, or some notary, or even McKemey himself, but any such was long dead when the fact mattered, wherefore it can only be said that the place of birth was in either state or, if the room lay just so, in both. As to his place of death, there are those that say it was *The Hermitage*, his home once and now a red star hard by Route 70 on a map of Tennessee. During certain hours of the morning and afternoon, the very bed can be seen within a rope wrapped in velveteen, and at its head a sign insists that his age at the end was eight-and-seventy years.

He would've been a bad bet to last that long. The way he drank, whored, fired up, and plumed around the Natchez Trace, he might well have cast his first vote in hell. Or, having got by Mike Fink, Sam Mason, and the Harpes, he could've died in the duel with Waightstill Avery over a side of bacon, or with the Dickinson fellow, who drilled him, or with the Benton brothers, who drilled him twice, or when he called out John Sevier (Nolichucky Jack) for blacking the name of his wife. He was odds-on, quite early in life, to wind up face-down in a puddle of mud.

He could've been killed by Tories under Tarleton, or by the small-pox he caught in a prison-camp, or by that drunk dragoon of children's stories (where else did he get the scar?)—he was fourteen then, and he could've been fourteen yet. And when he took after the Creeks to square the Fort Mims massacre, things had no brighter look—not with his arm in a sling from the Benton shoot, not with the trots making him lighter a pound at a time, not pointing an empty rifle at ranks stiff with mutiny. In the woods at Talladega, it rained Indians, and the same rain fell at Emuckfaw and the Horseshoe Bend (*The carnage was dreadfull*, he wrote. *The peninsular was strewed with the slain.*), but he didn't die at any of those places.

His time would come on another field, at Mobile, say, or when he fought for the waterway to New Orleans: Pakenham, with nine thousand men and naval guns dragged seventy miles upstream from the ships, Pakenham would do him in. He wasn't hard to find—sashed, cock-hatted, and ablaze with braid and epaulettes, he could be shot at day or night—but he was God damn hard to hit. As it turned out, Pakenham was hit, and they sent him home in a pipe of rum.

When cannon missed and pistol failed, life became the death he'd die of. He'd be carried off by the pleurisy of the Creek campaign (dyspnoea and a dry and coffin cough), or by the ball that was nine-teen years in his arm. His teeth would be drawn by snoose and chaw, and their juice, when mixed with Monongahela, would sear his liver, lights, and brain. The sight in his right-side eye would fade, his hearing would wane and his memory with it, and a dose might start his finish sooner. The Matchless Sanative would keep him alive (or so he'd think, for he thought it sovereign), and he'd drink it for his hemorrhage on the steamer *Vicksburg* and the edema that swole him up like a toad. Aye, for *Sharp Knife*, as the Chickasaws called him, the end of life was on the way.

There was some delay, though, because he lived to live in the White House. That became the ambush then, and in some hall would the footpad lie—not Big or Little Harpe of the Wilderness Road, but Death the knight of every road. He was past sixty when Marshall swore him in, and if he'd been lying down, they'd've buried him instead. All that wring-jaw and apple-jack, all that plug tobacco, all the ills and anger, the acorns eaten for lack of rations—they showed, and so did grief for the loss of his wife.

If he was dead, though, he didn't know it: he took more killing than a snake. Calhoun thought he had him cut up into the thirteen original chunks, but the tail still rattled and the head still struck. Nor was he crushed under the skirts of Peggy Eaton (*She is chaste as a virgin!* he cried of a chamberpot that her husband wore as a hat.). Nor did the Devil take him, meaning Old Nick Biddle, nor the infernal machine of Biddle's bank. He lived through dinners where the courses outnumbered the guests, and he drew a chance in a million when a lunatic's derringers misfired twice. There were wards on every flight of stairs, there was a thief for every landing and another for every door, and a bas-relief of seekers sought his favors from the walls, there were old soldiers, old neighbors, old friends, and new and old slave-drivers with their eyes on Texas—but having lived to live in that house, he lived to leave it.

His second term over, he went back to *The Hermitage* with ninety dollars in his pocket, and if he'd died the same week, he'd've come out even. But he stayed longer, and the duns made a din that his wife must've heard in her garden grave. He still wouldn't die, though, not then, nor when the house burned down and, to build again, he borrowed more, nor did it kill him that notes signed by his son fell due, or that his picked man Van got beat by Tippecanoe, and he survived kin, crony, broodmare, and many of his servants (which is what he called his slaves)—and at seventy-eight, he was down to being pure pain adrown in dropsy.

On a June day in 1845, a funeral was held that thousands came from far away to see, and they saw, before their journey home, two graves in the garden. About one of these, some always wondered, and in remote precincts. . . .

THE DONNER PARTY   *1846*

WINTER CARNIVAL

A man is a fool who prefers poor California beef to human flesh.

—Lewis Kiesberg

That's what they say he said, and since they're all dead now, the band that set out from Independence, it becomes the fact of the matter, or as near the fact as we're apt to get. They're all gone, those that died on the way of ills and Indians, those that made the summit of the pass and froze there in the drifts, and the rest, that ate the stiffs and lived to tell the tale—they're in hell now, one and all.

Hence, when you hear that this Kies- or Keysberg dined off the livers and lights of man, take it to be so, and credit too that he helped his meals to die, and for the fifty years they prolonged his life, hate him and call it a lie that he wasn't as black as painted: he was black, all right, as black as space. But if that's true, this is truer—there was damn little white in the party by the time it got through a winter in a dozen feet of snow. By then, who had not tried a slab of ass, or the tripes, or a kidney, or a fried brain, or a tit he'd had his eye on since Missouri?

They were human, the whole witch-held party, and they were up to anything going (name a deed, and you'll find a doer), wherefore, there being no Christ in the mountains, hungry Christians wafered-and-wined it off the body and blood of their kind. There was some stink about it afterward, but only among the meat-packers.

BUCKEYE JOHNNY APPLESEED

They say he first turned up in Ohio around about 1801—on Zane's Trace, it was, along Licking Creek—and they say he come leading a pack-horse loaded to the hocks with burlap bags, but they didn't say, because they didn't know, what-all was in the bags. Being he was a black-eyed man, a queer thing in those parts, and being he kind of kept to himself, which was all the queerer, he let himself in for a little side-watching, and no matter if he did overlook to bring a gun.

They say, the ones that made it their business, that he marched out onto a cleared piece of land and drawed something out of the topmost of his bags, which he buried it in a slew of shallow holes and went away, and when he was gone, it still being their business, they say they got down on their shins and poked about for whatever he'd cached (it figured, God knows how, to be gold). Only finding dirt as deep as they dug, they tried to pass him off as addled, but all the same they felt like chumps for being hankypankied by an out-of-stater.

They say this identical black-eyed man shown up next along the Muskingum, still with that pack-animal and still with those bags, and they say that there too he made some hocus-pocus over holes in the ground, and there too nobody got richer for scratching where it itched. And now the story began to get around, to pass from hand to hand like the gold they hunted and never found, and you heard that the black-eyed man and his monkey-shines had been seen wherever there was bottom-land—on the Scioto and the Hocking, on White Woman Creek, on all the Miamis and the Maumee, on the Big Walnut and the Black Fork of the Mohican. And you heard other things as well, how he played with cubs while the b'ar looked on or snoozed, how he walked barefoot and damn near b.a. in the snow, how he found his way just by following his nose, like a bee or a bird, and you heard how he'd douse his fire if insects flew too close to the flames.

After a time, they say people took to expecting him in the spring, looking forward to his freak but quiet ways, and when he would finally arrive—with his horse and his bags, but never with a gun—they would feel good, like they did about a rain, and they would talk to him sometimes, and some would be sad as he went about his fruitless work of hiding nothing in plain view of all. They dug no more now in the loose soil after he'd moved on: they let it lay, out of respect, you might say.

Fruitless? Not by a damn sight and a long chalk! Nobody said fruitless when the apple trees came, because that's what he'd had in those burlap bags—orchards for Ohio!

It's a good thing you're dead, Johnny. It's a good thing you didn't live to see what they did to your trees. They're gone, Johnny, the trees and all that grew from the other seed you scattered—catnip, snakeweed, hoarhound, dog-fennel, and pennyroyal. It's a good thing you're all done coming down the pike in your coffee-sack clothes and that stew-kettle you wore for a hat—you'd've been hot, Johnny, because there's very little shade.

They say you could stick pins in your flesh and feel no pain, but you'd've flinched for your trees if you'd seen them brought to their knees. They took fifteen years to grow and fifteen minutes to whack down, and even the axe was held to be slow—only one would fall at a time—and so the speed-crazy fell to using fire, and whole districks went to hell in a handbasket. It's a good thing you're someplace else now, Johnny, a good thing you're never coming back to a world held together by concrete and lashed down with steel rail and copper wire, a spoiled world.

They say you died up around Fort Wayne, and while they don't say where you went from there, a lot of us have a fair idea. We don't know the name of the state, Johnny—let's just say it hasn't been admitted to the Union yet—but whatever it's called, it must be pleasant up there under trees that'll never be snags or sawyers in some spring flood. Trees must grow better when they know they'll not be harmed: their fruit must be prime.

Are you running short of seed, Johnny? We could each bring a bag when we come. . . .

RALPH A. BLAKELOCK   *1847*

A DREAMER PERISHES

In the beginning the end, wherefore he must've been born with signs on the palm of his hand, islands on the lines, rings, mounts, a *via lascivia* to give the kind and cast of his mind, a crossing of creases to

betoken his first and last illness—his life. It must've been known, that
history-to-come, it must've shown on his plain of Mars that he'd bear
seventy-some years of pain and die.

From a queer father, this queer son—shy, tight-spun, a ten o'clock
scholar, a lover of olive-green and lonely places, a visioner, a sleep-
walker, a negative in a positive world, and as for his pictures, he'd *be*
his pictures, he'd be the shaded side of his trees, dappled by his
filigreed suns and moons, he'd be faint little rills, fainter wraiths,
he'd be paint in part and part painter. In time, it'd be only night that
he drew, and sylvan figures dressed in white, fauna, really, as seen
from afar, and no wind would preen the leaves, and even the streams
would seem to have paused, as if he'd invaded a dream and made it
stop.

It must've been there at the start, that his scenes would be hard to
sell. Some palmar arch, some flexion-fold of skin must've told how
he'd hawk them from door to door, a canvasser of canvases, how he'd
trade them for a meal, for a marriage service, display them in junk-
shop windows, deal for them in lots, thirty-three once for a hundred
dollars flat, and if that was written, this was too, his madness, and
how the sane would see him in freak clothes snacked with snickets of
trash, how he'd wear a dagger in a beaded sash and tear up blood-
won money, burn it, strew it in the streets.

In the beginning the end: twenty years in an asylum, a wall out-
side his wall. There'd be no more trees embroidered on the sky, no
more jabots of running water, no more rounds with rolls of landscape,
and gone the vivid turbans and tassels of defeat—the end, twenty
years of peering into himself, a dim and simple room. He'd be paint-
ing money then, million-dollar bills, and he'd be giving them away:
he'd be rich.

JOHN QUINCY ADAMS   *1848*

LAST OF THE SUPERBAS

My thoughts are running after birds' eggs, play, and trifles.
                                              —J. Q. Adams, age 9

They never called his kind again. They wanted thicker skin and thin-
ner qualms, and when he was gone, they got them—from porters and
surveyors, from storekeepers and buckeye doctors, from smiths and

preachers and log-cabineers, truepennies all but gents only in the *Gents Only* sense. He knew Dutch, French, Russian, Italian, German, and Greek, and he daily construed a page of Latin; they knew their own language, though for some it was spoken slowly and, when possible, with signs. Once each year, or twice if free, he made the Grand Tour from Genesis 1.1 to *Zuzims* in the Concordance; they saved their eyes for cards and bargains.

At fourteen, he was Secretary of Legation in St. Petersburg, and at eighty-one, a stroke on the floor of the House killed him off in two days. Between that beginning and that end, he served as Minister to England, Russia, Prussia, and the Batavian Republic, and in the time he spent at home, he was Senator from Massachusetts, Secretary of State, President of the United States, member of Congress for nine terms, and Boylston Professor of Rhetoric at Harvard.

He was lean early, fat late, and sour always, and he was known to boil at body temperature. Blunt, proud, mean-mouthed, and stiff, he hated Paine and Hamilton with equal passion, and among those he called liar were Jefferson, Lafayette, and the Czar. He was slovenly, waspish, vengeful, and snotty, a disdainer even when asking for the salt. From constant reading, his eyes teared all day long and while he slept, and he wrote his right hand into a palsy that must've been the last thing living when he died.

He was ten when he heard Bunker Hill from his father's Braintree lawn and eighty for his last swim naked in the Potomac, and he was there or hard by for the high hours of his age—the fall of Moscow found him on the Nevsky Prospekt, and he lucked on Paris for The Hundred Days. He gave dull dinners and attended duller, and he made time shrink by knowing Mr. Washington and sitting in the same Congress as Abe. He had no friends.

When carried on a couch to the Speaker's Room, he had two days left to go. He read no more at dawn, no Tacitus, no *Iliad*, no Ovid (he was about to learn a deader language), but in some unexploded part of his mind, he heard guns, a final echo from Charlestown or the sounds to come from Sumter. And then he put war away to run after trifles, and then even the thought of running tired him, and he desired to do nothing for a moment, just stand still, and that was when he died.

JOHN JACOB ASTOR   *1848*

THE LANDLORD

Has Mrs. So-and-so paid that rent yet?

—last words

He came from London with seven silver flutes
And some odds and ends of pounds and pence,
And keeping the coin as far as the grave,
At some place en route he gave up the rods.
His taste was for the till, a music-machine
That he could play all day long, never tired
Of the coloratura chime of chink on other chink,
A sound he found sweet when living soured,
And hired help had to haze him in a blanket
To spook the blood in his lukewarm heart.

He died at eighty-four, a few years more
Than were due him by the terms of the Book
And twice what a Sac trapper could look for
If, wambly on *voyageur* whisky or high wine,
He balked at pelt-prices, shorts, and shoddy.
The brave was brave indeed, that or cracked,
Who backtalked a factor or spat in his face
When given a frypan for a brace of blue fox:
Such a one left early, with a ball in his eye,
And over the plains, when an east wind blew,
His blown-out brains ran west with the dust.

Nor was life long for Astor's slow-pay tenants.
They too died in traps, at about the same rate
As the game he took in figure-4 and deadfall:
They died of fevers and of more scenic fires,
Of the shade of plague all the rage that year,
They died of milk-sick, of pox and marasmus,
Of struma, stone, quinsies, and peccant humor,
Of the malady that, when its name became known,
They could've cured *now*—by killing the rich.

But the flutes, what happened to the flutes?
Did he lose them, whose only loss was life?

ALTA CALIFORNIA

That's what the Mexicans called it, Alta California, and in Alta California lived the richest man in the world. A Switzer from Basel, he was, which made him a kind of a Dutchman, and all such being as queer as cats, when he first came to Yerba Buena, he had a body-guard of Kanakas with him, a gift from the King of the Sandwich Isles. Nobody knows why the Switzerman needed them: whatever he owned was in his hat.

It wasn't long, though, before no hat but God's would've held his hereditaments. He made a hit with Governor Alvarado and came away with a parchment that granted him a piece of land twenty-two hours square up along the Sacramento. The metes and bounds being tied to the clock, he was free to mark off the four sides of his *hacienda* anywhichway he liked: he picked fast horses, and in those eighty-eight hours, he rode a few to death. His holdings came to some seventy million acres, give or take a county.

He never did build a fence, because he had something seven mile better than a fence, a deed with enough reach in it to go from the Rio de las Plumas to Monterey. Over that sweep of land, he owned everything to the sky, and under it everything to the center of the earth. He owned the clouds when they trespassed on his air, he owned the shadows they cast and birds in passage, he owned the winds, the dust, the sweat that God let fall in the form of rain. He owned the Bay of San Francisco, he owned rivers stiff with bass, he owned mountain ranges where the timber stood as thick as hair. He owned granaries, vineyards, orchards, sweet wells, and ships, he owned a thousand hogs, two thousand horses and mules, twelve thousand head of cattle, and fifteen thousand sheep. He owned ferries, forts, bridges, roads, an army with brass cannon, and a distillery. He owned hides, tools, machines (he worked thirty plows at a clip), cloth, gunpowder, cordage, and a warehouse full of Mexican *reals*. He owned all and sundry—except a saw-mill.

His name was Sr. Johann Augustus Sutter.

When he got his saw-mill, it was due to James Wilson Marshall. This Jim W. Marshall was nobody particular, a carpenter, the story goes, a wagon-builder from the state of Jersey. They say he started west in '33 or thereabouts, somewhere in Andy Jackson's second term, and he knocked about in Indiana and Illinois must've been a good ten years before he took a notion to see Oregon. He blew in along about snowfall of '44 and wintered there, but next year he got to drifting again, this time southwards, and being what he was, he never set fire to much beside his pipe. He was a ordinary sort of man, nobody particular.

As stated, Sr. Sutter lacked a saw-mill. For a long time, the richest man in the world had been whipsawing redwood along the coast and shipping it to himself by way of the Bay and the Sacramento. Naturally, that was big overhead and slow work—wasteful. Now, if he had his own saw-mill near some of his own timber, and if a tote-road could be built straight overland to the fort, there'd be another smidgeon of profit, and the richest man in the world would be a smidgeon richer than before. He wanted a saw-mill, and you couldn't hardly blame him.

Where did this Marshall come in—Jim W. Marshall? Well, it happened that some time in the summer of '47, he was head wainwright at Sutter's Fort when the idea of that mill was riding the Switzer hardest, and one day he found himself packed off to the hills to scout for a site. Pushing up to the headwaters of Weber Creek, he made his way to the South Fork of the American and stumbled onto a little flat name of Coloma. It laid nice, with the river taking a swift bend around a gravel-bank, the whole shooting-match belted in by a stand of pine lush enough to stop a snake. There was Sutter's mill-site, and no mistake.

Back at the fort, Marshall told the Senor about his find, and the two of them entered into a Whereas: the Senor put up the money and the men, and the carpenter threw in his know-how, and when the mill got to running, the pickings would be parted down the middle. Around September of '47, Jim Marshall and his gang set out for Coloma Flat, and with winter coming on, first thing they done up there was raise them a double cabin, one side for the hands and the other for Pete Wimmer (some spelt it Weimer) and his wife, a woman brung along to serve up the salt pork and boiled wheat.

By New Year's Day of '48, the mill-frame was standing, and a brush dam and sluice-gate likewise. He knew how to get a job done, that Jim W. Marshall, and there was only one thing gave him even a little bit of trouble, and that was the tail-race. It hadn't been dug deep enough for the mill-wheel, so he put a bunch of Indians to chucking out the rocks, and at night he kept the gate open to flush out the dirt and gravel.

One afternoon late in January, Jim Marshall took a stroll along the forty-odd rods of the tail-race to see if it was coming to hand, and down near where it fed back into the river, his eye was caught by something laying on the bottom over against a slab of granite. He bent himself and stuck his hand in, and out it come again with a nubbin of yellowish stuff about half the size of a pea. . . .

Four days later, a clerk rapped on the door of Sr. Sutter's office at the fort and announced Jim W. Marshall, boss-carpenter. Ah, thought the Senor, the mill must be finished!

Soaking wet like a Hard Shell, and his eyes bugging like apples in a sock, Jim Marshall crowded past the clerk and slammed the door in his phiz. "I want two bowls of water!" Jim said.

Sutter shrugged and ladled them out of a bucket.

"Now I want a stick of redwood," Jim said, "and a length of twine, and two squares of sheet copper!"

Sutter asked him what all that junk was for.

"To make scales!" Jim said. "Scales!"

Scales? But the apothecary had ready-made ones.

"Send out for them!" Jim said. "Right now!"

"But, bitte," Sutter said, "tell me first of my mill."

"God damn your mill!" Jim said. "I want some scales!"

The clerk made a round-trip in the rain.

"Now lock the door!" Jim said.

"No more will I do," Sutter said. "I ask of my mill, and you demand scales. I ask again of my mill, and you order me to lock my own door. Are you betrunken, Americano? Bist du verruckt?"

Jim Marshall hauled out his poke and rolled the little yellow bead into his palm. "Look at this, you Swiss cheese!" he said.

Sutter looked. "Iron pyrites," he said.

"Guess again!" Jim said.

"Sulphuret of copper. Mica, maybe."

"Jesus please Christ!" Jim said. "It's GOLD! I struck GOLD for us —GOLD! What do you think of that?"

"What do I think?" Sutter said, and he turned to the window and stared out at the pouring-down rain. "I think the richest man in the world is now ruinated."

He was right, the Switzer Senor, right as that rain. Oh, he got his mill finally—when every other living soul was out snatching up gold-flakes, a band of Mormons stood by him long enough to finish it—he got his mill, all right. But what did his clerks do when the secret broke, and his field-labor, and his ferrymen, and his army? Did they hang around for their thirty bucks a year and found? They did, like hell! They dropped whatever they was lugging—pens, oars, reins, guns—and lit out for the diggings.

That was only a starter. In a couple of weeks, the Senor was over-run by every ball-bearing man in San Francisco, and six months later the tide came in across the plains and around the Horn. They took his grain, his grapes, his whisky, and his gunpowder; they took his horses, hogs, mules, and sheep; they took the deer from his forests and the fish from his streams; they took his three sons (shot one, made another shoot himself, and drowned the third); they took the birds from his air and the ground from under his feet; they took all that he owned between the Heavens above and the pit; they even took his God damn clothes. Maybe he should've built that fence.

He sued. The bill of complaint was thick enough to hide the judge, and it laid claim to San Francisco, Sacramento, and all the rest of that eighty-eight-hour Mexican grant, valued at two hundred million dollars American. Damages were prayed for from seventeen thousand named defendants, along with the accrued interest on those damages. The sum of twenty-five million dollars was cried from the state of California for confiscating roads that were private, bridges, water-courses, piers, and warehouses. Over and above all that, the United States of America was alleged to be responsible for failure to main-tain public order, resulting in a further loss to the plaintiff of fifty million dollars. Sr. Sutter sued everybody but the real culprits—God and Columbus.

Five years after the filing of suit, the highest court in California (Thompson, Ch. J.) rendered judgment in favor of the plaintiff, and a quarter of a century later, in the city of Washington, D. C., the plain-tiff dropped dead in the street: he was still trying to collect the first dime.

Marshall? What happened to Jim W. Marshall? Nothing special: he died too.

EDGAR ALLAN POE   *1849*

IN BRONZE ABOVE A DOORWAY

Little home of a great poet
                    —13 West Range, Univ. of Virginia

Did I live that life, the one just over, those forty years of dayless
days, and did I behave as they say I did, were such my ways, did I
write the hack and consequential work I signed, did I wear black to
match my blind-man's view of the world, a worldwide open grave,
was such my turn of mind? Did I stem from strolling players, did my
father cut and run and my mother die of lungs, leaving a few ringlets
and a miniature, so poor, so poor she sang and danced in motley till a
month before the end?

Was I given a home by Allan, and did he give or I take his name,
was I clever as a child, did I rhyme in Latin, recite to guests for
praise and watered wine? Did I love at fifteen, my first time and my
first Helen, and was she soon insane and dead and I insane alive?
Was it then I began dwelling on tombs and cinerary urns, on magical
radiances, compelling perfumes, ciphers and fascinations, dark-age
horrors, death gradual and intricate and sometimes by machine? Did
I know of drink then or learn its use at school (milk slings, they say I
took, and peach-and-honey—what was peach-and-honey?), and while
there did I lose three thousand at loo, debts of honor (whose?) that
Allan refused to pay?

Should I have starved when he cut me off, was it base to enlist as a
common soldier, a loss of face to eat my country's bread in the ranks,
and if so, why when appointed to the Point, did I dram it till they
drummed me from the Corps? Didn't it matter, didn't I care, did I
guess at twenty-two that there'd be no forty-four—those sudden tir-
ings, the troubles in my head, my shaking hands, and where was all
desire except when desire was safe, among consumptives, among
premenstrual misses and no longer bleeding maids?

Why did I marry my twelve-year-old cousin Virginia, whose
mother was nearer my age, and in the hovels we shared with a cat, a
bobolink, and a pair of canaries, did I ever see her naked, did I
surprise secret skin and shocking hair, and did I sink the sight in
opium when drink was slow to drug me? My aunt (Muddie, I called
her, and my bride was Siss), my kindly tireless uncomplaining aunt,

did she beg for us in shops and on the road, did she take in laundry, mending, lodgers (and lodge them where, on what part of the floor?), and when I went away, did she tend my wife in her lifelong dying and send me the fare to come home?

Did we move from place to place, we three with cat and birds, always to a smaller space, always taking fewer things, and if, as the doctors said, I had a lesion of the brain, explain my presence at the Springs while Virginia bled the bedsheets red? Did I lift material, pretend to erudition, puff jinglers for puffs in return (*R. H. Horne puts Milton in the shade*)? Did I laud empty lines, woo lady poets with reviews, give them valentines, was I *not myself*, was I high cockalorum when Lowell came to see me, did I court the widow Whitman and still unwidowed wives? Did I rave in my drunken manias, did I take poison and puke it back, did I, that winter at Fordham, warm my virgin's feet with her cat?

Tell me, did I die in the street or a Baltimore room, and tell me lastly this—some day, somewhere, in bronze above some lintel, please God will it say *Domus parva magni poetae*?

JOHN JAMES AUDUBON   *1851*

EVERY BIRD OF EVERY SORT

Every bird is my rival.

—his wife

When it came to making money, there must've been a curse on him. Some power, some will that swayed him, some spell made him choose the wrong chance, the wrong ally, the wrong thing to buy or sell— some evil eye, it must've been. Whatever it was, addled wits or lack of wisdom, he rarely owned more than he wore on his back. But he could take nesting birds in his hand (they'd lie there and let him fan their wings!), and he could make his dog perform at a nod, a glance, a thought, even, and he could dance as if in levitation, and he could play the violin and the flute and the flageolet, and he could shoot (they say he could snuff a candle and leave the flame!), and he could fence and skate and entertain with tricks of legerdemain, and he could plait willow and weave hair, and he'd walk for a week to stalk a falcon. He couldn't make money, though.

He could draw anything he saw, on the ground or in the air, fur or feather, poised or on the move, a tree, a moth, a whippoorwill, foxes, loons, grebes and gallinules, weeds, flowers, pools and streams, and he could draw faces too, posed or passing by. He was at his best with birds, and to make them live on paper, he killed them in the field. His rooms were filled with wired-up objects that seemed to hover, stoop, or run, and some mutely screamed or fed a spider to their young, and some, as if taking the sun, stood on stilts among dry reeds. He couldn't make money, but he caught those birds.

Rivals, his wife called them, and he pursued them for half his married life, kite and snowy heron, oriole and swift, showy creatures, as graceful as pendulums, bright, bold, perfect in flight and handsome standing still. Rail, ivory-bill, waxwing, and finch—every bird was a rival, she said, but if he heard her say it, he took it as meant, that his absent years were spent in high company. In the end, he came back, and she held his hand as he died. Or was he holding hers, one last confiding bird?

HARRIET BEECHER STOWE   *1852*

THE LORD HIMSELF WROTE IT

I was but an instrument in His hand.

—Harriet Beecher Stowe

Many an abomination has been laid at my door. Every clerk that rhymes on Sunday, every Rialto scrivener, every hack with the scribbling itch—all say that if they've sinned in words, they've sinned as me. Their sprung and stumbling rhythms, their daring dimmed by quotes, their Eureka!s among the known, their slow-motion wit—all declare these doings mine and doubt meanwhile my one Creation.

I didn't write this book, and I didn't use the woman as my fist. The fact is, I gave up writing a long way back, at the height of my powers and ahead of my time. Few read the stones I sent from Sinai and fewer my writ on the Chaldean wall, and all those few were Jews. Allow me this, though, that I used no blind; the name I signed was my own. Why hide now, then? And with the whole wide world to choose from, why behind a mother of seven, the wife of a crammer in Maine?

Her household smelled of smelling-salts, of six children (I took back the seventh, a year-old boy), of tansy, camphor, bacon-smoke, bound sermons, hand-me-down air, and, still faint and still afar, Bright's disease. I glanced through a window once and saw Mister conning the Scriptures and Missus dashing off a war, and the sight sent me home with the blues.

I never wanted that war (I didn't care a sneeze for the niggers), but she did, and she got it, and some five hundred thousand whites died for a book (in paper, cloth, or cloth full gilt, with discount to the trade). The only book that made more killing is the one that was written about me.

RUNAWAY SLAVE   *1854*

THE LAW MUST BE EXECUTED!

RUN AWAY FROM ALEXANDRIA, FAIRFAX COUNTY, choice young Negro Fellow, viz.: Anthony Burns, 20 years of Age, about 5 feet six Inches high, medium black Color, well made, a handy Sort. . . .

He belonged to a Virginian by the name of Suttle, a nigger-driver himself and a renter-out of niggers to be driven by anyone else. Burns could read and write—he'd been taught by children who attended school—and he could handle a tool as well as a white. He earned Suttle $125 a year, of which his cut came to 12½¢, but learning that third R, rithmetic, one night he grew tired of being hired out for a penny a month, and he greased, meaning morning found him far away. He was in Boston, though, before he lost the sound of the dogs.

From there, he wrote to his family (like a fool, some held, and some, like a fay), and when the letter came to Suttle's hand (did they ask him to read it? was it a family of fools?), he bayed his way to New England. The North had a few dogs of its own, and when he bade them *Bring!*, they brought him his fugitive slave. *How do you do, Mr. Burns?* he said, and, suave, he bared his head and bowed. He was saving the blacksnake for Virginia.

Burns didn't care to be defended—he thought he'd fare worse if he showed fight—but up there in Boston, some had blood that wasn't quite cold, and they spoke when told to save their breath. They broke into jail (a pastor led them), and in a rampant tooth-and-nail, they bled a blackleg marshal to death. *The law must be executed!* said President Pierce, and when troops were sent, the deliverers fled. That didn't end it, though.

To risk a walk now, Suttle needed a suite of Harvard southrons, or else, being still in the skin-trade, he'd've died in the street. And now flocks of replevins flew, and a habeas drew a black corpus to be denied in open court. Buckoes kept the peace within, and out in the air, there were marines, cavalry, two companies of artillery, and citizens so hot to kill that it didn't matter what.

The hearing took three days, and everyone was heard who had a right hand to swear with—that is, all but Burns, whose right hand was the wrong color. R. H. Dana appeared for the defense (the big Whigs were not to be found), and he closed with a four-hour speech that would've freed Jesus and both thieves, but all it got for his client was a free ride back to Virginia—when the people got out of the road.

Incur any expense! the President said, and the Adjutant General of the army was sent to Boston, along with soldiers from Rhode Island and New Hampshire, and fifteen hundred militia threw their weight to the police. For the march to the wharf, each man was issued eleven rounds, with orders to fire at the first interference. The procession began, and the further it went, the thicker the crowd and the louder the groans and jeers, and shouts of *Shame!* arose, and crowbars were thrown, and a horse was stuck with a bayonet, and flags were flown with the union down, and blows were struck, and lancers used their sabers on those that blocked the way.

There was lots of folks to see a colored man walk through the streets Burns said.

To get him aboard a revenue cutter, it cost the country $100,000.

That night, Dana was waylaid by a tough, and, as the phrase went, he was given his corn, an iron rod on the side of the head.

CHARLES SUMNER

THE HEAD WHICH IS GOLD

I have read your speech twice over carefully. It is a libel on South Carolina and on Mr. Butler, who is a relative of mine. . . .

—Preston Brooks to Charles Sumner

Sumner was at his desk in the Senate—reading, perhaps, or writing a letter, or construing Juvenal, or he may have been scanning a list—and those on the floor who saw and heard say that Brooks began civilly, as required by the Code. *Mr. Sumner*, he said, and then came the rest of the words, after which he did his best to brain a man with a cane. *I gave him about thirty first-rate stripes*, he stated later; *I wore my cane out completely but saved the Head which is gold*. It was all done quite properly. A Georgian was there, a Mr. Toombs, and such quality would've noted any falling off.

Some, though, held the golden head to be on Sumner, not on the cane, and now that pain had tangled it, from whose mouth would come those philippics against the South? In Charleston, they called it sham pain, and Brooks was given another stick, this one inscribed *Hit him again*. In the Senate, Sumner was honored by having his chair kept three years vacant, and certain stains were cherished on the floor. The war, long on the way, was nearing the door of the chamber.

Epilogue

Brooks never used the presentation cane. A croup or quinsy choked him to death in the Dred Scott year.

Sumner lived to sit at Lincoln's pillow when he died. Mrs. Lincoln, with her usual flair, sent him her husband's cane.

DRED SCOTT   1857

LIKE THE SAP IN A TREE!

I was born in the Old Dominion, mother of presidents, but I never got to be president, and for that matter, I never even got to be a Virginian. I happened to be black, and my state was slavery, and wherever I went, a piece of it followed me, the piece I stood on, or so Master Blow told me when he took me to Missouri to work for his living. He died there, the stars were bad, and along with a lot of trash, I was left to his spinster daughter. She used me till I must've gone out of fashion, or else she needed cash, and I was knocked down to a man from Jefferson Barracks, a Mr. Doc Emerson. He carried me off across the big river to Rock Island, Illinois, the first free soil I'd ever set foot on—and in a twink, that freedom began to flow up my legs like the sap in a tree.

Like the sap in a tree!

The arms I had grew longer, and I grew new ones, like branches, and I owned forty hands of forty fingers each, and when that freedom-juice gave me speech, I spoke in words that only whites and flights of birds had used before: I said *I'm free!* I said it to myself once, trying it for flavor and finding it salt, and then, aloud, I said it to a cloud, to trees and smoke-stacks, to steeples and cornfields, to railroad tracks and dozing dogs, to people—whites, blacks, and in-betweens—and in the end, I said it where it hurt, to Mr. Doc. Hurt me, I mean, because he filled my face with dirt for it and took me back to Missouri. It was Illinois dirt, though, and it made me free. I spat on the Show-me state and said *I'm free!*

I said it to slaves, to Lovejoy's friends, to Osage braves, to boys in the street, to stars and walls and stern-wheelers, to the plains, the straight-down rains, and a flood of mud, the Mississippi. I said it for twenty years, ten of them to meeching Christers who looked the other way or laughed, and ten more to a raft of shysters scared stiff by the South. I said it to deaf ears, plugged ears, and what was left of ears slit for lying. I said it to the well, the sick, the dying, and the dead. I said it—*I'm free!* I said—to frontier pimps and waterfront ginch, to sloe-gin drunks and greasy gunmen, to hound-dog handlers and easy marks, to brass-knuck toughs and squatter-sovereigns, and now and then, meaning once or twice, to someone nice enough to call me Mr. Scott.

The Supreme Court said otherwise in '57. It said I was a nigger (it used fancier guff), and a nigger, if he acted bardacious, was apt to end on a tree with a bigger neck than when he started. It said I was inferior. It said I was a chattel. It said I had an owner—or, worse, the owner had *me*—and it said he could sell me, swap me, or stick me like a hog and eat me. It said all this clack about being free would have to stop. It said I'd be free some time, but not this side of the grave. It said my case had been tried, and still being alive, I was still a slave.

But I said *I'm free!* and I never quit.

The word was like the sap in a tree!

LINCOLN-DOUGLAS DEBATES   *1858*

TWENTY-ONE HOURS IN ILLINOIS

Hon. S. A. Douglas
Will it be agreeable to you to make an arrangement for you and myself to divide time, and address the same audiences during the present canvass. . . ?

—A. Lincoln

Hon. A. Lincoln
I will speak at Ottawa one hour, you can reply, occupying an hour and a half, and I will then follow for half an hour. . . .

—S. A. Douglas

They chose seven sites, one in each of seven counties, and to all those places the people came. To Ottawa, where the Fox and the Illinois joined, they came dredged in the brown flour of the prairie, and they came afoot and astride and on the trains of the Rock Island, and drawn by pairs of steppers they came, and by teams on loan from the plow, and they flowed down both streams, and even these wore the dust of the road. The square began to fill at cockcrow, and by eight o'clock, the all-around grassland seemed to burn and smoke, and brass twelve-pounders spoke in turn, and in the din and churn, flags flurried and bands drowned, and rubes razed the roof of the speakers' stand. Judge Douglas led off at half past two in the afternoon. . . .

And the people came to Freeport, which was midway up the Pecatonica from the Rock. They came by the cars if they could, the Galena & Chicago Union and the Central of Illinois, but in the main they came in rolling-stock of their own. They came from Eleroy and Afolkey and Lena and German Valley, and they came from nameless quarter-sections in between. They came from the cellars of houses about to be built or lately blown away, they came from dugouts, caves, and barns, and a handful came from mannered halls. They came with food, dogs, dolls, and sucking infants, and they came with their old and some with their dying. It was cold that day, and off and on it rained, but they say sixteen thousand were in that grove when Lincoln rose to speak at two in the afternoon. . . .

Jonesboro was in far-south Illinois, or Egypt, as the few that lived there put it, but few or countless, it was come one come all, some from Cairo (Cayro, they called it) and some from Thebes, and they came, if by rail, to Depot Anna a mile or so off. For the rest of the fifteen hundred, it was footback to the fairgrounds, where a cannon fouled the air. Douglas himself opened fire in the early afternoon. . . .

Twelve thousand came to Charleston (some set it higher), and they came from near Mattoon and from the Wabash fifty miles away. They came in league-long parades, one such headed by thirty-two girls on horseback, a girl for each state and each sporting the red, white, and blue of all. They came behind eighty-foot banners and plumed and spangled bugle corps, and with them came a sailing cloud of soil. Lincoln took the stand at a quarter to three in the afternoon. . . .

And the people came to Galesburg, and once again they rallied in the rain, a fall that froze in a wind off the Muscatine bend of the Mississippi. They came Micks and Macs, and Danes came, and Dutchmen, Swedes, and Swiss, and mixed with all that salt came a peppering of blacks. They came cross-country, the twenty thousand, to the lawns of Knox College they came one on a horse, two on an ox, and three, if small, on a mule. At two-thirty in the afternoon, Douglas spoke into a blow that sometimes flew his words away. . . .

Quincy stood with its feet in the big river, and the people came there, up, down, and over that running yellow street. From Iowa they came, and from Missouri, some of these from Hannibal, wherefore one might have been Twain. And they came on CB&Q iron and along its right-of-way, and with lamps in every window and torches out-of-doors, the town saw daylight before it saw dawn. Under a clear sky, at half past two in the afternoon, Lincoln spoke. . . .

The *City of Louisiana* carried both parties downriver to Alton, seventh of the seven venues, and the people came there too, in other bottoms and alongshore and in a coach with Mrs. Lincoln on the special Springfield train. The final meeting was more subdued than the rest. The Little Giant appeared to be tired (he had spoken fifty-five times in the campaign), and the other giant might have been thinking of Lovejoy, shot dead in that place for saying what was about to be said again. Douglas got up to speak at two sharp in the afternoon. . . .

In seven places, in the sun at times and at times in the rain, the people stood and listened through seven afternoons. They had come, some a far cry, to hear words that seemed familiar, as if spoken or dreamed before. They had come booted and barefoot, and the sick and the well were there, and the wild ones came, and the tame, and some lugged a jug and some a tired child—all to see mouths move that might have been their own. And now and then they laughed, or looked for a laugher to lick, or spat and stomped the spit, or clapped their hands, or slapped a handy back, or at some hit scored by their man, said *Good for you, Judge!* or *Give it to him, Abe!*—but mostly they listened, and it was mainly himself that each of them heard.

No one took it hard, therefore, when both the Judge and Abe said *nigger* instead of *black*: north as well as south, *nigger* was the going name. And no one thought it odd that the Judge and Abe held niggers to be less than whites: niggers were inferior, to the Judge and Abe alike. And when they said the same say about the peculiar institution—that where they found it, there would they leave it—no eyes stared in surprise. They scorned the blending of blood, they said, in wedlock or otherwise, and neither one balked at returning a fugitive slave. They saw as one on the franchise—none but a white might make his X—and lastly, they agreed with Jesus Christ that a house divided could not stand. And the people shared these views.

All the same, there was a difference, and the two giants, big and little, knew it, and the people who heard them knew it, and the house divided knew it, and the difference was this—that in speaking of slavery, never did the Judge call it wrong, and never did Abe call it right.

The Judge said: *I believe this government was made on the white basis. I believe it was made by white men, for the benefit of white men and their posterity forever.*

And Abe said: *We have in this nation the element of domestic slavery. It is a moral, a social and a political wrong.*

All through those twenty-one hours in Illinois, that was the difference between the Hon. S. A. Douglas and the Hon. A. Lincoln, and on a 4th of March to come, the difference would show, for Abe would be swearing to defend the Constitution, and the Judge would be holding his hat.

AT HARPER'S FERRY   *1859*

OH, DEAR DANGERFIELD

If you do not get me somebody else will. Come this fall without fail, money or no money I want to see you so much: that is the one bright hope I have before me.

—Harriet Newby

Dangerfield was her husband, half-nigger and half-Scotch, six-two barefoot and both feet free to come and go: if he wore a collar, he also wore its key. But she was still a slave, his Harriet, and about to be sold down the Rappahannock, and she wrote *Buy us soon, dear Dangerfield,* and his own bright hope became old John Brown.

A Mr. Richard Washington shot dear Dangerfield in the yard of the Armory at Harper's Ferry, using a rifle that fired a six-inch spike. It took out gullet, jugular, and part of the jaw, opening the throat in a grin like a broken watermelon. For souvenirs, a mob cut off dear Dangerfield's ears, and then they cut off twos of anything else he had no further use for.

JOHN BROWN   1859

HAD I SO INTERFERED IN BEHALF OF
THE RICH

. . . it would have been all right.

—John Brown

You're on the far side of the grave, Dred,
A year gone and freer dead than I am living,
But I'll bear you company in an hour, friend,
And I'll end as black in the face as you:
They're going to hang me—but I'll rejoice
At drawing a last breath where you drew a first,
And I'll be grateful, as though given a choice,
That my place of death was your place of birth,
Virginia.

I could've lived to be older than fifty-nine,
I could've lasted out this bastard century:
I had the frame for it, if not the frame of mind.
If I'd been blind to you and deaf to God,
If I'd loved myself more and money most,
If I'd kept my nose clean and my soul snotty,
If I'd valued my skin, if I'd thrown no stones
At the sin of slavery, if I'd passed the buck
And left such truck as bravery and broken bones
To fools—in short, if I'd been a sleeping dog,
They'd've let me lie till the nineteen-hundreds.

I die sooner, with nothing done that I'd undo
If my life were spared: the slavers slain
On the Pottawatomie would be slain again,
All five and more if found; the battle
Once won at Black Jack Oaks would be twice won;
The raids made on Sugar Creek and the fight lost
On the Marais des Cygnes would be made and lost
In the future as they were in the past;
The same slaves would be taken by force
From Messrs. Hicklin, Larue, and Cruise,

Of Missouri,
And Cruise would be shot dead a second time
If he cocked his Colt in his second life;
And lastly, the same treason would be committed
At Harper's Ferry, and when brought to book,
I'd give the same reason that I gave
In Kansas:
Nits grow to be lice.
Knowing that delay would merely change
The number of the day and the name of the month,
Knowing that at some later date, as the same
Traitor, I'd dance on air for the same crimes,
I say let them crack my spine now and here.

Commend me to your only Master, Dred, and mine.

JOHN D. ROCKEFELLER   *1859*

petra, **rock**+*oleum,* **oil**

God gave me my money.

—John D.

There were pits of the liquor near Babylon and pools in the Isles of Greece. Strabo spoke of it, they say, and Herodotus, and Pliny, and it was found in Ecbatan and Sicily and known as *burning water* in Japan. Marco Polo saw it in the Caucasus, where it sweated from the ground, and Raleigh, discoursing on Trinidad, noted its springs of pitch, and in Rangoon too it rose and ran, and on Barbados, and in the Carpathians, and even in the state of New York. Tar, the ancients called it, and earthbalsam, and the oil of St. Quirinus, but always it was a gift of nature, like flowers of the field, like rain, an upward-falling rain.

It was drilled for first up along the Allegheny, a bit drawing blood (black, green, brown, blue) sixty-nine feet down into Pennsylvania. Before John D. had time to come from Cleveland, a few drops spilled on the still-clear stream. They spun in the eddies, they broke on the falls, they went with the current and were lost in shallows of sand. That was not to happen again.

His father was a cancer-quack and his mother was Dutch Reformed. At school, they dubbed him *Deacon*, a nickname that, behind his back, became *that stick*, and he was thought reserved, grave, quiet, the sort little given to idle play or loitering while he walked. Drink, cards, sports, the stage, these he shunned, and if ever he danced, it was only a *pas seul* after making a killing. He steered clear of loose women and, for a time at least, of tight, and what he spent when he spent at all went for psalms and alms (*$0.25 to a poor man in the church*). Wary, exact, exacting too (*to a fraction*, a partner said; *if there was a cent due us, he wanted it*), and, to gain an end, patient enough to make Job look rash. He was the save-all type, a shaver, a pincher, and in private he may well have tried coins with his teeth. He came softly and as softly went, his tone was mild and his manner humble, and he dry-washed his hands *à la* Heep. He talked to himself (*Look out! Go steady!*), he left notes for himself (*Don't make any more such covenants!*), and when it came to wedding, he couldn't've done better if he'd married himself: his Missus wouldn't even write a letter on the Day of Rest. He had no friends, he joined no clubs, he dined at home—that stick! that strict and sterile stick! But as with the almond rod in Numbers, it came to pass that he came to life, and when his wife was lying in, he read her the Word of God from his own side of the bed.

Once the Deacon reached the scene, no more oil (black, brown, green, or blue) would seep back down or wisp away on some gyrant stream. It would flow to him, not some but all, and the day would come when he quit pissing like a man and began to piss kerosene. Mourned by those who were paid to keen, he would go into a dry hole at ninety-eight.

ABRAHAM LINCOLN   *1861*

ILLINOIS CENTRAL CABOOSE

That winter afternoon, the train to Mattoon was late, and, his connection gone when he got there, he had to ride a way freight to Charleston, a dozen miles off across the prairie. How many stops were made on the run no one knows now, and none can say whether he sat at a window or stood outside as track paid backward on the snow, nor has it come to light that someone at some crossing saw him and spoke (*Man there might've been Abe*), and someone else replied (*Smoke turns purple this hour of day*).

They're all dead now, the brakemen, if any were in the car, dead those who might've watched beside the right-of-way, and dead and gone Abe and the lilac hour of that winter afternoon. *What went through his mind in that hour, what words, what sequences of scenes, what fancies in color and fears in black and white? Did he think of the seceded states, see them as sisters lost or sisters strayed, did he dwell on death and the two faces he made in the glass?*

Tomorrow, in Charleston, he would visit an old woman he had loved a long time, his stepmother Sarah Bush, and they would talk of forty years back (paid-out track) and of the inauguration, still forty days ahead, but of that hour at the end of a train, nothing would be said, and it would remain a secret known to one until, in broken bone and scattered brain, it became unknown to all.

ABRAHAM LINCOLN   *1861*

FIRST INAUGURAL

Mr. Lincoln is to be President of the United States some day. If I had not thought so, I would not have married him, for you can see he is not pretty.

—Mrs. Lincoln in 1846

He was a cartoon to her too, a stork in a stovepipe hat, a hook-nosed Hebe, a treed coon. She saw what the sketchers saw, the rat, the hayseed, the knockkneed jester capped and belled. Mr. Lincoln, she called him, but she beheld only the pen's inkling, ape, swine, serpent, six-four something from a nether world. She saw the wens and the stickling hair, the loose and lizard skin, the deep roads, the wear and tear. She saw the scarecrow clothes, the teeth (or where teeth had been), the pale eyes, gray, they say, and she said *You can see he is not pretty*. All the same, there were some who thought otherwise, some for whom, coming, he lit the room and, going, left the lamp.

TALL TALK IN SOUTH CAROLINA

THE CONFEDERACY TO P. G. T. BEAUREGARD:
If you have no doubt of the intention of the Washington Government to supply Fort Sumter by force, you will at once demand its evacuation, and, if this is refused, proceed, in such manner as you may determine, to reduce it, etc. . . .

P. G. T. BEAUREGARD TO R. ANDERSON:
I am ordered by the Government of the Confederate States to demand the evacuation of Fort Sumter. All proper facilities will be afforded, etc. The flag which you have upheld so long, etc. I am, sir, very respectfully, etc. . . .

R. ANDERSON TO P. G. T. BEAUREGARD:
I have the honor to acknowledge receipt of your communication, etc. It is a demand with which I regret that my sense of honor, and of my obligations to my Government, prevent my compliance. Thanking you, etc. . . .

P. G. T. BEAUREGARD TO R. ANDERSON:
Useless effusion of blood, etc. . . .

R. ANDERSON TO P. G. T. BEAUREGARD:
I will not open fire on your forces unless compelled to do so by some hostile act against this fort or the flag of my Government, etc. . . .

P. G. T. BEAUREGARD TO R. ANDERSON:
Honor to notify you, etc. Will open fire on Fort Sumter in one hour, etc. . . .

R. ANDERSON TO A SOUTHERN GENTLEMAN:
If we do not meet again on earth, I hope we may meet in Heaven, etc. . . .

The stipulated hour ended at 4:20 in the morning, at which time the lanyard of a 10-inch smoothbore Columbiad was tendered Mr. Roger Pryor in recognition of his rhetoric: *Not only is the Union gone,* he had intoned, *but gone forever.* And yet, strangely, Mr. Pryor shook his head, nor was this all of him shaken, and he said *I could not fire the first gun of the war.* The high honor now devolved on Mr. Edmund Ruffin, another Southern man of the mouth, older than Pryor—sixty-seven, he was—and of colder blood, and his eighteenth-century hand was quick to grasp the cord. The gun—elev. 5 degrees, range 1,200 yds.—spoke.

ROBERT E. LEE   *1861*

CHIVALRY vs SHOVELRY

Duty is the sublimest word in the language.
                                                              —R. E. Lee

There were spend-alls in his top and bottom lines (his sire was Light Horse Harry and his dam a Carter when the Carters were rich), but as the tin went, so went the taint, and his blood came to him pure, running blue and drying even bluer. He admired the ladies, they say, sought them out, wrote to them, flowered in their presence, but it was quite harmless, that leaning of his, and all Virginia knew it. He was the reverent kind, and owning the bed that Washington had died in, daily he knelt beside it and prayed in the shade of his abiding beau ideal. It was hard to fault him. He took his wine by the sip, simply for the savor, and a glass or less would last a meal, nor would he dip snoose, chew, or make other use of the bronzed weed. A good son, a good father and husband, a good friend (perfection, the man was!), a good master, soldier, citizen: *Duty is the sublimest word*, he said.

He was only doing his duty, of course, when he took John Brown and swung him for his crime of Harper's Ferry. In days to come, at Sharpsburg, at Spottsylvania, at Cold Harbor, he'd do worse than the old crank had ever done, but he'd get away with his blue and gray murder, and rightly so—his aim was different. He wasn't out to change things; he was doing his duty and keeping them the same.

HENRY THOREAU

A CALL OF NATURE

Ask me for a certain number of dollars if you will, but do not ask me for my afternoons.

—H. D. Thoreau

He said his say against the peculiar institution, and now and then he bedded and fed some runaway slave; he gave and gathered freedom-money, he wrote his share of touchwood words, and here and there in his Journal, a note throws light on where his heart was and its shade; he made himself over that he might remake the world, a perfect one to perfect the many. But in the end, it came to this, that never was he in danger: he threw no stone nor had one thrown at him.

Oh, it was a marvel, the way he could reach into a hole in a tree and bring out a screech-owl—and she with young in the nest! It had to be seen, his trick of luring fish with his hands, bream that would nibble at his fingers and let themselves be lifted from the stream. And mice would come and feed at his feet, and crows would eat from his mouth and frogs lie supine to be stroked with a weed, and he spoke the kind of woodchuck that woodchucks could understand. Birds came and went at his chirped command, and the same for squirrels and, it almost seemed, for rain. Flowers opened and closed for him, clouds appeared and were blown away, and arrowheads grew where he pointed at the sand. It was a miracle, what the man could do, an eighth wonder, you might say, like a pyramid, like a hanging garden, and children had faith in him, as if he were their eyes.

Still, he was never brained with a cane, and no one rowed across a river to kill him, or towed him through the streets with a rope, or shot him behind the ear, or broke his neck with the knot of a noose. He slept well, they say, that one night he spent in jail, and come morning, he went his way when his bill was paid by a party in a veil. His aunt, it may have been, but no one ever knew.

J. PIERPONT MORGAN   *1862*

A LESSON IN BUSINESS

Financier and banker, prominent member of the Protestant Episcopal Church, enthusiastic yachtsman, notable collector of books, generous benefactor. . . .

—Encyc. Brit.

He was twenty-four when the Civil War came, but he took good care not to fight in it. Like as not, he'd've been issued one of those defective guns he'd palmed off on the Government, and he wasn't the kind to let blow-back take his thumb off, not when it could do the same for someone else. The field simply wasn't the place for a man able to buy condemned carbines from the Army and sell them right back to the Army at a yield of five hundred per cent.

At Antietam, a body was found in Bloody Lane fifty-seven times hit, but it didn't belong to Morgan. The chances are, he never saw Antietam, or if he did, only from a private car, when someone might've pointed out the East Woods and the West Woods and the Cornfield and the Sunken Road near the Dunkard Church. He was a buyer of incunabula by then, and he owned the Baltimore & Ohio. It's hardly likely, though, that he was shown the grave where more bullets were buried than bones.

ABRAHAM LINCOLN   *1862*

AT THE TELEGRAPH OFFICE

My God! What will the country say!

—A. Lincoln

He couldn't stay away from the place. Day after day, he'd put on that tweed shawl of his and that tall black hat and cross the street to the War Office, and there he'd be when news came in—from Malvern Hill, it might've been, from Antietam, Shiloh, Chancellorsville. He'd be standing at a window or folded to fit a chair, but wherever he was, he'd be silent or saying little sadly when the sounder began to play in code. Somewhere, in a wagon or a tent or the open air, a hand on a key would be making and breaking a circuit, sending word in Morse for a loss of lives, for death at a stone bridge, at an unheard-of church, or where two roads met in a wood. And to the man at a window or choked in a chair, it would be as if he were with those dead as each one died, and each on going left less of him, and the day would come when the last of him went, and he'd die there, in the war being fought in that room.

VICKSBURG   *1863*

HUNDRED YEARS' WAR

When you write of the South, don't remember such running off at the mouth as Pemberton's: *When the last pound of beef and bacon and flour, the last grain of corn, the last cow and hog and horse and dog shall have been consumed, and the last man shall have perished in the trenches, then, and only then, will I sell Vicksburg.* He sold it a damn sight sooner, but don't hold the old gascon to his brag, and when you write that we still had food when we showed the white flag, don't say that only those ate who could pay on the nail.

Dwell, if you will, on our slurred speech and bird-free lives, on our hot blood, our cold pride, and our lukewarm wives, but don't mock us, don't abase us, don't make us read our own disgrace: *If you can't feed us,* many soldiers wrote, *you had better surrender us.* Would it be a disreputable act, would it be wrong to conceal the fact that we were still thirty thousand strong when we threw in the sponge? If so, play yourself false, look the other way.

And why harp on the private bomb-proofs of the elite? Granted we kept some caves for quality, but wouldn't it be kinder to say that when shelled by the fleet, we all of us took cover—slave, slaver, and trash alike? And why dwell on the cowards who cowered under fire and raved *I want my mother?* Say this instead, that Vicksburg knew none who whimpered when hit, none who didn't curse the day we quit, none who was laid by the heel or shot in the britches, none who wolfed a Union ration or wept at such compassion as you blue sons-of-bitches tried to feel.

Leave us something. You've taken the City of a Hundred Hills, the gold, and the bacon that was never consumed because it was never sold, and you've got a dozen batteries of still artillery, the silent cheers of our would-be mutineers (*If you can't feed us, you had better surrender us*), sixty thousand stand of arms, and our women and those charms of theirs that never move. . . . Leave us something. You've got it all.

Leave us the legend that one Reb and ten Feds are a fair match; that we eat fire and spit sparks; that we're half eagle and half catamount, and with a pinch of Scratch and a dash of God, we're the hope of the Old World planted in the New; and, last, that these states are too damn good for the nigger, the Pope, and the Jew.

Leave us a little: we'll make it bigger.

SOLDIER, UNION ARMY   *1863*

THE BLUE AND THE GRAY—AND THE BLACK

Dear Joe: By the time you read this scrawl
(The slurs are blood or mud or maybe Java,
And if I blur some word or pink the paper,
Remember I'm writing on a fresh-killed ass,
My out-of-doors desk in the gasiform rain),
I'll be a spy. When they call the All-Quiet,
I'll shuck blue faded here and there to gray,
I'll give away my Colt and two-buck carbine,
And then I'll slick between pickets into Dixie.

If I'm lucky, I'll still be free at sunrise;
If otherwise, I'll be a short while dying,
And I'll be lying not with honor in a grave
For pilgrims to vault the bulge I raise
And weep salt savor to my skull—Jesus, no!
I'll be taken apart by the inch, like a snake,
And left to rot where the sundry inches fall.

I tell you all this not to make small of it
Or to prove my valor; I simply want to speak

Before I die and say that this, *this*, was why
I showed a hand when a show of hands was made:
It was not enough to pine when sold for knives,
Beads, and wine, or to maim or take our lives,
Or to kill for the cold favor of being killed;
And it was not enough to plot a servile war
And be cured like a ham or shot like a pigeon;
It was not enough to get religion secondhand
From some back porch, and, praising de Lawd,
Understand that only He made only me a slave;
It was not enough to take freedom-papers after
Forty years of *Massa* and forty-one of beans;
It was not enough to run away from the music,
Or to own my own mouth if the South remained
To deaden my voice; and now it's not enough
To lie on the fringe and send lead envoys in.
I go in—and if they catch me by the toe,
I hope they don't eeny-meeny-miney-moe me;
I hope they destroy me before I can holler.

THE ADDRESS

1863

CEMETERY AT GETTYSBURG

We are met on a great battlefield.

After the speeches were made, after the drums were rolled and the dirges played, the crowd dispersed and strolled the ground. What blood they found was four months old, browned by the sun and run by the rain, and, eating fruit, they walked where shot-off feet had taken one last stride through the wheat, where nine thousand had died in three days, and they picked over the notions, the knickknacks of war, buttons, buckles, numerals, kicked the sixes and sevens of the North and South, and they drank from Spangler's Spring, and they tried the rifle-pits and the lunettes, only a little less deep than they were before, and they heard the distant cough of artillery, and they saw Pickett coming and fought him off.

Nine thousand dead, in the Den, on the Round Tops, in the Orchard and the Angle, and what had they won who'd lost their lives? A common grave, a holdall for blue and slaver, as though cold soldiers were all the same.

GENERAL N. B. FORREST   *1864*

LOW COMPANY IN TENNESSEE

If we ain't fightin' fer slavery, I'd like to know what we are fightin' fer.

—Gen'l. N. B. Forrest

Before the Rebellion, he ran a nigger-yard in Memphis, a line of work that barred him from the *bon ton* tables of the South: it might be all right to buy his meat, but you simply couldn't seat him with the pink. It never did wear off, the stink of his business. It must've been under his skin somewhere, and it came on the air with his sweat, his breath, his presence, even. To the elite, it didn't matter that he couldn't spell or sign his name, but how did one dine with a seller of slaves?

He shucked the trade when the war came, and he did so well at killing that he rose in grade almost by the hour. His third star very nearly made him respectable, but there was still that whiff from Ft. Pillow, where two hundred black Federals had surrendered, and he'd let his men shoot them to blue rags. Their blood, dispatches read, had dyed the river for an eighth of a mile—and the river the Mississippi! He just never got out of that nigger-yard.

INQUIRY INTO A MASSACRE

. . . wearing the uniform of the United States, which should
be the emblem of justice and humanity. . . .
                                    —Sen. B. F. Wade, 38th Congress

MAJ. SCOTT ANTHONY: There was one little child, proba-
bly three years old, just big enough to walk through the sand.
The Indians had gone ahead, and this little fellow, perfectly
naked, was following after them. I saw one man get off his
horse, at a distance of about seventy-five yards, and draw up his
rifle and fire: he missed the child. Another man came up and
said, "Let me try the sonofabitch; I can hit him." He got down
off his horse, kneeled, and fired at the little child, but he missed
him. A third man came up and made a similar remark, and
fired, and the little fellow dropped.
    QUESTION: Those were men of your command?
    MAJ. ANTHONY: Of Colonel Chivington's.

He commanded the 3rd Regiment of Colorado Cavalry—hundred-
day men, they were—and with no Rebs to kill in the Territory, time,
as he heard some say, seemed to stand quite still. He saw their blue
wear thin at the seat and knees, and he saw it fade in the sun and run
in the rain, but there was no gunfight nearer than Georgia, and soon
they'd turn in one-shot Sharps fired only at the butts, pristine sabers,
and bayonets blooded in a scarecrow's guts, and none would know,
none be aware of, the comradery of lead, and then he remembered,
as always when he somewhere itched, the Indian.

. . . holding the important position of commander of a military
district. . . .

Black Kettle the Cheyenne, he thought, the friendly to whom he'd
given two flags, one white and one American, with orders to fly them
from a pole if taken for a hostile. Black Kettle, he thought, and he
could almost see the brave on Sand Creek, where he'd sent him to be
safe among his own people and Left Hand's band of Arapahoes—

friendlies all, and with their true colors to show if the blue soldiers came.

To the 3rd, he added a battalion of the 1st at Fort Lyon, and they rode all night for Sand Creek, forty miles away. In the morning, five suns rose there, one from the hills and four from field-guns: the Cheyenne camp was blown awake and then to blood and bits of bone. A few fire-eaters made a show of fight, got out their reject rifles, and tried to bag cannonballs in flight—but not Black Kettle, the white man's friend with flags to prove it. He ran them to the top of his lodge, where the wind shook out their folds, and then he waited for the firing to stop. He didn't have long to wait, only seven hours.

Who can say what the soldiers saw through the smoke and dust? The white flag might've been taken for a towel, the stars and stripes for stars and bars, but whatever was waving there across the stream, they kept on shooting until they'd laid two hundred Indians dead among the alders. They stacked arms then and drank to the day's work. According to an officer, it was work done well.

LT. JAMES D. CANNAN: In going over the battleground the next day, I did not see a body of man, woman, or child but was scalped. I heard one man say that he had cut a woman's private parts out and had them for exhibition on a stick. I heard another man say that he had cut the fingers off of an Indian to get the rings on the hand. I heard one instance of a child a few months old being thrown in the feed-box of a wagon, and after being carried some distance, left on the ground to perish. I also heard of numerous instances in which men had cut out the private parts of females and stretched them over the saddle-bows, and wore them over their hats while riding in the ranks. According to the best of my knowledge and belief, these atrocities that were committed were with the knowledge of J. M. Chivington, and I did not know of his taking any measures to prevent them.

. . . and therefore having the honor of the government to that extent in his keeping. . . .

MATHEW BRADY   *1861-5*

WAR FOR ALL TO SEE

His pictures teem with phantoms, the steam remains of men in motion, and spectral trains go past on ghastly wheels. Through them can be seen the posed platoons and the guileless postures of the dead, and streams flow flat and seem solid, and ironclads draw no water, like the toys in a war-room game. Trestles grow stick on stick, jackstraws played with pines, and hundred-pounders point at space, naval guns in land emplacement, and mortars too besiege the sky. Shot trees lie where fallen, along a wall and across a run, and some become *chevaux-de-frise*, and picked-off snipers cure in the sun. 4-4 engines sport their names in gilt, and tricked with brass and flowers, they swagger standing still. An embalmed stiff smiles in his sleep, calmed by his chemical blood, horses swell among future souvenirs, and on the *Monitor*'s deck, sailors sit at checkers but never make a move. And there are tethered mules, there are wagons with their peckers down, there are sail and sidewinders on the Rappahannock, artillery parks, stacked supplies, corpses with mouths open at O, blacks waiting for nothing in sight, pontoons, bent rail, raw wood, maimed soldiers smoking and hale ones playing cards. And there are pictures of war after war's end—chimneys show the height of former floors, piers step creeks without a span, but no dogs appear, no birds, no blurs that might've been a man.

ABRAHAM LINCOLN   *1865*

SECOND INAUGURAL

Fondly do we hope—fervently do we pray.

—A. Lincoln

There was a spell of rain that day, a light fall and rather fine, they say, but enough to weigh on flags and strain festoons, and in the mousse it made of the going, skirts grew stiff, and boots and shoes seemed uppers only. It kept none off the avenue, though, and long before the swearing in, the lawns were paved with faces to a distant line of trees. A slow descent of rain, it was, measured, sheer, like crepe de chine, and it settled on plume and braid, on sequin, fur, and pelerine. It stopped—all took note of the odd conjunction—just as he began to speak. The rain stopped, and the sun shone on the fallen drops, and each became a sun itself and burned. An omen, the people called it, and they gave heed to the words that were streaming toward the trees.

Seven hundred words, there were, and with them the South lost the war, and they knew as much when the speech was read in Richmond. There was no comfort for the Rebs in that seraphic final paragraph—their cause was gone before he ever got there. *With malice toward none*, he said, and in truth he felt no enmity of heart, no spite for those who'd laid five hundred thousand dead for the right to eat their bread in other men's sweat, other men's sorrow. He hated no one, even as Matthew and Matthew's master, but woe had been promised those by whom offenses came, and woe would come. They knew that in Richmond. They knew it was more than a promise in seven hundred words. It was a prophecy, grave but somehow glowing, and a multitude fled in dread of doom.

FALL OF RICHMOND   *1865*

APPOMATTOX, 95 miles

From City Point, he was taken up the James on the steamer *Malvern*, and when it went aground near Rockett's Landing, a barge brought him off for his one-hour turn in the streets of Richmond. He had an escort of twelve sailors armed with carbines, making thirteen to kill if the rebels willed it. A stone flung, a shot fired, a wrong flag shown or a right one wrong, and Lincoln would've been guarded by a dozen dead and dead himself.

But with Petersburg gone, the capital knew it was going next, and sooner than surrender, it blew itself up. In ones and twos and block-long rows, the roofs of Richmond took the air, and with them went their stores of flour, and kites of lath and plaster flew, and floors and stairs, and toys and books, and now and then a dog or an old man—

and when the town came down, it burned. It burned in ranks, and it burned at random. The trees still standing burned, and the window-frames in fallen walls, and the paper past of Virginia burned, and, catching a likeness of the fires, the James burned too.

When the last grayback had headed west, the civilians followed suit, a few with pets and keepsakes and the rest with mismatched loot. They ate it, drank it, played with it, tried it on if they knew what it was, and threw it away or wore it, and as they went, they swapped on the run, a plume fan for an embroidered sheet. They ran with dance-favors and Jeff Davis dollars, they ran with canaries and incomplete sets of spoons, some of them pausing to stare at a small party of Federals, six before and six behind a tall stranger in a plug hat.

No one threw a stone or made a show of colors true or false, and no one fired a shot. The tall man, whoever he was, was suffered to take his walk. A few watched him go where their great had been and tread on tomorrow's shrines, and then they fled down a road toward the end that was in the beginning.

THE SURRENDER   *1865*

ARMY OF NORTHERN VIRGINIA

They weren't much to look at—they'd never been much, but they were less so now. They wore butternut, some of them, and some wore bombazine, all of it rags, and they'd gone from half- to quarter-rations, from parched corn to parched cobs, and their flags were old bandages, ravels of silk, ravels of air. There were damn few rounds for the guns in the train, there were bare wounds, staring eyes, pain, visions, bloodspots in spit, and the stink of the trots, but the men in their minds were as good as new, full of piss and pizen, and with Lee to give the word, they'd've fought him another fight. But he couldn't give it, couldn't cry *Never say die, boys!* not again—they'd died to that for four years, and all still alive were dead on their feet. He couldn't face a last day's dying (*useless effusion, etc.*), he couldn't send them out for more blue murder: they were beaten, bitter verb for bitter end.

R. E. LEE TO U. S. GRANT:

I suppose, General Grant, that the object of our present meeting is fully understood. I asked to see you to ascertain upon what terms you would receive the surrender of my army.

U. S. GRANT TO R. E. LEE:

The terms I propose, etc. The officers and men surrendered to be paroled and disqualified, etc. The arms, artillery, and public property to be parked and stacked, etc. This will not embrace the side-arms of the officers, nor their private horses or baggage, etc.

R. E. LEE TO U. S. GRANT:

This will have a very happy effect, etc.

U. S. GRANT TO R. E. LEE:

Unless you have some suggestions, etc.

R. E. LEE TO U. S. GRANT:

There is one thing I would like to mention. The cavalrymen and artillerists own their own horses in our army. I would like to understand whether these men will be permitted, etc.

U. S. GRANT TO R. E. LEE:

You will find that the terms do not allow this. Only the officers, etc.

R. E. LEE TO U. S. GRANT:

No, the terms do not allow it. That is clear.

U. S. GRANT TO R. E. LEE:

Well, the subject is quite new to me. I take it that most of the men in the ranks are small farmers, and as the country has been so raided by the two armies, it is doubtful whether they will be able to put in a crop, etc. Let all the men who claim to own a horse or mule take the animals home with them, etc.

R. E. LEE TO U. S. GRANT:

This will have the best possible effect, etc.

And now Lee said something about notifying Meade, and Grant said something by way of apology for turning up without a sword (*no disrespect intended, etc.*), and Lee said something about the two armies being kept apart (*personal encounters, etc.*), and then Grant suggested something or other, and Lee mentioned something about something else—but who remembered? It was over, it was all over.

There were some spoken words to be taken down, of course, there were some names to be signed, some token courtesies (the bowing of the principals, the salutes of the aides), there were coughs to cough and quickly kill and a pause to fill and soften with goodbyes—but it was over for the C. S. A. There were some odds and ends of defeat outside, but why report the prying eyes of the Union staff, the half-minute wait for *Traveller* to be bridled, the queer way Lee stood striking and striking his hands, the misfortune of Grant's appearing on the porch and covering the moment by baring his head? Why mention such things? Why pay attention to a paroled officer riding a gift horse back to what was left of the Army of Northern Virginia with the five years that were left of his life? Look away! For God's sake, look away!

Item: Phil Sheridan paid twenty dollars in gold for the table used by Grant. Lee's went to Cresap Ord for forty.

This will have a very happy effect, etc.

JOHN WILKES BOOTH   *1865*

PLAY WITHIN A PLAY

Ah, you've a bad hand; the lines all cris-cras.

—a fortune-teller

The hand held a single-shot brass derringer firing a .41 caliber ball. . . .

What was the hand's history? Where had it been, what had it done, in the twenty-seven years of its age? Had it trifled with the sun and moon, with lone stars and Charles's Wain, with the beaded bars of a crib? Had it caught at straws of sound, a bell-tone, a tick of time, the sharps of a passing bird? Had glass cut or fire burned it, had it learned the trick of turning pages, had it picked the eyes from a shag tiger? Had it borne a flag, a toy sword, a toy horn, had its skin been pricked by a pin, a thorn, or (from within) a broken bone? Could it take a fly on the wing, cast a stone, wring a neck, could it make music wave from wire? Was it dry or damp, was it steady holding cards, deft at pouring wine? Did it slap backs and pound tables, did it play in public gardens, or was it found in private parks? Did it make a tight fist, did it write fine, and what oaths had it sworn, what bargains struck? Was it coked by callus or a soft touch for children and other things of silk and smoke? Did it sport rings, hair, scars, was its blood still short of the fourth generation of those that hated the Lord. . . ?

The derringer weighed half a pound. The ball weighed half an ounce.

MARY LINCOLN   *1865*

GOOD FRIDAY AT FORD'S THEATRE

He'd die the next morning, in the Peterson house across the street, but she'd beat about the world for another seventeen years before she lit and lay down beside him on that hill in Illinois. It'd be the same shot, though, that did for both of them, him in a matter of hours, her a long road later and hard going every yard of the way.

She was an odd make, God knows, a pustule of woman, a sty, a sore, and you could hurt her with a word too many, one too few, or none at all, with a bow more curt than she thought her due. A cough out of season, a glance, sass, soft soap, even, and she'd storm you to shame though your name was Abe. She was vain of her blood, a rare vintage, she deemed it, claret from a peerless year. It galled her to be on the sawed-off side, squat, she seemed, and it served her not to put on airs: her feet still touched the ground. A short blue in the tall grass, she was, a better among worse, and with feuds outnumbering friends, she became a pigeon for her image in the glass: she bought six hundred pairs of gloves, shawls that cost in the thousands, pearls, diamonds, gowns, feather and ribbon bravery, traps, stuff, things, bought till buying alone was the end she sought. Still and all, money was her one and panic dream, money or its lack, and the shadow cast by plenty assumed the shape of need. She hearkened to diviners, to readers of signs, bell-ringers, beaters of drums in the dark. She was a nest of whims and pique, of spleen and dander, and a fire always smoldered in her grate. She was a suite of ills and pain, with chambers for chills and fevers, for the migraine, the uterine lesion, and a curse that came in spates, and before the finish there'd be fluid in her tissues, sugared urine, swellings of the hand and foot, and she'd suffer loss of weight, failing vision, an impairment of the mind, a fall from a chair. . . .

A long road, hers, and she'd die it by the inch. She'd have little at the last—a pair or two of those gloves, some rags of *mousseline de soie*, a torn fan, a balding fur, no friend, no feud, and one damn son who'd sworn her mad. And yet, what would she have done to be brought so low—lived near the light and not been lit? Would that be her crime, that she'd never glowed, that she'd lowered Abe's day with her night?

ABRAHAM LINCOLN   *1865*

SEVEN CARS IN BLACK BUNTING

As the trucks began to spin out track, to the dead man in the seventh car, it might've been the depot that departed, the train that was standing still. To him, not he but the world was going away—but who can speak for the dead, who can say? To the living, he was on the move, and over the same seventeen hundred miles of rail he'd ridden once before. They were in reverse order now, and the last mile was the first, and the first would be the last, and the things and places passed—creeks, towns, telegraph-poles—the book of things and places would read backward, from the right. Seven million faces would be deployed between the District of Columbia and the state of Illinois, and there would be fires in the night, limp farewells from rain-soaked flags, and gloom doled by guns and bells, and famous men would be there behind plumed pairs, and unknowns, a week on the march to see seven cars come, would watch for a moment and see seven cars go.

ABRAHAM LINCOLN   *1865*

MARSE LINKUM

Tell fewer of the funny stories I told
And make no further mention of my plug hat,
My rolled umbrella, and my outsize shoes,

Bury the legend that I was a bastard deep,
Let my mother's sleep be that of the just,
And if you must be heard, speak briefly
Of my wife Mary and my wife's madness,
But speak not a word of my spoken-for Ann
Nor say that I loved her all my life.

Forget my arms and legs, my awkward ways,
And the guffaws I caused when I sat a horse,
Forget the catnapping pickets I pardoned,
Forget my Four-score speech, my Bixby letter,
And my six-mile walk to refund six cents,
Forget the first house I lived in (let it rot
And let all the others, but not the last),
And build me no more monuments, nor cast me
But as pennies for children, for small change.

Say not that I saw two faces in my glass,
One like my own and one strange, as if bled,
And dismiss my dreams of a terrible end
Such as many now dead dreamed of and found
Before the sunken road at Fredericksburg,
Make little of my anger at little McClellan
(Outnumbered! With two blues for every gray!)
And less of the lie that the slaves were freed,
Because you know better, and so do they.

Say naught of my high voice and my sad eyes,
Throw away my relics (the watch and key,
The muffler, the ox-yoke, and the rock
On which I scratched my name and Ann's),
And retain but a pair of my photographs,
A Brady for the hard evidence of my looks
And a Gardner for the books of learned fools,
And now that only my coat can be pilfered,
Stop moving my coffin from place to place
And let the ghouls unfrock these bones.

Such are the slight favors that I request,
Yet if it please you not, grant me none:
Get my old chestnuts off your chest

Should they still strike you funny,
And if you like, praise me as Honest Abe
And raise a log-cabin Christ with nails,
Re-engrave this grave and homely face
On your money, preserve the box at Ford's,
And make cold fact of the cool fiction
That my father's name was In- or Enlow,
Wring more tears from women on the floor
For bounty-jumpers and last-remaining sons,
And count the ones that kissed my hand,
And if your tongues are slung in the middle,
Then keep Ann and my love for Ann green
While you hail the hell I had with Mary.

Small favors, and done without with ease,
For I doubt there's much I much require
To lie decently dead save your living long,
And you will so live, and I will so lie,
If you know the truth: it was you, not I,
That Booth was hired to kill, it was you,
The Union, that he fired at in firing at me,
And since I died of what went wide of you,
Please remember all I stood for when I fell.

CHINESE IN CALIFORNIA   *1866*

THE PIG-BUSINESS

Every branch of industry in California swarms with Chinese.
We appeal to the working man to step to the front and hurl
back the tide of barbarous invaders.
                                        —speech at a Union meeting

At Hong Kong and Macao, they were put below decks, stowed away
hundreds to a hull, and they never saw daylight till Frisco showed on
the beam. The pig-business—that's what they called the coolie traf-
fic, but of course no offense was meant. They were human enough,
the Mongolians; it was just that they stank like swine when the
hatches were opened and they swilled out onto the Embarcadero.

We kind of liked them at first. Being mostly up at the diggings, we had to hire somebody to wash our drawers, to hew the wood and fetch it to the fire, somebody had to do the swink—and who better than the Chink from China? A dollar a day, they'd work for, and they made it pay for the seaweed they ate, and for their grass shoes and grass hats, and it covered their fan-tan bets if they happened to lose on the beans, and, damn their cockeyed eyes, two bits out of eight went back to Asia!

Still, we didn't call them heathen in those days, we didn't find them dark, vain, peculiar, cruel, we didn't say they practiced all the nameless vices of the East. Instead, we gave them the glad hand, brought them home as house-boys and let them rule our roosts, and if they turned an odd penny on the side, if they learned to spin wool and weave it, to can shrimp and dress stone, what did it count against pay-dirt in a pan? We even looked the other way when they took over the shirt-trade, the whole jimbang, and nobody cared about the cigar-trade, either, or the boot-trade, and who was hurt when they grew zinnias in the sloughs and truck on the dunes, soil where us whites would've simply grown old? We didn't fear them at all.

Things looked good then. Up there in those brown hills, we just stood in the shade and waited for riches to flow down to us from up-stream: they'd never play out, we thought, not so long as water ran. We were wrong, sad to say, and the day came when it hardly paid to fill a cradle, and we had to quit our claims and grub for wages. Our house-boys, damn their slanting souls, they made livings off our leav-ings! For them, there was gold in the pickings of a nose.

And now we were afraid of them, and none the less so when they showed us up on the Donner grade. It was mile-high work, laying CeePac track, and if the black powder didn't kill you, the white snow would. It was no job for boomers, that one, hanging from a cliff and hacking its face for a place to stand, it wasn't for us, a winter under forty-foot drifts, it wasn't for a mule or even for a nigger—but the damn yellow devils, they never came up for air! Crocker's pets, we called them, but they built him a railroad down there in the dark. It stunned us, the way we caved in, and those grinning little bastards lasted till spring.

We cut the ropes on some of them, and we shot a few when we were out for deer, and we knew a trick or two about starting a slide, and when May came and the snow was going, we spotted them below Cape Horn and Cisco. A thousand feet down, they were, small stiffs in blue, some still holding a pick in their hands. We had to do it, you understand, we were only human. . . .

THADDEUS STEVENS   *1868*

THIS QUIET AND SECLUDED SPOT

Finding other cemeteries limited as to race, I have chosen this.
                                                          —Thaddeus Stevens

Caliban, they called him in the Cloak Room, and then they gave him the frailties that sorted with the name, all but the clubfoot. He got that from his father, who was either a cobbler in Vermont or, as they said behind a hand in the House, Père Talleyrand. A big-domed man, bald as a bubble, he died in his wig at seventy-six, mourned at his bedside by his mulatto mistress. If others wept, then or when they put him under an out-of-the-way piece of Pennsylvania, their tears were shed within: he had no friends, he left no kin. There were many at the grave, but they'd only come to see that he went.

He lived as if he had a lifelong feud with the human race. Where he had been, hatred stayed, smoke from a passing train, and sprayed sparks were the words he spoke—*I now yield to Mr. B., who will make a few feeble remarks.* He believed in no God, no family of Gods, no one who pissed standing up and no one sitting down. He drank, gambled, plunged and paid up (two hundred thousand once for a bankrupt partner), and his black love referred to them as *we.*

But beyond cards, pot-pleasure, and chambering lay his real and red-hot passion: the hanging of the South, master, mister, and trash in gray. For him, no banjos, no chinquapins, no skirts that sailed on coonskinned lawns, nor had the War for him been a hard-fought game: it had been treason and murder, and the traitors were slated to pay. He meant for them to swing, the way Brown had swung, and, with their blood attaint, their land would go to other lords, the blue-gum one-time slaves.

He came within a vote of bringing it off.

THE LOBBY   *1869*

THE NAST PEOPLE

There are too many pigs for the tits.

—A. Lincoln

They thronged the streets, the stairs, the presence chambers, they
plucked at sleeves in whorehouse halls; they swelled fairs and balls
and queues that formed for shaking hands; they stood at curbs and
crossings, they met steamers, stages, and the cars, they swarmed
hells, bars, stunt-shows, stags; they frequented solonian floors and
cloakrooms, and they were meek when spurned from *pissoir* doors—
they merely turned the other cheek.

They were there for franchises, routes, grants, letters patent, *cartes
blanches* to all in sight and delights as yet unseen; they were there
for rights-of-way, sinecures, a mountain range if one was unspoken
for, or a time-zone, say, or such small change as lay around loose. It
added up, the much and the little: it came to the U. S. A.

UNION PACIFIC   *1869*

DESERET*

In the Book of Mormon, a coined word meaning land of the
working bee.

The Shoshone on the butte did not call it that, nor did he call it Zion,
or Utah, or anything else. He had names for snakes and streams and
rain, for other braves and other horses, and for his own and other
dogs, and he knew how to summon spirits and tick off certain birds,
and he had terms for time and thing and place, and in his tales of the
chase and war, the names of the dead would come alive. But this
roundabout him was the world, and he could make no sound, no
small word, that would take it all in.

Far down, near the great still lake of brine, the diamond stack of
Jupiter and the straight one of *119* sent black smokes into the sky,

and they wrote a sign that he understood who could not read. Die, it told him: take your people and your people's bones, take your no-account ponies and your greasy ginch, take your smell and arraigning eyes, and go away and die—but not too close to the railroad line. That was the sign written in engine smoke.

Under each mile of track, 2,640 ties had been laid, and north and south of the right-of-way, no oak now stood for fifty miles, no cedar, no fir, no ash or cottonwood. Buffalo, shot for their tongues alone, rotted in the sun and starlight and stank both hot and cold. The pronghorns had fled the steel bees and, stung, died on the dead run, and bear were robes now, and gone the four-stripe chipmunk and the porcupine with yellow hair, and in the salt sea, loon and teal were pickled feathers now, killed not for the pot but to kill an afternoon.

A spike-maul spoke in the distance, and small waves broke on the butte: the golden nail was going in.

R. E. LEE AND *TRAVELLER*   1870

A PAIR OF CONFEDERATES

Virginia is my country.

—R. E. Lee

A gray with black points, the horse was, and his rider rode him from lone deaths on picket to death in rows on redolent fields. Gray himself, himself gray roan, he rode no end of miles among his bayonets, slants of sunlight, they may have seemed, and many more miles he rode in the rain, and then another few, the longest ride, to surrender. *Traveller*, the mount was called, and after Seven Pines he was there for all of it, all the high-water marks, all the sunken roads and bloody angles, all four years of plural and singular killing, and he was there too, rubbed to a shine and wrought with ribbons, when the gray rider died—close by he stood, just outside the door. They're bones in boxes now, those two, relics in a shrine, as though they'd given up the ghost, like Jesus, exalting the name of the Lord. Saint and saintly steed they've become, instead of graybacks dead in a grailless cause.

GEORGE CATLIN   *1872*

PAINTER OF THE PAINTED INDIAN

Oh how I love a people who don't live for the love of money.
—George Catlin

When he was born there, they were still talking about the Wyoming Valley massacre. They were still plowing up powderhorns and now and then a mildewed moccasin, still finding buckles and bits of faded cloth, and the swamp where the womenfolk fled still yielded the odd set of bones. It was only a dozen years back to the day the British and the Mohawks attacked from the north, to the stand that was made at Forty Fort, and the night of killing after the fight was lost. He must've heard the story young and often: they were still telling it to each other, those that survived, as if once they stopped, they'd stop being alive.

Dwelling on how prisoners were cooked on coals, fried in their own fat, he could've grown to hate the Indians more each time the tale was told. It would've been easy to say hell was too cold for the kind who pleasured in their victims' pain, who were quick to madden and slow to be satisfied, who were two-faced, malign in the mind, stiff with pride, and born with a craze to kill. You'd've sworn he'd hold, as so many did, that no Indian was any good, not even a dead one.

He never believed that, though. To him, the whites were the thieves and murderers, the whites were the perjurers, the cheats, the makers of war and in war the savages, it was the whites who had jails, poorhouses, locks and keys, and law. He said *Nothing short of the loss of my life shall prevent me from visiting their country and becoming their historian,* and he did visit them, Sauk and Mandan, Assiniboin and Cree, and on his little canvas reservations he kept the red man green. And he never really lost his life: he gave it away to a people who died without Jesus but lived without greed.

HENRY WARD BEECHER   *1874*

ON A COUCH IN THE VESTRY

I gave her a paroxysmal kiss.

—Henry Ward Beecher

It beat the band, how he stuck his gun up all those skirts. A preacher and a preacher's son, he was, and you wouldn't've thought him a candidate for the hell his father promised and the hell he promised himself. You'd've supposed that some. of the fears he raised were his own, and that though his eye was ever open, he'd keep his fly closed. If so, you'd've had it bass-ackwards.

As a boy, twice he was sent to schools for girls, one he among forty shes, and he got to know them early, their smell, their sound, and, under the cellar stairs, perhaps their taste and feel as well. He was barely of age when he married that Eunice of his, and he kept her on her back for some-and-twenty years. He did the same for others— there were other beds, other tables, other floors, and there was that dee-vine divan behind the vestry doors.

Women rumored him, he was current in their murmurs and airs, forwarded by glances, palpitations, sudden quiet, and always in his presence you seemed to hear the sibilance of silk, as if his mistress of the day were rushing to keep their tryst. There were many such—a Betty-something, fourteen when he showed her the ceiling, and Sarah, the slave he bought and installed so close to home, and the wife of the man he owed his pulpit to—a congregation of whores, he had, some coming at him in furs to the chin and some in ready-mades.

And then, turning a page, you reached Libby Tilton, mother of five but half his age and twice as lewd. Her hair, drawn down flat, was an embrace, a black bracket for her face, and as you stared at that sphincteral mouth of hers and her heavy roll-top eyes, you thought of the bolted vestry and its lowered blinds, and you saw those dark glims loving upward in the gloom—and all at once your envy of the devil-dodger died. It was you, not he, between her and the sky.

FRANK LLOYD WRIGHT

GIFTS FOR HER SON

All are in my fingers to this day.

—Frank Lloyd Wright

When she opened the box, what met the eye was a rhapsody of things. Toys, they might've seemed to some, the blocks and cylinders, the rings, the paper wafers and paper diamonds. *Kinderspiel*, the cubes, the cones, the painted balls, the gaudy sheets to cut and fold, and they made an iridian falls as the box was tilted and they spilled to the floor. The boy knelt before the bright disarray, but not as to pistareens, beguiling picayunes. To him, the turned wood and tinted pasteboard were the integrants of a world he'd build on the world that was known, they were geometries that his mother had poured at his feet, and with them he'd improve on the six days' work of the Lord.

He'd live to see some of his wonders undone and others in danger —alas the day, he'd be a builder of mortal monuments. If that box had informed a smaller art, one that might've adorned an altar, a wall, the newel of a spiral stair, it would've still been there for the final fanfare. But no structure would hold him: he was for the open air, to be contained and cold-shouldered by the *nouveaux riches* next door, to be leaned against by loafers, a striker for matches, a surface for *affiches*, to suffer the wear of the seasons, to bear the indifference of dogs and other passersby. He'd stand till he stood in the way.

SEQUOIA GIGANTEA 1875

THE MIGHTY FALLEN

He offered to bet that he could fall it with an ax in thirty days or better—a month's pay, he said, for a month's work—and he was covered. The stake didn't come to much, a hundred dollars, maybe, give or take, nor did the parties in their persons make the little seem a lot: to tell the truth, nobody ever rightly knew their names. What sweetened the pot was simply the size of the tree.

It grew near Dinkey Creek, a tributary of the North Fork of the Kings, and it'd been growing there since the Year One, meaning the one in 1 A. D. At the rise of Christ, therefore, it had thirty-three plies, and it comprised seventy-nine for Pompeii. Fire scarred it when Roland died betrayed on the Pampeluna road, and drought and flood tried it, and heat and freeze, and it stood off moth, disease, sapsucker, and the pest that fed on seed, and it lived through lightning, fork, sheet, chain, and ball, and through wind and rain and all the crescent hazards of age. So tall was it, some swore, that it touched the face of the moon, and to band the base, it took a ring-around of twenty men. *The Old Gentleman*, the stick was called, a good deal of wood to bring down in thirty days.

Three feet thick, the bark was, but like a sponge, and the blade bit it free in henna chunks, and then the cambium layer went, showing the alburnum, after which the going got harder. In a week, though, there was a knee-deep rut in the chips about the tree, and in two weeks, the bole appeared to rare up from a pit of old-rose smithereens: the man himself was out of sight. All day and part of the night, flakes of history flew, and time ran backward as the evergreen's time ran out. Oolong steeped in Boston Bay, and the Maid became a saint on a spit. King John signed a screed in a Surrey meadow, a Crusade began and failed, and heartwood grown when Rome was sacked scaled through later air. The wafer was taken by Constantine, and seven miles from Naples, a spew of cinders, stone, and ash. . . .

The tree went down as the fourth week ended, crown, trunk, butt, and all. At the core of the stump, a sliver was left, a spicule as old as the Calvary cross. In a moment, the man would break it off and use it to pick his teeth.

CRAZY HORSE   *1876*

HOKA HEY!

This is a good day to die!

—Crazy Horse

There were soldiers along the ridge, and there were soldiers in the wood and on the bluff and backed against the stream, and we killed them in all those places, though they fought bravely and lived till

Death came to take the dead away, late in the afternoon. Beside the Little Big Horn, much fine killing was done that day, wherefore truly had Curly spoken when he called it a good day for dying: when whites died, it was always a good day. But what we did not know then, savoring their blood and wearing their hair, was that we too were now dead, not some of us only but all, those of us still under horses in the high grass and those singing in stolen hats and the tops we cut from the soldiers' boots—all. It was a good day to die, Curly said, and thereafter we never lived again. It was the end of living for us, that victory in the hills where the Tongue River rose, and the Rosebud ran.

GEN. GEORGE CUSTER   *1876*

ON THE LITTLE BIG HORN

The guide said, ". . . They have told you that the Sioux scalped every man but Custer that day. They have told you that the Indians, fearing his bravery even in death, permitted him alone to wear his hair to the end. But Custer was not at any time a man of greatness to us as an Indian-fighter (Crook, yes, but not Custer), and if, as some said, he once had taken the field against the Cheyennes and Arapahoes on the Ouachita, few here on the Big Horn knew his name, and of those none trembled when our scouts brought it in at dawn: he was only a white soldier, to be met, to be fought, and to be killed. He died with fine bravery, for there was much of it in his body, and therefore we desired it, but there was much also of false pride, and it was for this, not the other, that we refrained from eating his heart and taking his hair: we refused to taint ourselves with the rashness, the disdain, that had made him attack four thousand with six hundred. Always and under any conditions, we had attacked man for man, and so often as to make us despair, we had attacked one for two, but we knew that one sent against seven must die, and we thought this Custer very bold in the mind, very proud, to offend Death as he did that afternoon: he must have known that Death would be displeased. Not only were the Sioux before him in great force, but also they were laden with ammunition and repeating-rifles of a good pattern, and more than this, they were weary of being run like game from whatever country the whites thought good for Gold; they wished ardently for one place from which they would be harried no more, for one place in all this land that did not promise to hold the Yellow Powder the whites so deeply cared for and killed so much to obtain."

The guide looked out over the groundswell toward the Rosebud Mountains, saying, "This place on the Little Big Horn was such a one as our people had longed for. It was a lost country then, as it is now, and there was much game in it, of which little is left but wolves. It was far from the reservation in the Black Hills, but the whites themselves had forced my people out when the Yellow Powder was found there, and they thought that it would serve them well to go once and forever to where they would not again be compelled to move their houses while the whites dug up the floor for buried bones. When the Dakota earth lay dead, with many holes in it, the whites invited my people to return, but they were unwilling, for they could not live where they had been defamed—and Custer was sent out to bring them in."

The guide squatted on his heels alongside a lone stone in the waving grass, and uprooting a few stalks that brushed its graven face (U. S. Soldier 7 U. S. Cav.), he said, "He did not know that eight days earlier, Crazy Horse and twelve hundred Sioux had fallen on the Gray Fox, as Crook was called, and defeated fifteen troops of cavalry, five companies of mounted infantry, and two hundred and fifty Crow and Shoshone scouts. Nor did he deem it necessary to wait for Gibbon's column to come up with its battery of Gatling guns before throwing himself on the largest Indian village since the days of Montezuma, although he was warned of it by his half-breed, Mitch Bouyer. And finally, he did not think that my people would fight hard enough to hurt him if he divided his command. He detached Benteen with three troops of cavalry to flush the hills on the left, and they were gone from the field; he sent Reno and three more troops against the center, where twenty-five hundred Sioux under Gall and Two Moon cut them to pieces as soon as they deployed; and with five troops for himself, Custer rode off to the right, or straight toward us along this ridge. Every man that rode behind him died within an hour, one for each of these stones. They fought bravely, and they drew much Indian blood before they fell, but they had come to kill us with guns, and having guns ourselves, we killed them, and they died. . . ."

THE MOLLY MAGUIRES   *1877*

CLASS STRUGGLE

They all protested their innocence and all died game.
                                             —Eugene Debs

They swung eleven of them—Boyle, McGeghan, Munley, Roarity,
Carroll, and Duffy at Pottsville, Lanahan at Wilkes-Barre, and
Campbell, Doyle, Kelly, and Donahue at Mauch Chunk—eleven.
There were those, though, who made it ten, and if ten it was, which
one lived to wind up in a canal, or under a train, or while serving a
lag in the pen? Who drew the long straw, the pebble, the numbered
slip, who held the charm—Lanahan, Munley, Kelly, Roarity? Who
broke jail, who sang before his last supper—Boyle, Campbell, Dona-
hue? Who beat death by taking his life, who died even as they came
to kill him, who was never caught and never tried—Duffy, Doyle,
Carroll, McGeghan. . . ?

What had they done, the ten, the eleven? Had they croaked some
member of the multitude, a clerk in a store, a teller, a sorter of let-
ters, a girl they'd ganged, or were the micks all hanged for stiffing
their betters, did they bomb some Silk Hat Harry, a man or men with
monograms, is that the kind the Mollies paid for, a Boss of the Pits, a
lienor, a turner of the screw, or were they scragged for bagging a
nothing at all, a Pinkerton, say, a shack, a powder monkey, a com-
pany snitch, a scratcher of backs for the hard-coal rich?

Which one got away? Was it that McGeghan. . . ?

BOSS TWEED   *1878*

WRONG-WAY ALGER-BOY

Politics were always dishonest. A politician in coming forward
takes things as they are.   —William Marcy Tweed

He has gone to dwell in that place where the worm dieth not, and
the fire is not quenched.

He was buried in Greenwood Cemetery by the Palestine Lodge of
the Free and Accepted Masons. Over his grave-clothes, he wore his
lamb-skin apron of innocence.

At the age of fifty-five, he died of diabetes and heart disease in New York's Ludlow Street jail. With him for the last rattle were a son-in-law, a physician, a friend, a warden, a lawyer, a daughter (just then arrived with ice cream), a black servant named Luke, and, over in a corner, Azrael, the Angel of Death.

Tried before a jury under an indictment containing two hundred and twenty counts of misprision, he was found guilty of two hundred and four. Had his sentences been made to run consecutively, he would have served one hundred and two years in the coop. He was put away for only two, though; he got a century off for cash.

In a span of thirty months, he stung the City of New York for $200,000,000.

He said *What are you going to do about it?*

He built a courthouse, and for every dollar it actually cost, he rigged a bill for five. *Tammany! Tammany!* His plasterer (Andrew Garvey, Prince of Plasterers) was paid $2,800,000 for his work, which would have been a fair figure only if he had put the same three coats on the state of Arkansas. *Tammany! Tammany!* For three chairs and forty tables (or was it three tables and forty chairs?), he approved a charge of $180,000. *Tammany! Tammany!* Six reams of foolscap, two dozen pen-holders, and four bottles of ink came to $10,000 on the nail. *Tammany!*

He said *What are you going to do about it?*

When his daughter was married at Trinity Chapel, sports, hangers-on, whores, and fancy men sent her gifts worth $700,000.

The books of the city were examined by John Jacob Astor (Prince of Calciminers), and they were found to be in order. He did not question a voucher for $66,000 endorsed by one Philip Dummy and another for $64,000 bearing the signature of a T. C. Cash.

He said *What are you going to do about it?*

He offered Tom Nast half a million dollars to go abroad and study art—and forget cartooning.

In his shirt-front, he wore a diamond as big as a blue eye.

He kept his pussy at his coachman's house.

He married into his employer's family.

He was industrious, frugal, respectful, frank.

He had a head for names and faces.

He shook hands warmly, often adding his left.

He smiled readily, seldom with cold teeth.

He weighed 260 pounds.

He did not smoke.
He did not drink.
He took his wages home to Mother.
He said *What are you going to do about it?*
And he was born.

THE KING RANCH   *1885*

THE RUNNING W

*Be it remembered that Richard King deposited his Brand and
Ear Marks for Horses & Cattle in Book B for Registry of
Brands.*

— County records, Texas

For all anybody ever knew about him, his life began at the age of
eleven in the hold of the *Desdemona*, a sailing-ship a few days out of
New York for Mobile. He was a stowaway, and when found, he gave
a maybe name and mightbe date of birth, and then he quit talking as
if there were nothing more to say. It came to be a paying habit, that
one, keeping his eyes wide open and his mouth nearly shut, and in
the sixty years he lived he hardly missed a trick. He hardly missed a
hectare, either, or a cow, or a hog, or a mustang mare, and by staying
mum, he departed rich, this Richard King that *Cristo* knew where
he came from, and *Dios* knew where he went.

He was well-nigh half a century between the Nueces and the Rio
Grande, and next to the fief he put together there, the surest thing
about him is that he wore out lawyers in spans of two and teams of
four. In fact, he demoted them to notaries, and it was their lifework
to attest the rights, the *derechos*, he bought up from the Eusebios
and Faustinos who still held a share in a Spanish grant, a *poco* thirty-
second or a *poquito* sixty-fourth. What parchment they must've con-
sumed, those *abogados*, what seals and tape, what ink! What palms
they must've crossed to quiet titles, what gifts made to scribe and
appraiser, to *jefe* and registrar, what compliments paid to *niños*,
in-laws, the crucifix, and Bolivar!

It's all but lost now, the cost to King of a Texas league, seven
square miles of hock-high grass. The numbers are under lock and

key, they're in sequestered libers and impounded minds, and there are deaf ears and blind stares, and questions fly with no dry land to light on. But someone slipped once—King, was it, or King's counsel? —and the truth is on file in the County of Starr, a far cry from the first parcel the man took in fee simple. It's in the Mendiola grant, and for one time, by a few words only, too much is said. For *three hundred dollars, the receipt of which is hereby acknowledged*, it conveys to King forever and a day all that part of the earth known as the Rincon de Santa Gertrudis—fifteen thousand acres for the *gringo*, two cents apiece for the Mex!

Cancer of the stomach killed him, but before he died, the *patron* of the Running W owned more ground than fast mounts could ride him around in a week. A million acres were his, together with all their trees and game and grain, all the water that rose, all the rain that fell and ran. All the space between heaven and hell were his, all the flies and ticks and flowers and dust, all the wild horses and the half-wild spics. And, as his title-deeds pray, much good, much good, much good may it do him!

U. S. GRANT   *1885*

LAST IN PEACE

In his early pictures, you lost the person and saw the clothes, wrinkled, dusty, and doubtless stained, and after a while, you came to know that the man too was in need of pressing. But even so, with his creases sponged, he'd still smell of old smoke and cold and mildewed rooms; even in his best, lace frill shirt, sprigged vest, and smooth tile, you knew you'd find a trace of bacon grease, of harness and a long-ago cigar.

He lived a four-year life, the length of the war. The rest of it, before and later, was only time ticking toward a day at Mount McGregor, when it ticked itself away. First he failed for forty years. Whatever he tried came to little if he was lucky and less if not: where he farmed, nothing grew; where he kept store, there was no gain; where he bore arms, others shone. For forty years, he put his hand to this and that, and finally something seemed to wane in him, his will, maybe, or maybe his blood, and he was dead wine, flat champagne, as if the fizz had gone out of him or never been in.

Then came those four years when he went from two bars (retired) to three stars among the blown shapes in the dumps of war, the wrung parts, the hard rags, the iridescent flies and fat. He wore three gold stars on his coat in that house at Appomattox, but when, after certain punctilios, he rose to bow his blue to gray, suddenly there lay ahead of him only a fourth star and twenty-one guns, more honors to splash, more medals to cover with ash and disgrace, sixty thousand more cigars, and a tomb on Riverside Drive. But he'd've died years before his date of death, and what they'd put away in marble was a long-gone and shopworn stiff.

THE VANDERBILTS   *1885*

MONUMENT TO MANURE

Still enjoyed by the family is the story of how the old Commodore was bested by his son in a business transaction. William, it seems, desired to purchase from his father a load of fertilizer. . . .

Dutchmen, they were, and they got their start on Staaten Eylandt, Moravians from Utrecht, dull-witted fellows, farmers most of them and the rest ferrymen, but what they knew best was the value of a guilder or guelder or whatever the hell they called their money before the day of the dollar. A close kind, the Van Der Bilts, a niggardly strain of man, pinchfisted and pinched in the mind, a string-gutted breed with a creed that had to ring true and a God they bit first and then believed in.

By the time he died and left it all behind him, William had run that load of shit up to two hundred millions' worth, enough to bury Staaten Eylandt a mile deep and him deeper, for he lies six feet under New Dorp, a spit from where he was born. His tomb is romanesque, with twin domes, like miters, and buttresses and pillared arches and, above the main portal, seven slender windows, a candelabrum of lights for the soul of the dead shit-merchant. The pile, it's said, was suggested by a chapel at Nîmes honoring St. Giles, a holy man who'd given his goods to the poor and who lived, they say, on herbs and the milk of a hind which came to him at certain hours of the day.

EMILY DICKINSON *1886*

REVENGE OF THE NERVES

the doctor calls it. —Emily Dickinson

A sickbed phrase, garish words for pallid days, but in his journal he wrote *Bright's disease*. From a long-sunk Anatomy, some bubbles of lore still rose, and on a remembered renal section, he saw the Malpighian pyramids, the columns of Bertin—*Bright's disease*, he thought, and he reached for a pen, but the pen was in his hand and his finding on the page. He knew what was killing her, and he could almost set the time. He knew from the color and kind of urine, from the pains in the back, the fever, the hydroptic hands and feet, he knew from old books, old cadavers—*Bright's disease*.

It was a high wide world, the room she lay in, and the sights it held he never descried. There were wilds inside the wall, there were rare shores and private ports of call, and he strode unaware among flowers, flights of bees, birds achant in a virgin mode. In that world of hers, he breathed love, not air, but what he sought there was Bowman's capsule, and what he found was a name for death—*Bright's disease*.

THE HAYMARKET, I *1886*

A JUROR: *I'D HANG ALL THE DAMN BUGGERS*

Not the ones who sold the Army defective guns
And worm-eaten hulls that wouldn't hold a nail,
Nor those who made paper shoes and blue shoddy

That faded to gray and fell apart in the rain,
Nor the peddlers of tainted beef, death in cans,
Nor the ghouls who cashed in on gullible grief,
Shipping mule-bones north as the Union's slain,
Nor the dry witches walking on watered stock,
Nor their one-star shills, the brazen brigadiers,
Nor the trained animals in their act on the Bench,
Nor the pastors and the pastor-masters, the rich.
I'd hang all the damn buggers, the juror said,
And he meant the eight framed in the Haymarket.

The ritual of the law consumed a Chicago summer
Habitually reserved for croquet at Lake Forest,
A bit of garter at one of the better beaches,
And muskellunge on light tackle off Charlevoix,
But Judge Gary (Joseph) made the best of it.
He entertained ladies of fashion behind the Bar,
Executing sleights of hand for their amusement,
Feeding them bonbons, and telling droll fictions
To beguile their minds from the luminous passion
Of eight dirty radicals on trial for their lives.
In general, the fillies and mares were charmed,
And the prosecutor's wife whiled away the time
Covering sheets of paper with knots and nooses.

I'd hang all the damn buggers, the juror said,
But he was given only five—only four, really,
Because Louis Lingg smoked a stick of dynamite
That a policeman concealed in a nickel cigar,
And you couldn't snap a spine that you couldn't find.

THE HAYMARKET, II   *1886*

PATROLMAN MATHIAS DEGAN

It's still there. If you go west on Randolph, four blocks after you cross
the Chicago River, you'll get to the Haymarket: it's where it always
was. But this time, nobody you know will be spellbinding a crowd

from a wagon-tail or listening entranced in the rain; the faces of a certain night in May are gone now, a life or two away and nearly out of sight downstream. If voices are heard, they won't be saying what they said then, and you'll not be stirred to shake your neighbor's hand, or make a fist at the sky, or cry *No!* and *Never!* for some firebrand, Parsons, maybe, or Fielden, or Adolph something (Fischer, was it?). There's no hay on sale in that place now and nothing to show it was ever sold, not even a telltale trace on the air, and where the bomb fell and sixty-six bluecoats bled, the ground has been sixty-six times paved.

If the seven that died have slipped your mind, you can read their names on a stone, from blown-up Degan down. When they lumped his drabbled driblets, a lung, a kneecap, ten or a dozen teeth, a hand without a thumb, when they trumped up a head and stuffed a new suit full, when they bought a box and put the forcemeat bull on view, all Cook County came for a walleyed look, the poor, the poorer, and, poorer still, the rich. To these last, he was a godsend. They lagged eight dreary little foreigners for his murder—bottom dogs, steerage people oddly tagged (Neebe, Spies, Engel, Schwab, Lingg with a pair of *g*s), shiny-coats, Rooshian scurfs, sheenies off some teeming shore —and put them on trial for their shabby little lives.

In talk and print, though, in the written word and the word on wire, they were in Dutch for a higher crime than murder: the affair was called The Anarchists' Case. Well, they *were* anarchists, and they'd said as much in their greasy gazettes (daily in *Die Arbeiter* and every other week in *The Alarm*), confessions that went at a penny apiece. In black-letter bold, they told the police all:

> Damn law and order. We have obeyed law and order long enough. The time has come to strangle the law.
> The law is your enemy.
> Lay hands on it and throttle it until it makes its last kick.
> Throttle it. Kill it. Stab it.
> Arm yourselves. If you do not, birds will sing May songs on your graves.
> Force is the only way.

Fashionable gash was there to stare at a lower grade of meat. Judge Gary stood treat to comfits and creams, and when his guests began to jade, he fed them again, with bon mots now and leger-demain.

Dynamite is the power with which to gain our rights.

Every man must learn how to make and use dynamite.

Of all the good stuff, this is the stuff. Stuff this sublime stuff into an inch pipe, plug up both ends, insert a cap with a fuse attached, place this in the immediate neighborhood of a lot of rich loafers, and light the fuse. A most cheerful and gratifying result will follow.

A pound of this good stuff beats a bushel of ballots.

It took three summer weeks to pick a jury. The bailiff called a panel of nearly a thousand, some from off the street, they say, and some from a special list. When the weeding out was over, for cause or otherwise, the State had twelve friends tried and true (one said *I'd hang all the damn buggers*) and the eight defendants none.

The next issue of *The Alarm* will begin the publication of a series of articles concerning revolutionary warfare, viz.:

The Manufacture of Dynamite Made Easy
Manufacturing Bombs
How to Use Dynamite Properly
Exercises in the Use of Dynamite

It took five more weeks to put the evidence into the record. Scenes were laid by mouth, map, and almanac, writings were read and pictures shown, and ticketed bits of metal and bone cast silent stones of blame. Cases were cited and rulings made, and piquant legal Latin went on the chic Chicago air. Toward the end, a smell of burning filled the courtroom, as if the city were again on fire.

The simplest and surest way to explode dynamite is by fuse and percussion cartridge. The cartridge should reach into the explosive material two-thirds of its length. When the fuse burns to the cartridge, it explodes the latter, and that the dynamite. . . . °

The greatest force of a dynamite explosion is in the direction where it meets the greatest resistance. The best shape for a bomb is globular, and the stronger the shell, the more splendid the result. Placed under the table of a gluttonous dinner party. . . .

°This and the quotations that follow are from *Science Of Revolutionary War*, a manual by Johann Most.

To manufacture dynamite, add one part of nitric acid to two
parts of sulphuric acid, mix, then add one-eighth of their total
of glycerine. Purify with soda lye and stir briskly, keeping the
windows open. . . .

Gun-cotton is more easily manufactured and has an innocent
appearance. Take unglued cotton wadding. . . .

Fulminate of mercury consists of equal weights of mercury,
sulphuric acid, and alcohol. Once blended, the product is
spread on tissue paper to dry, a little potash being added. . . .

A particularly effective weapon is fire. Buy yellow phosphor,
cut it into small pieces under water, drop pieces into bisulphide
of carbon. . . .

The best substance for poisoning is curari. It is absolutely
fatal, but it is high-priced. A red-hot dagger hardened in rose
laurel is fatal. So with verdigris. So with cadaver poison and
prussic acid. Pulverized seeds of stramonium baked in an al-
mond cake. . . .

The wagon was defined inch by inch, from the seat to the tailboard
and then back through its bed to the shafts and the horse, whose
color and age were sworn to, as were the number of spokes per
wheel. The time of night was ticked to the second, and the arc
described by the fuse in flight was described again in words, and
then the bomb was made to burst in court, as it had done among the
police, and, last, mortal wounds were cast for place and scored for
size, and the bone and iron bits were passed before ready, willing,
and able eyes.

Still, nobody knew who threw the bomb. It might've been any of
the dirty eight, it might've been one of the crowd in the square, or a
provocateur, or the Mayor of Chicago, who earlier on was there; it
might even have been the horse. No one knew. But all the same, it
was held that, having written and spoken death, the dirty eight in-
tended death, and the hand that worked it, known by name or not,
was their own. The Judge too intended death, and to his world's
delight, he bestowed it on five of the eight. By one road or another,
all five died. Four swung, and the fifth lit a loaded cigar and blew
up, along with his double *g*.

T. S. ELIOT

THE VERDICT

this Birth was
Hard and bitter agony for us, like Death
—T. S. Eliot

A life sentence of seventy-seven years, on condition that he spend it as if condemned instead to death: die daily, die all the way, die of the horror outside the skin, the deadly disarray, the I-disease, and die of the horror within it, the mal for another time. He'd've given up being to have been in some myth, the distant kinsman of a god, the custodian of some minor power, sung of rarely and then but in Greek; or he'd've settled for an odd something in the Concordance, a name with a single mention, a bystander, say, a beholder; or, these denied, he'd've squired in this or that Crusade, a braider of manes, a cupbearer, an epicene, even, if such would've made Jerusalem fall; or, because Paradise might've brushed his rags, he'd've been a beggar at the Arno wall. But he drew a bad time for living and a worse one to die.

PAUL BUNYAN

LEGEND WITH ADDED MATERIAL

Trouble with Paul was, he had the big head. He got it from knocking over all those Michigan saplings, and before long he was thinking he could do the same to everything made of wood. In Michigan, maybe, but not in Oregon. You ever hear the story?

He come out here a while back to make an estimate on a logging operation, and he no sooner seen his first stand of Douglas fir than he said, "I guess I should've brung m'lawn-mower." That didn't go down quite like he expected: nobody laughed. We just stood around waiting, and I'm here to say that when an Oregonian waits, he can outwait the Final Judgment.

Paul couldn't take that long to show off, and after a week or so, he said, "Well, what does a man have to do to get a 'Gee-whiz!' out of you Modocs?"

We kept on whittling, and he got sore, and taking out a jackknife of his own, he grabbed the top of the nearest tree and said, "Y'know what I'm going to do? I'm going to snip this sprout clean through the butt!" and *slaunch!* he made a cruel swipe at that fir. A long strip of something peeled back over his fist, and he stuck out a finger to stop the tree from falling. Nothing fell. What'd peeled off was a layer of the knife-blade.

"Must be that diamond-wood I hear about," he said, and *strink!* he took another slash. That time the blade broke off and flowed away red-hot. "Hard stick of wood," he said. "Wants to be drug out by the tail." He got a good holt—only one hand, of course—and he give an honest tug. The tree didn't budge enough to shake the smell off it. Paul was owly-eyed by then, and he tried to hide it by saying, "Must've lost m'balance," but we noticed that when he clapped a fresh grip on, he was using both his graspers.

We'd heard that when Paul really fastened onto a pole of wood, it begun to ooze, like he was squeezing cheese, but this one, he couldn't dent it enough to make a weevil uneasy. With both arms around the butt, he foamed and faunched till Oregon spun twice counterclockwise underfoot, but nothing else moved except a stream of pure block-salt down Paul's back. He looked bad.

We were still waiting for something out of the ordinary to happen, and finally Paul put on a silly sort of grin and said, "No damn hands at all," and down he knelt and went to work with his chewers. He gnawed for two hours and a half, but all he had to show for it was a hogshead of tooth-tartar. Somebody let out a laugh.

That was all Paul had to hear, and cupping his hands, he bellowed, "Babe, come on out here to this unnatural state and bring m'private ax!"

He must've used two lungs—before the echo died away, the Blue Ox was in from Michigan with the ax in his mouth. We moved in a little for a look at the tool, and there's no denying it was the finest double-bitter ever made. The blade'd been tempered in a forest fire and a tidal wave, the cutting-edges'd been ground so keen they only had two dimensions, and the helve was one whole petrified hickory.

"I'm just going to use the flat of it," Paul said. "That'll be sharp enough." And *squinch!* he swang. The side of the blade cut a hole in the air that hasn't healed yet, but that's all it did cut, and a couple of people yawned. "Oregon's sure hell for rusting tools," Paul said. And *splinch!* he swang a second swing. All that happened was, that ax-head puckered up like a bottle-cap and fell off.

Paul laughed, but the laugh was so full of hollow that there wasn't any room for the sound to make a noise in, and it come out silent. "Only been horsing all along," he said, and he turned to the Blue Ox. "Been saving this weed for you, Babe. Push it over and let's get on home."

I'll say this for Babe: he was ready. And I'll say this too: he was willing. But that's all I'll say, because he wasn't able. He set his poll against that fir, and he shoved so fierce that his hind legs passed his forelegs, and he had to move backwards to go forwards, and all of a sudden he quit moving either way and sat down. Paul rushed over to see what the matter was, and it didn't take him long to find out. "Hernia!" he said, and he laid down and started to cry.

Right then, the sun skipped four hours and set in four seconds, and we were about to go home for supper when a voice come out of darkness so dark you had to light a match to see whether the match you just struck was lit. The voice said, "You ought to call in another man, Mr. Bunyan."

Paul stopped crying long enough to roar, "No other man can do what I can't, and if there was, he'd be me!"

The voice said, "They tell some pure things about a natural man from down south."

"Can't none of 'em be true," Paul said. "There never was a southern man could work his way out of his mama's belly."

The voice said, "The one I got in mind has quite a name down home."

"Local boy," Paul said. "Couldn't heft a boxcar."

"That's no lie," the voice said. "I'd tip over. I got to have one in each hand."

"*I!*" Paul said, and he sat up. "That means you're talking about you!"

"Name's John Henry," the voice said, and then the darkness moved aside and got out of the sun's way, and what we seen was a nice-looking colored lad dressed in a fresh suit of overhalls. "Pure proud to know you, Mr. Bunyan," he said.

"By the jowls of the Great Hog!" Paul said. "A junior eight-ball!"

"A Negro," John said, "and a natural man."

"Natural man!" Paul said. "Just how old are you, son?"

"Eleven, going on twenty-two."

"Holy Ham Hock! You ain't even learned to count yet. For your benefit, *twelve* comes after eleven."

"That's Michigan-counting," John said. "I don't grow a year at a time. I double."

"If so, you started at eleven," Paul said. "You trying to tell me you was eleven years in the stove?"

"Naturally," John said. "I'm a natural man."

"Well, you ain't going to look so natural when you get back to New Orleens," Paul said. "Put up your feelers and square off!"

"I don't want to fight you, Mr. Bunyan."

Paul's lip curled back so hard that his teeth curled with it. "I thought you was black," he said, "but I guess you're a colored boy of a different color."

"Oh, I'm black, all right," John said. "I'm a natural black man."

"Black, nothing!" Paul said. "You're as yellow as a quarantine flag!"

"I was brung up not to hit a old man."

Paul got madder than God ever did at Old Horny. He swole up like a toad, and he kept on swelling. He pumped rage through his system till his hair split nine ways and knotted itself like a whip. He began to sweat live steam, and he ground his grinders so hard that his spit turned to glass, all the while stomping with such power that he made footprints through his calks. He sure looked put out.

"You're black," he said, "but that's only a crime in Dixie. And you're just a pukey boy, but that ain't a crime nowhere, only a misdemeanor. But you don't have respect, and that's a felony even in hell. I hate to do it, son, but I've got to learn you better, so wrap yourself around something and hold on tight: I'm going to put the clouts to you."

Paul snaked off his belt, and while he was taking a few practice-swings, the black boy walked over to that troublesome fir, and without so much as a wheeze, he yanked half a mile of it out of the ground. Paul was dumb-struck.

"It's in kind of snug," John said, "but it ain't pure stuck," and again he pulled, and another nine hundred yards of timber came up.

Paul put on his belt again. "Typey type of tree," he said.

"It ought to be rooting out real soon," John said, and now he fell to drawing the tree up hand-over-hand, like it was a fish-line. But the more that came out, the more there was left, and the going got worse all the time. The boy took to unscrewing it, and that helped for a while, but it wasn't long before he was sweating water in sheets, like plate-glass. Paul swabbed him off with his shirt, but when he come to wring it out, it was bone-dry. "I don't sweat *out*," the boy said. "I sweat *in*."

But now the tree wouldn't even unscrew. The boy tried it first one way and then the other, and it seemed to be jammed for fair. He lost his temper, and drawing back, he cocked a fist and threw it at the contrary trunk: it only went in elbow-deep. "Like a little old pecker-wood!" he cried. "I must be losing my natural power!"

"Listen," Paul said. "I been measuring this wood you've tore up, and it comes to a good seven thousand miles. If that's losing your power, you ought to be glad. If you had it all, you'd kill yourself just by staying alive."

But all the boy could say was, "Only eleven years old, and I'm losing my power!"

"You ain't *losing* it," Paul said. "You just ain't *got* all of it yet. When you're full-growed, son, you'll move the globe without a pry."

Well, Paul might've been no great shakes as a logger any more, but that was a fine remark even for a has-been, and it pleasured the boy. "Maybe you're right, Mr. Bunyan," he said. "Here I been thinking all along I was a natural man. I guess I'm still only a natural kid."

"And kids get wore out," Paul said. "I just wanted to see how long you'd last."

"I still got some kid-power," John said. "Now, if I only had some man-power to help me, I could fall that tree yet."

Paul teetered, looking up at the sky. "There's quite a few men around," he said. "Pick yourself a good one."

"How about you, Mr. Bunyan?" the boy said.

"Shake, Mr. Henry!" Paul said, and they shook.

At that, they joined hands around the tree, with Paul saying, "Count off, somebody. At *three*, we pluck this stick like a straw from a broom."

I hadn't counted that high for a long time, but I took the chance.

"One. . . ," I said, and they closed in tight.

"Two. . . ," I said, and they got set.

"*Three!*" I said, and they made a muscle.

They must've made more than they meant to, because it boiled out of their arms like lava and flowed away smoking. They put so much pressure on their legs that the kneecaps wound up behind the knees. They took in air so fast they had to breathe in and out at the same time. And then the tree began to give!

There was a scraping, gnashing, cracking, tearing noise—and *thunk!* out came that fir like the world's cork. We all felt a draft and looked down. At our feet, there was a hole straight smack through to China! It was like Paul to go and pick the one tree the Chinks had planted upside-down, and it sure put the kibosh on him.

Or didn't it?

RUSSELL SAGE   *1891*

THE GO-BETWEEN

The bag I hold in my hand contains ten pounds of dynamite. If I drop it, it will explode and kill every human being in the building. I demand $1,200,000, or I will drop the bag.
> —Laidlaw vs Russell Sage, 158 N.Y. 73

The words were neither low nor loud, for they weren't spoken. They were printed on a paper handed to Sage by a man named Norcross. Sage read the note—read it twice, in fact—but he said nothing; instead, he folded the slip, the sheet, the torn-out page, and put it in his pocket. There were others in the office at the time, callers and clerks, but none of them knew the nature of the message, and none was aware that he sat or stood in the presence of death, capricious and presto. In eyeshade and sleevelet, therefore, scribes worked on at books and bills, ticking figures, penning pin-point entries, licking a pencil, and one, perhaps, frowned, or sighed, or soothed a mustache with a thumb.

One of the callers was Laidlaw, and as the clock ticked toward the fateful tock, it found him near a window, where, with his back to Norcross, he was gazing down at Trinity churchyard. He was a person of no particular value, this Laidlaw, a cashier, possibly, a flunky somewhere at thirty or less a week, and he was here in the Sage office on some flunky's errand, to pay or collect a fee, to bring some crumb of commerce or take some crumb away. He was a nobody, a used man, a soul in a secondhand suit.

To Sage, the hundred-millionaire, he was worth his every bond, his loans, his lands, his chattels, his estates at will, his rents and stocks and rights-of-way, his brownstone on the Avenue, and his twenty-room box at the beach; he was worth his spans and tandems and fours-in-hand, his now and future whores, his ready cash, and most certainly his wife. Laidlaw was Life to him, that prettiest of pennies, that one and precious pearl.

Sage behaved as if the carpet-bag contained ten pounds of maraschino cherries. Quite *degagé*, he turned away from Norcross, making some vague gesture or some faint remark, and strolled, drifted, one might say, toward Laidlaw, who was still rapt in slanting stones and sunken graves. *Mr. Sage put his hand on my shoulder and took my left hand in his left hand. I was conscious of force being used sufficient to move me. It was gentle. It was not violent.* It was a lover's touch that moved him ever so gently, that placed him just so, as though for some delight, a gift, an embrace; it was a lover who, quite without violence, used him as a shield against violent death.

The bag fell, and in a trice Norcross became a charred head, a pair of shoeless feet, and a Brooks Brothers suspender button; he also became a fresh coat of paint on the ceiling and the floor. A scrivener named Norton was blown through a wall into the boneyard below, and he was closely followed by a typewriting machine, all forty pounds of which landed on his face. He died at a gallop in a horse-ambulance.

The blast drove Laidlaw into the arms of Sage, but alas, love had fled, and the lover no longer yearned, not for a nearly naked body that lay on his chest and bled from a severed artery. Sage shoved him aside to lie sprawled on the floor until someone slipped in his gore and shipped him off to die at St. Vincent's. By some freak, he squeaked through, but Sage never called on him, never wrote him a line, never sent a dime or a delicacy, never gave a sign of regret. He simply didn't have the time: he was on his second hundred million.

Laidlaw sued for damages, but after four trials and four appeals that consumed eight years, he limped through the Great Door well before Sage did. The loan-shark lived to see ninety.

THE STRIKE   *1892*

HOMESTEAD, PENNSYLVANIA

*We will want three hundred guards for service at our mills as a
measure of precaution against interference with our plan to
start operation of the works.*   —H. C. Frick

The party assembled at Ashtabula and went by train to Bellevue,
where it boarded a tandem of barges. An hour or so after midnight,
these were taken in tow by the tug *Little Bill*, and a start was made
for the Carnegie docks thirty miles away up the Monongahela. There
was no wind, and the stool-brown stream hardly broke the lights laid
down from shore. A shag of mist scrimmed the Golden Triangle, and
when the flotilla passed, Fort Duquesne could not be seen. But even
if the time of day had not been night, even if the sun had brightly
shown the old blockhouse, few aboard the scows would've known its
history, and none of those few would've cared.

*We anticipate some demonstration upon the part of those
whose places have been filled.*   —H. C. Frick

What the Pinkertons foresaw was a round of cold-cocking, and that
was about all. They were jailbirds in the main, or chaff at best, bruis-
ers, roughraff, and sent against a caboodle of locked-out Hunkies,
they meant to do some sapping for their five a day and found.
Walled in by armorplate, they squatted on cases of Remingtons, or
they sprawled in slumber on the decks. They were taking it quite
easy, even the seven whose number was up.

*We think absolute secrecy essential in the movement of these
men.*   —H. C. Frick

It was about as secret as a Bessemer in blow. The whole county
was in on the cruise, and when it got to Homestead, a good four
thousand met the Pinks at the pier. They met them without flowers
and streamers, without speeches and music, without the city's keys.
They met them with rifle-fire, rafts of burning oil, bombs made of
blasting powder, and a cannon cast for the Civil War. They met the
Pinks with death.

As soon as your men are upon the premises, we will notify the
Sheriff and ask that they be deputized.   —H. C. Frick

The Sheriff got near enough to smell three hundred pairs of pants,
but that left him a long way off, and if he swore in anything, it
wasn't the Pinks; it was their shitten-britches. Bagfuls, they were, the
hired sons-of-bitches, and for a day or more, they waddled around in
those iron-clads, skidding in bilge, crap, and gore till five a day and
found lost all its sweet for some (the seven dead ones) and some of it
for all. Let Frick do it himself, the live-and-kicking said, and up went
the white flag, the last clean shirt-tail left. The Hunkies agreed to let
them land—if they first took off their hats.

When these works resume, it will be as non-union, and employ-
ees will have to apply as individuals.   —H. C. Frick

When the Pinks came down the planks, they had to pass through a
crowd grown to twenty thousand, and if they were tough at the start,
they soon enough got soft. Curses alone would've made the going
bad, but stick and stone made it worse as the little parade went by. It
was pissed on and smeared with dog-drop, and dead cats were swung
and thrown, and a woman's umbrella poked out an eye. There were
broken noses and noses broken twice, and one of the Pinks was two
balls short when he got to the end of the hike. There were forty
thousand hands in that Hunky gantlet, and those that ran it were
lucky to live, except maybe that slob with blood on his fly.

The U.S.A. is a great and growing country. (This is confidential
and not for publication unless name is omitted.)   —H. C. Frick

Later, of course, the soldiers came.

JAY GOULD   *1892*

ALWAYS FOR ERIE

In a Republican district, I was a Republican; in a Democratic
district, I was a Democrat; in a doubtful district, I was doubt-
ful; but I was always for Erie!

                                                    —Jay Gould

Toward the end, he'd walk the streets at night, spitting blood into a
handkerchief: with his tb. at a gallop, he'd fail to stay the year. From
that brownstone pile of his at 47th, he'd wander up the Avenue
through cones of gaslight and the in-between gloom, and he'd pass
other mansions, other ruins, and there'd be high-wheel hansoms
going by, there'd be twos en route to Del's and bed, but all he'd be
aware of was the ghost at his side or, at most, a step away.

With the grave in sight, he'd not be thinking of his eight thousand
orchids, or his Palace cars in the Jersey yards, or his yacht the *Atalan-*
ta that carried a yacht-sized gig, nor would he dwell on his Western
Union poles, his shares in the Iron Mountain and the Wabash, or his
Rosa Bonheurs and Bouguereaus: as he brought up stain on those last
few rounds, all he'd entertain was death.

It didn't pain him, in the days at the close, that he had nothing to
bequeath but numbers, no name, no deed, no words wise or other-
wise. The chapel, the chair, the fund, the prize—what were they but
the partial restitutions of the rich, the loud return of an emptied
purse? To hell with monuments! he must've said: he meant to be
always for Erie dead; he meant to die with his stolen numbers whole.
And he did.

WALT WHITMAN   *1892*

A HELL ON WHEELS

The long brown path before me leading wherever I choose. . . .

—W. Whitman

To him, this must've been a flat world, where roads ran without end and always away from a place called here. There must've been no rim around it beyond which nothing, there must've been more than seven wonders for him, more than four winds, more than a three-in-one God and a solitary sun. He was hardly in his grave when they that trust in chariots began to pave it, along with his winds and wonders, his triune Gods and suns.

Did he dream down there of the last tree to go, the last seed of the last stand of grass? Did he hear the last gasp of the last mouse or mole, did he see the last house fall, the last hole fill, and the long brown path, did he know it was six feet down, with him?

AN EMIGRANT   *1892*

ORIGIN OF AN AMERICAN

In one of the smaller towns of Kovno Guberniya, there dwelt a certain Sinai Gruenberg, locally known as a Talmudic scholar. Let it be quickly owned, however, that what absorbed the philosophe for ten hours a day in the bookroom of the synagogue was not his meditations on the *Mishnah*, no, nor on the two versions of the *Gemara*. It was, blessed be the name of the Lord, the pastime, the game, alas, of chess—aye, the board of sixty-four squares where armies warred with sixteen men.

Providence for the family fell by default to Gruenberg's wife. On her earnings as a wig-maker, the woman contrived bread for the mouths of five daughters (as needful as blows on the head!) and Herschel, a climacteric son. Life was hard for her, life was bitter, a galling of the spirit, and yet she'd not have found it so—indeed, her lifelong toil would've become a lifelong *mitzvah*—if there'd been no such thing as a queen, no such piece as a rook. She hated the carven figures, she blamed them for her lot, and often she was heard to curse them thuswise: "Eighty-eight black years on the little pieces of wood!"

Herschel's father died when the boy was nine, died, it may be admitted, in the act of moving a knight. The hopes of the Gruenbergs now centered on the son, wherefore, quite unschooled, he was apprenticed to a journeyman cobbler, and soon few were the byways of the province that knew not the master with his tool-sacks and rolls of leather and young Herschel with the silver trumpet that announced their calling as they came.

Twice in the year, they made their tour of farm and village, mending along the way such boots and harness and kindred articles as had fallen into disrepair during their absence. Apart from letting the boy herald their approach on the horn, the master conceded nothing to Herschel's youth, and between flourishes, the boy was forced to learn the trade and earn his keep. He learned well. By the time he was twenty years of age, he possessed a route of his own, a set of tools, and a *cornet-à-pistons*—and but for an odd circumstance, now about to be related, he might've lived out his life blowing occasional fanfares across the Lithuanian countryside.

The circumstance was this. He returned from one of his circuits carrying all his equipment in an almost new Gladstone bag, and being observed by a friend, he was asked the following question: "Herschel, where did you obtain such a stylish box?" There was no more to the circumstance.

Now the truth was, the stylish box had been acquired in a manner that reflected little credit on Herschel's business ability, and being proud, he was too ashamed to be frank. In the great city of Suwalki, he had labored for some days in the service of a certain merchant, using the best of his stock of leathers, neglecting other customers of longer standing, and even, very recklessly, devoting the sum of his skill to the fashioning of a gift, a pair of Morocco slippers in a lady's size. All this—naught is hid from the Lord!—all this because the merchant's daughter, a curving girl with slanting eyes, had come to the work-shed a dozen times a day on this errand and that, never speaking to him, but always passing close enough to be smelled, and, smelling sweet, she'd gone to his head as though she were wine.

And then one day, his labors done, Herschel had presented himself to the merchant for payment. Regretfully, the man had informed him of trade fallen upon evil times and coffers that held no cash, and he had besought Herschel, therefore, to let his claim be acquitted with merchandise. Sensing what was in the wind (the girl was! she spiked the air!), Herschel had hastened to agree, and, bemused by the fumes of love, he had even produced the slippers. But how far from his dreams had been the quittance offered—a Gladstone bag as good as new! For this, Herschel had had as much use as for an iron anchor, but he'd given his word, and he was bound, and ruefully he'd left the great city of Suwalki and set his face toward home.

The question, "Where did you obtain such a stylish box?" remained, and Herschel's reply, if not quite candid, was entirely honest. "It was given to me in the great city of Suwalki," he said, and he continued on his way.

A little further along, he encountered another friend, and this one said, "Herschel, what are you doing with that stylish box?" and Herschel, unable to explain, explained nevertheless. "As you can see," he said, "I am carrying it by the handle."

At the town's edge, he was accosted by a third friend and asked the most perplexing question of all. "Herschel," the third friend said, "are you traveling away somewhere with your stylish box?" Herschel gave what he thought was a perplexing answer, saying, "People come, and people go," and well pleased with his skillful parrying, he tarried for a moment to treat himself to a glass of peppermint seltzer.

The delay was fatal. It gave rumor time to grow into fact, and Herschel reached home to find his mother, his five unmarried sisters, and all the neighbors gathered in the road, and his mother was rocking herself and crying, "Eighty-eight black years on Columbus! My son is traveling away!"

And Herschel, trapped by his proud nature, was compelled to say, "Aye, with this stylish box, I will travel away to the American States."

AN IMMIGRANT   *1893*

ELLIS ISLAND

Aye, with this stylish box, I will travel away to the American States.

—Herschel Gruenberg

Eighty-eight black years on Columbus! his mother had cried, but too late the curse of pain perennial, the lifelong thorn in the side—her son had gone and with him (a pox on it!) the Gladstone bag. They'd fared far, the man and the box—still nearly new, it was, and strained but little by the little it contained—and now the two stood together, a mile or so away from the American States. As he watched a ferry tread down-bay from the Battery, the man wondered what awaited him ashore, what lay in store beyond the smoke and stone horizon.

There were others on the pier—he was merely one of a staring crowd that lined the stringers or craned from behind—and they too tried to read the rest of their lives from a book that was being written a page at a time. They found only the blank of tomorrow, and what would fill it none of them knew, not the Swede with the cardboard grip, the Serb with the hamper, the gypsy, the Galitzianer, the Kovno Jew with his portmanteau.

Below him, the river swirled the long green hair of the piling. In the current, fractions of the new world flowed, fingernails, wax, phlegm and embryos, blood, sweat salts, bile pigment, urinary sugar, schools of rubber fish, and, under all, a silt of melted stools. It was as if he were entering a house by way of its outfall, and passing in small instalments were its cast and spew, its rot, its day- and night-soil, its eaten and its not, and now and then a cork went by, riding high and heading back toward Spain.

As the ferry crawfished into the slip, he felt the crowd condense about him, and he breathed a mix of unfamiliar flavors, a migrant allspice, and with it the septicemia running past him in the stream. He reached up and felt for the ticket in his hatband—it was there, his permit, his paper key to the American house, and soon now he would go inside. To what? he thought, and again he wondered about the life that would start when he opened the door.

Years would spend, almost all he owned, before he knew that it had mattered little whether he came or stayed away. For one or two, a few at most, his journey from the Niemen would have changed a course by a hair, suggested a choice, provoked a focus of the mind, but for the rest, it would have been as though he'd lived his days within the ring of eleven forts that barred the road to Vilna, gotten old there with his Gladstone bag, never used and out of style. Instead, he'd find, he'd aged here, and with the end close, he'd think back to the day on the pier, remember the hampers, the bundled bedding, the allspice smell, and the shawls, and he'd wonder then where the crowd in black had gone, to what Brooklyn Calvary across the road from what Beth'el.

JOHN ALTGELD   *1893*

EIGHT DIRTY RADICALS

I want to do something, not just make a speech. I want to get hold of the handle that controls things. When I do, I will give it a twist!

—John Altgeld

When the verdict of the jury was read—guilty, it found, guilty all eight—he did as he'd said and never spoke a word. And when judgment was passed, when seven were doomed to the black cap and the trap, the voice of the people was heard, but his was saved for a safer occasion. Others cried out then and there, certain of the cloth and literati, the odd blue-blood, the odder banker, a one-time partner of Lincoln's, even the master of the Northwestern road, but not the careful Dutchman: he never showed the color of his mind. At the C&EI station, myriads signed round-robins, balladeers sold penny laments in the Loop, talesmen told of lies and bias, and even the trial judge filed a mild, a milk-and-water, appeal, but the lawyer from Hesse-Nassau kept his face shut for seven years: he was waiting for that handle.

He didn't get it until he was Governor of Illinois, and by then five of the eight were dead. The other three, two of them by commutation, were caged in Joliet, staring at barred sunlight on the walls, ladders they were not yet crazed enough to climb. *I want to do something*, the stickler had said, but now that he could do anything, now that he could twist the handle, he seemed to twist himself instead.

You could almost see him writhe in his clothes, thrash inside his head: he stood quite still and floundered. *I want to do something*, he'd said, but he lost his nerve when he counted the cost, and for six more months, the sun played its tricks on those walls. *I want to do something*, he'd said—and in the end, he did it. When the pardons came, Schwab was binding books in the prison library, Fielden was breaking rocks in the yard, and Neebe, in the kitchens, was holding a dish of prunes.

He twisted the handle finally, and it finished him. The three he'd sprung may have drunk him a health, and maybe even their kin and kind, and someone may have written a memoir about him, cited him in a sermonet, made him an addendum to a footnote, but his name was mud in most of the world and all over Illinois. He was due to die in another ten years, and he must've spent the time wondering what had imbued him. What force had he met that moved him, or had he found the force inside his skin? It was more than he could understand. What, he must've marveled, had made him trade places with three dismal and censorious strangers, what had stirred him to imprison himself and set them free? Who were they, those upsidedowners, that he'd clung to them and thrown the world away? If they were his brothers, killing brothers was all the rage, the now and eternal thing. What passion, therefore, had changed the fashion for him, drawn him to the Cross to die for them?

MARK TWAIN   *1893*

GIVE A DOG A BAD NAME

Given under my hand this second day of January, 1893, at the Villa Viviani, village of Settignano, three miles back of Florence, on the hills.
                              —Mark Twain: *Pudd'nhead Wilson*

In the tale as told, two children were born on the same day to the Missouri household of a certain Percy Driscoll. The mother of one was black in a sixteenth part of her blood and therefore, under the laws of the state, black in all eight pints of it. Her son, got by a white father, was black only in a thirty-second part, not nearly enough to dinge his skin or kink his hair, but he was no less nigger than his mother and just as much a slave. *Valet de Chambre* was the name she gave him, after a phrase she'd heard above the stairs, but he answered to something lower-flown: *Chambers* would always fetch him.

The other child born that day came from the groin of Mistress Driscoll, and he was as white as God's laundry, the clouds in the sky; he was white from the outside-in and the inside-out, white from A to izzard and halfway back to A. His name, which his mother was allowed but a week to delight in, a week to speak before she died, was *Thomas à Becket*, a big handle for a little blade.

Chambers and Tom, infant slave and infant master, alike in age, place of birth, and actual color, which was the cameo-pink of canned salmon—both now were fostered by the mulatto woman. They sucked the same pair of tits, they cheesed up the same sour curds, they shiced themselves in the same brown carefree way. On many a spring and summer day, they sat face to face in a toy wagon, gumming bacon-rinds, reaching for sounds, smells, and flash until sleep sank them without warning. They were hard to tell apart. The elder Driscoll could distinguish them only when they were dressed: his own child wore ruffled muslin and a necklace of coral, the other one a tow shirt and no *bijouterie*.

Now to the Driscoll household, hard lines came. Thrice had small sums of money been stolen, the dollar bill, the odd coin, or thrice had they walked away, and on the fourth occasion, the slaves were summoned and told that unless the thief owned up, all would be sold downriver and no two to the same master. All, of course, confessed, the mother of Chambers along with the rest, and for the moment, Driscoll's hands seemed tied. But with danger past, she knew that danger remained. One more loss of loose change, or none, for no reason was needed, and her son might end in some far-south field, a hand, a man named Boy. No long-tether times for him then, no rafting or fishing, no soft touches won by foxing the whites, no slow-speed days, no skim off the *crème de la crème*—and in sudden dread, she switched the halves of the Driscoll whole. The muslin and coral went to Chambers, and the tow smock went to Tom, and together with the clothes went the names.

There were queer consequences. Before the switch, the children had been like as drops of rain; afterward, strange to say, in no way at all were they the same. The great change took place in the new Thomas à Becket, the Valet de Chambre that was, almost as if magic resided in the unfamiliar name. If so, it was evil magic. No sooner did the little slave sit at the little master's end of the wagon than he became odious. Five months old, abruptly he turned spiteful, cranky, and base: a bully, a glutton, a crooked stick, he cried without cause, held his breath and blued, spilled food or threw it away, pounded, scratched, ruled with an iron hand no bigger than a doll's —a nigger doll's.

What did all that, you understand (and made for murder later on), was that dash of black blood, that taint, that tinker's damn, that metastatic fraction, that thirty-second part.

JACOB COXEY   *1894*

COXEY'S ARMY

We will send a petition to Washington with boots on.
                                        —Gen. Jacob Coxey

He was a good salesman: he could've sold the Kickapoo Indian Remedy to the Kickapoos. To the old, the poor, the laid-off and the landless, the pus of the pimpled rich, he spieled that if they made the trip, they'd grow by merely going and reach the flowing tit a hundred thousand strong—and the Simple Simons bit. They set out on Easter Sunday in bygone shoes and rags, and though on fallen snow fell rain, they flew their flags from the Tuscarawas to the Monongahela and beyond. They endured cold, they trudged mud, they stumbled over rocks, and there were mountains to climb, creeks to wade—and after five weeks on the road, the ignatz crusade was on the Capitol lawn, stone-bruised and blained, lank, funk-footed, and raw from the running squitters. They'd come to claim their country back.

Army of the Commonwealth of Christ, it was called (*Peace On Earth!* its banners said, and *Death To Interest On Bonds!*), but only two hundred had left Ohio, and they'd drawn no kindred legions on their twining line of march. Where the parade ended, it was met one-for-one by the bluecoats, who bled a dome in every four and sped the three unbroken home. On the way in, some may have seen the Monument, and on the way out, some the Mint, but if so, that was all they ever saw of their own. They'd come a far cry for a fair share of the milk and honey, but aside from a scab on the head, none took away any more than he'd brought: the two hundred, alas, had come without guns.

An odd ike, the General, the sort it was hard to fault and harder to favor, as if he were a shake short on the pepper or a pinch long on the salt. He led his troops from a carriage, and he slept the nights in a bed, but when he got his comings, it wasn't for raising an army: it was for walking on the national grass. They fined him a fiver and cooled his ass for twenty days.

PULLMAN STRIKE, I   *1894*

KINGDOM COME, ILL.

Pullman is a model little town, artistically planned, scientifically constructed, and consisting mainly of neat workmen's houses. Among the chief features is the Arcade, a building which includes shops, a tasteful theatre, and a library (8,000 vols.)   —Baedeker

Pullman is a model shit-house!   —Mark Hanna

The town was on the west shore of Lake Calumet, about twelve miles south of the Loop, and it belonged first and last to a man named George Mortimer Pullman. He owned it in bulk, and he owned it by the pound—the devil and all, he owned it. He owned every worm in it, every stone, every underground grain to the core of the world; he owned the air and the space above it to where space ended; and on the surface, he owned every brick, stick, and quill of grass, he owned the leaves on the trees and fallen leaves, he owned dust, snow, rain, birds while they lit and droppings when they'd flown away. He also owned the neat workmen he paid a wage.

They hated him and, more than him, the town. They cared nothing for his tenements, lettered A through J, his one-tap flats, and the one-stool toilets that five flats shared, and he could shove the library (2,073 vols. in the poetry stacks alone), the pools and pleasances, the stores, and the Florence Hotel, where he fitted plutes and whores for private cars. They'd say *sir* as he came and *sir* as he went, but they hated him only a snick less than the town—and for the benzine stare they fixed on his back, he hated them.

One thing mattered to them, and that was the thing they made, the gilt and walnut palaces, the inlaid domes they built on wheels. These they rode but once, on the shakedown runs, and on such occasions, they'd play at being their betters, feigning Cuban smoke from two-for-five cigars, fishing for fancied garters, dumping wheat, cornering gold. . . . And then they were back in their cold-water flats (A through J), and coup and killing went up the flue.

A town from which all that is ugly and discordant and demoralizing is eliminated. . . . —Pullman *Journal*

Not quite all. Gene Debs was still there or thereabouts, six-two of hard lean stuff, a tamping-bar of a man, a first-class rail from Terre Haute, and as long as he stayed out of jail and spoke, there was going to be a shaking underfoot, as if a train were coming. All told, he must've made a speech from every stack of ties around Chicago. He'd just walk the track and climb up there, and he'd bend forward from the hip, a way he had, and let the words rip. He had a lot of faith in that voice of his. He was sure it carried, sure it was heard far beyond his little gangs of unioneers. He liked to think it was a wind, one that would blow the top down and the bottom up, one he could change the world with. He missed, but he didn't miss by much.

He shook things—chandeliers swung, crystal chimed. In the minds of the rich, a train *was* coming. . . .

PULLMAN STRIKE, II   *1894*

IF CHRIST CAME TO CHICAGO

Why, the average wage being earned is $1.87 a day!
                                              —George Mortimer Pullman

If Christ came to Chicago, He would say Mr. Pullman has done his part.   —Rev. E. Christian Oggel

It was a tight year, '94, one of the tightest yet, and with dividends down to 8% and profits barely six million net, Mr. Pullman had to lighten the load of the rich. He did that by firing some of the help and grinding 40¢ a day off the rest. He kept rents where they were, though, which was half as much again as they were outside the fence.

The rent! That's where their pay all went, to meet the God damn rent! He skimmed it off their weekly wages, and what came out of the cashiers' cages was the copper that was left. (*I have seen men crying because they got only three or four cents. I have seen them stand by the window and cry.*)

They sent spokesmen to Mr. Pullman, but he spoke first, saying, "There is nothing to arbitrate," and then E. Christian Oggel spoke, he from Psalms 8.5, and he said, "Thou hast made him a little lower than the angels," and finally three thousand workers had their say, and it was short. They said Mr. Pullman was not only lower than angels, but also somewhat lower than their ass. Thereupon, he locked them out of his shop and went home.

Debs was brought in from Terre Haute, and though he looked and listened, it was much too late to stop. He knew it was the wrong time for a strike—the Company was strong and the union puny—but the men wanted it, and he didn't have the heart to make them call it off. He too thought he heard a train coming. It was, of course, but not the one he had in mind. . . .

PULLMAN STRIKE, III   *1894*

THE BIG TRAIN

Has anybody ever heard of soldiers being called out to guard the rights of workingmen?

—Eugene V. Debs

Mr. Pullman withdrew to Elberon, enjoying on the Jersey shore the airs that blew in from Portugal and the spices they bore from further east. Behind his back, forty thousand miles of track grew rust, and slow snows of dust settled on the 4-4s of the Marquette and the Wabash; food spoiled along the Burlington docks, and, pizzle-deep in shit, steers died in the pens of the Rock Island; rails spread, and signals lied, and when Monon trains went up in fire, smoke ghosts tormented Chicago. Mr. Pullman bathed daily if the weather was mild.

Nothing entered the city, neither the living nor the dead nor the U. S. mail. There was a stillness over the prairie, as if the town had gone down in the swamp it stood on: *the onion-place*, the Indians called it. In the yards, sleepers snubbed the common run of cars, gondolas, reefers, hoppers, crummies, but all, varnish or otherwise, were rolling-stock now standing still. They were winning, the strikers thought.

They hadn't heard of Richard Olney. He was a Bay State man, and being a little short of blood, he was the sort that ran on cruder fuels, gall, bile, and insulin from an island of Langerhans. He learned his law at Harvard, after which, for thirty-some years, he championed the cause of the ill-used, among these the Old Colony Trust and the Boston & Maine. It was said of him that he read aloud pleasantly and that he was a swift walker, but it was not for these excellences that Cleveland named him Attorney-General: Mr. Olney had heard of the strikers.

He caused a writ to be issued that estopped Debs, on pain of contempt, from addressing the workers in any manner, whether by writing, speaking, tapping in code, or pissing out a message on the ground; it banned the frown, the nod, the wink, the sign of the hand; it commanded him to remain as he was, sitting if the writ found him seated, standing on one foot if he happened to be putting on his pants. What the writ failed to do, though, was move the mail, and Mr. Olney called for the regulars. Cleveland said *If it takes every soldier in the United States Army to deliver a postal card in Chicago, that postal card shall be delivered.*

No troops were sent to Elberon, and from its poops and oriels, no tent was ever seen, no campfire, no furled or flying colors, no sun on a stand of arms. Down below, skirts swayed and parasols twirled as croquet was played on the hand-picked lawns. The shots were fired a thousand miles to the west, and when thirteen strikers fell, they went to hell with the music on the east wind, laughter, a mallet on a ball, polite applause.

Has anybody ever heard. . . ?

A WORD FITLY SPOKEN

. . . is like apples of gold in pictures of silver.

—Proverbs 25, 11

W. J. Bryan: *Picture of Silver*

His father was a wet-all-over Baptist, and three times a day—four if
fair—he'd get down on his knees anywhere he was, in a courtroom, a
town square, a county road, and offer up a prayer to the Lord, or, He
being out, to whoever was in at the time. A straight-cut man, the old
Judge was, with eight corners and twelve edges, like a brick, and
there were guesses about a rectilinear prick and a four-square pair of
balls. From a common hell, he claimed, came Abe Lincoln and Satan,
and he kept a fourteen-acre deer park to state his station to Illinois.
Such a one nonetheless begot himself a son who, when he spoke,
stirred men to rend their clothes and cry aloud, as though some Mes-
siah had been heard.

Well, a Messiah was needed that year, and he was needed as much
in Chi as in the prior promised land. Found in the Street now instead
of the grass, the enemy was still the same old snake. It was never
Black Hawk, never the green *jager* or the red grenadier; it wasn't the
spic or the nigger, the jew or the mick—it was the rich. There was
none but that snake, and the poor fought it with a Savior who hailed
not from Heaven but Omaha. A tin Jesus, he was, but he made a
silver speech that people as they tore their garments swore was the
word of God.

The next morning, Altgeld said *What did he say, anyhow?*

Wm. McKinley: *Apple of Gold*

His father ran a furnace—a foundry, some called it—at Niles, Ohio, a
thank-you-ma'am on the road to even less: he was no judge, except
maybe of charcoal. In another kind of fire, he made himself the sire
of nine, of whom a son when hardly sixteen found a dented God in a
sawdust aisle. The ironmaster, if that's what he was, marked the
youth for the ambo then and there, but it never came to pass: Sumter
fell, and the Seminary lost him for four years, which meant forever.
He proved to be brave at Opequan and Winchester, and they say

that at Antietam. . . . But it's all on a plaque somewhere around Sharpsburg. He went in a private and came out a major, and he kept on rising, but he had one big hole in his coat: you couldn't find him in a crowd unless he carried a flag.

Mark Hanna knew what to do about that: *give* him a flag. First, though, he wanted to hear a word about gold. . . .

MRS. STEPHEN CRANE   *1896*

CORA, *MI CORAZON*

If thou and thy white arms were there,
And the fall to doom a long way.

—Stephen Crane

In Jacksonville, her joint was spoken of as a boardinghouse, but it must've been a borderline boardinghouse, because if you could buy a bed and meals there, you could also, with the wrong sort of luck, buy the clap. *Hotel de Dream*, she called the place, a sweet name for the same old stew, and it drew the inkhorn trade, among them the skinny wonder who wrote for the New York *Press*. One of his books had shown up sooner than he did, so in a way madam could claim she'd met him before. She was no reamed-out whore, though, that Cora Taylor, no emptied bag of tricks, and he found that out, and more, on the first trip he made to her room. His fall to doom was four years off and far away, but she was still with him when he fell—in the next century, it was, at Badenweiler (spa, Kurhaus, equable climate, park of 15 acres). After that—well, where for her but Jacksonville, where else but that dream hotel?

AT HAVANA   *1898*

U. S. S. MAINE

Displacement: *6,682 tons*   Coal capacity: *900 tons*
Length overall: *319'*   Armor: *12" maximum thickness*
Beam: *57'*   Main batteries: *4 10", 6 6"*
Draught: *21' 6"*   Secondary batteries: *7 6-pdrs., 8 1-pdrs.*
Horsepower: *9,000*   Torpedo-tubes: *4 14" (surface)*
Speed: *17 knots*   Commissioned: *1895*

All those numbers blew up one night, and the *Maine* became sunken
hunks of guessed-at junk. None of the 6-pounders was ever fired
again, none ° of the coal was ever burned, and the twin screws
turned no more nor shoved the hull another knot. There was no
power now in the nine thousand drowned horses, the dimensions no
longer fit the ship, and through breaches in the armor dog-sharks
cruised. One day, the mainmast would go to Arlington and a capstan
to somewhere else, an anchor would end in the Keystone State, and a
plaque made of deck-plate would mention Teddy R. Of the two
hundred and sixty-four men who went up and down with the wreck,
none would have a name that finished out the year: dead, they were
merely one of the numerous numbers. To hell with Spain! the jingoes
cried, though none was sure what Spain had done—and Spain was
sent where the *Maine* had gone.

THEODORE ROOSEVELT   *1898*

IT HAS BEEN A SPLENDID LITTLE WAR

Did I tell you that I killed a Spaniard with my own hand?
                                             —T. Roosevelt

It was splendid for the ones tapped for Bones.
It came between semesters, a bother, you know,
For it did me out of a final whirl at end-rush

° See THE SHIP THAT SANK TWICE, page 218.

And a rather sporting girl that I had in view,
But by and large, it was a bit of high-jinks,
A lark I wouldn't have given up for 'varsity
Or a soubrette's bloomers in the chandelier.
Ran into Dick and Reggie on the dock at Tampa
(By Gad, you'd have thought it was Mouquin's!),
Both in blue, of course, and both so *sans peur*
You simply couldn't dream one marked for death,
But a Mauser dumdum had Dick's number on it,
And he'd sung his last rousing "Boola-Boola":
He fell a hero, with spic blood on his blade.
As for me, a nick or two, a touch of the fever,
A scout behind enemy lines (cited in dispatches),
And there you have the long and short of it—
Something to make nothing of if Pater makes much.
Tell him it was a perfectly splendid little war.

It was splendid too for the Hearst circulation.
DOES OUR FLAG PROTECT WOMEN? the *Journal* cried,
And it ordered a pen-and-ink from Mr. Remington
To show Spaniards stripping them to the buff:
Three days later, by an uncommon coincidence,
The *Maine* went up in a puff of Havana smoke.
The *Journal* offered a reward of fifty thousand,
Crying THE WARSHIP *MAINE* WAS SPLIT IN TWO BY
AN ENEMY'S SECRET INFERNAL MACHINE (diagrams)!
It knew a splendid little war when it saw one.

It was equally splendid for Theodore, who wrote
"The clamor of the peace-faction convinces me
"That this country (read *Teddy*) needs a war,"
And using his drag with Mr. Lodge, he got one
Made to order, and he fought it singlehanded.
He landed at Daiquiri, ate lead at Las Guasimas,
And with the foe in front and the press behind,
He ran all the way to the top of San Juan Hill,
And then he faced about and ran all the way down,
And when he reached bottom, he ran some more,
And faster: he was headed for the White House.
Czolgosz took three years to evict Mr. McKinley,

But Mr. Lodge was patient, and so was Theodore:
It'd been a splendid, a really bully little war.

And lastly, the Cubans thought it splendid also.
In God's wisdom, they continued to die of tb.
At the rate of three or four dozen per hundred,
But it consoled them that their hacked-up blood
Was now for the kind *hacendados* of Wall Street:
They died practically free, thanks be to Jesus,
Rarely owing more to the Church and Sr. Morgan
Than their grandchildren would be able to repay.

ERNEST HEMINGWAY   *1899*

THE BLOOD-LETTER

You'd remember, on the day he died, how surprised you were at his age. Only a little over sixty, he'd be, a low number for all that noise and motion, all those bottles and executions, for so many words on paper and spoken words, a low number for all his goings-up and comings-down, his wrecks and wars and afternoons in the *sol y sombra*. Near the end, he'd look older than he was, and his gait would be older, and his voice, and he'd *read* older, write as if sixty were already sixty years behind him. His friends would learn what his ex-friends knew, that he had a mean streak in him: he'd get between you and a bear, but when the bear was taken care of, as like as not he'd turn on you. You'd learn to keep mum when he ran himself up and others down, when he planned one of those games of his, those campaigns to make something living become something dead. You'd take no trips with him, or none but the first—he'd run the show, he'd choose the roads and rooms and tell you how your days would go. You'd steer clear of his dromes and cirques, his armorers, and the sporting bars where he held soirees. That mean streak, it would always transpire through his much-man grace, and it'd be wise, you'd find, to let him blow about a mind and eyes that never lied and such exactitudes as *lovely*. You'd wonder at such a world, where all that mattered was how you took the slug, the gaff, the sword, the horn. You'd all be fair game there, for him, for death: if you were brave and stood ill luck well, he'd slap your back and score you high; if not, he wouldn't even crap on your grave. He'd be big, fast, tough, and dumb, like America, and he'd last till his dying day—and before he went, he'd take his limit of unicorns, German browns, and you.

STEPHEN CRANE   *1900*

HIS NAME WAS HEART'S PAIN*

None of them knew the color of the sky.
> —Crane: *The Open Boat*

He liked the waifs and strays of the world, the loose leaves. He liked foundling cats and dogs, on-the-towns, boes with burlap underwear and newsprint in their shoes. He liked the hand-to-mouth kind, those with nothing for the dry or rainy day, the ones they fished from the river or found in a drain, snowbirds, paregoric drunks, hatcheries for the spirochete. He liked the skim, the slough, the eyesore, the round-the-corner queer. They were the last of the free.

He too traveled light, as if he knew the way would not be long. He took his Cora, the whorehouse madam, he took his bad teeth, his tubercle bacilli, his six-shooter, and his pack of mutts, but no maps and no other load than such phrases as *wounds in the rain*, and he went from start to finish at high speed. He died at thirty in the Black Forest, but unlike the clockwise living, he knew the color of the sky.

---

*Title from Poem XLI, *The Black Riders*

THEODORE ROOSEVELT

THE AMERICAN

Britain must be kept up to the mark.

—T. Roosevelt

Damn the Dutch.

—T. Roosevelt

Those Dagoes will have to behave.

—T. Roosevelt

Look at those damn Spanish dead.

—T. Roosevelt

I am alive to the danger from Japan.

—T. Roosevelt

When the telegram came, he was about to kill something in the Adirondack woods, a deer for its hatrack or a bear for its robe, or, lacking nobler game, he was taking aim at frogs, preening sparrows, fish asleep in pools, but whatever the prey, he was poised to slay it when the telegram came. As the wire ran, it was touch and go with McKinley, or touched and going, for Holy Willie had gangrene, and by dawn, it read between the lines, he might be dead and gone.

They hauled Teddy down off a mountain and hacked him fifty miles to the railhead, and then, by special train, they sped him west toward a bed in Buffalo. Long before light, though, he was merely bound for the White House by a roundabout way. They swore him in that afternoon, and he said *in spite of the terrible blow*, and he said *the honor of our beloved country*, and he said—but what was in his mind, not what did he say, what did he see behind his one good eye?

Was it a gun, a Remington he'd brought from Dakota, say, or a Krag from Kettle Hill, or was it the express he'd used on the Upper Nile, which? And was he watching the ninth of his nine lions twitch, the first of his five elephants, or any of his thirteen rhinos and seven hippogriffs? Was he kneeling near the wrecks of leopards, was his hat on right, did his belly-fat show, was the sun too bright on his specs? Or did he dwell on the Czolgosz pistol—and that reminded him! He moved into the Mansion before Mac's widow moved out with her fits, and he tried keys and chairs and Cleveland's wine, and he sneaked a few winks in Lincoln's bed. . . .

You must always remember that the President is about six.
                                                —Cecil Spring-Rice

He was forty-and-change that day in Buffalo and half as much again when his brain blew up (*Remember the Maine!*) at Sagamore Hill, and, all of a piece, his days were less a life than a lifelong gasconade. He was a lover of livery and the livid phrase, a clap-sword and a double-dare-you, and they drew him as a four-eyed Buster Brown dragging a toy cannon in the street. Where he went, there a roar arose, as from a crowd, and he seemed to need more space than a place allowed him. He was always in motion, always *doing*, and always he'd paw and pound and mill around—Teddy, the one-man herd. He'd grin and bare his teeth, he'd wave his arms and crank the wind, he'd strike his palm, lay down the law, like the snot that owned the bat and ball.

He was smoke, steam, and fizz, and he seemed to hum, as if filled with bees, and where others strolled, he strode, and where they spoke, he screamed. He was all cut and shoot, and he entered a room as through a breach in the wall, and though brave enough at fisticuffs and twisting Chile's nose, the rich when they whistled could always make him heel. He was a skittish friend, a now-and-then liar, and a tin soldier to the end, when the little flag broke off and the paint wore thin. He was his world, and outside his skin, there was only applause. When it stopped, he died.

AT KITTYHAWK   *1903*

THE MACHINE

After running the engine and propellers a few minutes to get them in working order, I got on the machine. . . .

Gulls were there, and they saw it. They were in the air over mile-long curls of surf, they were in the stays and rotten rigging of wrecks buried to their decks in the shore, they were in the sedge and the cord grass, the rice and rye and celery on the dunes. They saw the shovel too, and the pot and stick (glue, like as not), and they saw the pi-shaped stool and the wired box, but these were on the sand and stayed still. It was the machine that ran and ran and rose, a little like a fledgling, and then, tired or frightened, fell. The gulls screamed at it down the twenty-knot wind and turned to other things, to food flung off by the Stream, to snow geese and goldeneyes, to highfliers, divers, waders spearing for shrimp in the foam, to the thin blue shell of the world.

> *The machine lifted from the track just as it was entering on the fourth rail. Mr. Daniels took a picture. . . .*
> —Diary of Orville Wright

JOSIAH WILLARD GIBBS   *1903*

WHERE NO ROAD RAN

> *Mathematics* is *a language.*
> —Josiah Willard Gibbs

There was a stillness about him, as if his life were one of those walks he took alone. He'd ride the cars to the edge of town, and where no road ran, he'd go among the trees, naming such as he knew, and he'd wade through sun and shade, and he'd note birds in a river's reeds, clouds on the current, like foam, the flowers on certain weeds, and he'd seem quiet in the quiet he found, a house where the only sound was the murmur of the world outside.

Within, though, a frenzy of magnitudes, powers on the boil, symbols tumbling and palpitant, a commotion of primes, equations, signs, all whirling around some calm and focal eye, and on occasion, the componental rage would reduce itself to one, as if aimlessness had lit by chance on aim, and then time would mark time while, as on another Sinai, a commandment was handed down.

THE DITCH WHICH HE MADE

Those Dagoes will have to behave.

—T. Roosevelt

Those contemptible little creatures in Bogota.

—T. Roosevelt

They'd wrought in gold, those little creatures, before Christians learned to pick a nose. Contemptible, Teddy called them, but they were already reading when Spain arrived, they were praising God, the Woman of the Lake, and a man-child led by the hand, they were paving roads, their towns were planned. In their laws and lives, in the store they set by honor, they rivaled the Incas, but to the kind of mind that Teddy had, they were Dagoes, and they had to be taught to behave.

We didn't own Darien, where Teddy wanted to dig his ditch. He'd offered a few pin-pricks and pistareens for a cut of it, but those mix-bloods, those griffes, they were balking him, they were talking big as Cuffy, those niggers, they were standing in his way. He hadn't asked for much of Colombia, only a slice ten miles wide and fifty long, swamp, most of it, and skeeters the rest, hissing hot and jungle-rotten, a pesthole, a hell on earth, and worth at best a dime an acre. They told him where to stick his picayunes, and he got sore, roared as though he'd done as bidden.

Oh, say can you see we sang as gunboats steamed, and freedom rang when the people rose and shot a Chinaman. A barefoot handful, the people, in cotton suits and bandoliers, and after cheering whoever was *presidente* that week, they went back to sleep for another hundred years.

Teddy had a place for his ditch.

THOSE EASY AIRS FOR EVERYMAN

On the pianos of 28th Street, a numerous daylong music plays in particles, sprays of sound all but lost in that of drays and cars and passing feet. From window, door, and transom, notes and bars of ballad pour, ions of rue and longing, and they spin and tumble in the wind, they sway and swing and drum, and some seem to sort themselves, to touch and cling, to join and fly away, and soon the world will sing the thin tones of the tin tunes made on an upright eighty-eight. These shrill and facile chansonets, these valedictories for the tongue-tied, these ready-to-wear regrets for the threadbare back of the common run—what do they hold that the *Misereres* lack?

ALBERT EINSTEIN   *1905*

A WANDERING JEW

It is strange to be known so universally, and yet to be so lonely.
—Albert Einstein

In the legend, he was one of those who lined the way walked by Christ behind the Cross, and they say he taunted the Son and urged Him faster, crying *Go on! Go on!*, and thus, they say, did the Savior answer: *I go, but thou shalt stay and no wise taste of death till my return*. So runs the tale, and many are they who claim they saw him, the mocker, *der Ewige Jude*, snapper at the heels of the Lord.

If ever onesuch was, this creased, this slack and often shoeless, this mild and wild-haired little Jew could not have been he, for despite the high hand holding him, he'd be gone before the Second Coming: he'd be dead, he'd die in his sleep in another fifty years; he'd sigh a last few words in German, his aorta would explode, and he'd die, never having known where Calvary was nor stood beside the road.

All the same, there'd be some who'd vow that he was the Jew the ages knew at Leipsig, at Ypres, at Altbach and Astrakhan—he'd died, they'd allow, but in doing so defied the Will, set aside his sentence, and gone before the appointed hour, and seeking the secret of his power, they'd relieve him of his brain, together with the meninges that invested it, and burn the rest and strew the ash on a running stream.

The brain they'd test in other fires. They'd observe it first, each fissure, each convolution, and then they'd wield their calipers, weigh it, palp it, and describe its color, texture, conformation; to inure it, they'd steep it in brine, arsenic, alcohol, formaldehyde, whatever would firm it while staving off decay; and then it would be dissected, stained, and microscoped, it would be pulverized, it would be titrated and centrifuged; and always it would grow smaller, their prize, it would be spoiled in part and partly mislaid, it would be left in trains, stolen, played with, flushed down drains, it would be shelved between semesters and regimes, it would be forgotten during illnesses, vacations, wars, hurricanes, and there'd be demises and retirements, there'd be new Christs or none and rumors of an old vag haunting the streets of Brussels, Prague, Valladolid.

And so seven years would pass, and though still there'd be some of that Jew's taciturn brain and someone still to twist the screws, it would not speak, it would not confirm, and no agony would ever break it, no shame. It would occur to no scientific team to try eating it, to accept, as savages would've done, that they'd thus absorb its properties, its arts and inclinations, and therefore when the kilo of matter was down to a gram, they'd tire of the minikin lump, and they'd throw it away, let it go as the body had gone, wandering down a running stream.

HENRY ADAMS   *1906*

THE EDUCATION OF *PTERASPIS*

One must not try to amuse money-lenders.

—Henry Adams

His book wasn't meant for the public any more than he was. A hundred copies were printed, and they went to a hundred friends—a private affair, you might call it, something for the Magi, for the Back

Bay blues, and not even all of those, for many made gelt in the three-ball trade, commonly the field of the Jews. But among the best of the best—not the richest, mind you—all along Beacon, the best praised that book of his until not they but death gazed through their ripple-glass eyes at the Common.

There were presidents in his line, his father's father and that one's too, but there'd be no third, and he knew why when he wrote the book: he hadn't grown, he hadn't evolved, he hadn't *become* anything. He was the same ganoid fish that the first Adams came from, cousin to the gar and kin to the shark, but it wasn't enough to have teeth if you had no taste for blood. Blood didn't draw this last Adams, it didn't excite him from afar, feed an appetite, fill a need—in fact, it offended him, as if he lived on thought, on his name, on air, which he didn't, because from somewhere came the cash to pay his bills, some till, some tap he seemed unaware of all his life. Those sail and steam excursions he took, those coaches across the Stelvio, those fairs attended, those seasons here and there—the Nile, the South Seas, Russia, Rome—all those comings and goings that way-wore the mind, someone sprang for them, and for his D.C. house and the St. Gaudens figure on the grave of his wife, someone made the tin for him, and someone paid it out.

Maybe that's why he never tried to make State Street laugh. Maybe that's where he got the ready for his tailor and the rent, for the fees and fares, the alms, the tips, the copper trove Kanakas dove for. Maybe he wanted fools to think him wise. The wise never thought him a fool, though. He wrote what the whole hundred would've written had they deemed it worth their while—that a new man had come to rule the world, and that he glowed like that Other One, shone. The differences were small: this one turned wine to water and bread to a stone, and in his creed, a camel would pass through a needle's eye.

HARRY K. THAW   1906

ONLY THE POORER GRADES OF MEAT ARE FRIED

You have ruined my life!

—Harry K. Thaw

There was always something wrong with him. When he was three months old, he had what his mother described as *a congestion of the lungs involving the brain*, and after that he was never right. Sleep came seldom and soon left him, and night and day he'd lie staring, perhaps at a murder still thirty-five years away, and wearing out each of the strong young women hired to be his nurse. In his time, he wore out most of the women he knew, some of them with whips.

When old enough to sit, he sat for hours glaring out at the world through those sewn-on eyes, and being puny from puking back his food, and having a big head to go with that puckered gizzard, he looked rather like a kewpie gone bad, a mean and meager doll. He had chorea more than once—a sort of insanity of the muscles, it was —and all his days he walked and ran as if about to fall. He was never really right, that Harry.

If crossed, he'd scream, hide his face, and pitch himself on the floor, the street, the grass, whatever was underfoot, and for his first six years, he spoke a stammered and spastic language that only his governess could apprehend—a dummy-sound, it might've been, a kind of drowned hullabaloo. When sent to school, he let no day go by without a scene: there'd be a sudden cry over some trifle, a centrifugal to-do, and then a headlong sprint around the room.

He made a small gain at Harvard. He came to know a few hundred words, nouns in the main, and he used them to demand the things he wanted more of: fine food, champagne, girls, boys, nine-tailed cats, and cocaine. On the eighty thousand a year that his mother allowed him, he rarely had a desire he was unable to name; he could even hire Sousa's band to play him under the table at Maxim's.

You have ruined my life! he shouted (or, as some heard it, *wife*), and into one Stanford White, who was seated over bread and wine, he fired three shots, two by way of the shoulder and the third by way of an eye, whereupon White did abandon his meal and die. Harry stayed alive, though, for another forty years. His mother spent one or more of her many millions to keep him out of the Chair, and she must've spent the money where money talked, because higher-grade Harry was never in the pan, never on the fire.

THE FIRST BROADCAST   *1906*

THE WORD IN SPACE

Angels once were on the air, and on the rare occasion, God Himself would shoot the breeze. They say He spoke to Paul on the way to Damascus, and to Peter from a bright cloud—*This is my beloved Son,* He said—and those in flight heard Him through the dreamsome screams they fled, and on the pyre, saints replied to the Unseen Word inside the fire. But it was others, not I, who had the gift of ears, and thus I thought that where no face was, no mouth could speak, no tongue could cry—until from space that Christmas Eve, this: *Adore and be still!*

No snow fell that night, and no rain: it was so clear you could see the constellations in the groundswell. We were off the Carolinas, not too far from the Stream, and wearing my head-set, I stood in the open doorway of the shack. The eye of a storm, I was, of a swarm of dots and dashes from other ships and the shore—and then came this that Christmas Eve: *Adore and be still!*

I didn't know the phrase was Gounod's and the voice a man's: for a moment, I suffered the joy of hearing God. *Adore and be still,* I fancied He'd said, and for a moment, a single moment, I did as I'd been told: I stood where I was and looked upward, and I saw spars write our roll and pitch on the sky, and the wires between them were strung with stars.

It turned out to be that fellow Fessenden up at Brant Rock. He'd been singing in an empty room, as God did before the beginning, but for a moment, for one wondering moment. . . .

EX-GOV. FRANK STEUNENBERG   *1907*

A MURDER IN IDAHO

They say he neither smoked, drank, nor swore, which alone would've
made him a crank, but he had an even odder wrinkle: he never wore
a necktie in his life. Union-card typographer, sheep-rancher, twice
governor of the Gem state, he always displayed a collar-button, but
he balked at bows and knots. For fifty-four years, that brass link
shone, and then one winter afternoon in his dooryard, it was blown
away by a bomb. In cap and gown he'd worn it, in sack suit and
mackinaw, in shirtsleeves and vest, in wedding clothes and Sunday
best. Now he was a caboodle of mucous giblets, and he died in twenty
minutes. No one seems to have known if he was decked in neckwear
for the grave.

The bomb had been rigged to his garden fence with a length of
fish-line, so that when the gate was opened, the string drew the stop-
per from a flask of sulphuric acid and doused a stack of blasting-caps
—whereupon gate, fence, duck-boards, and about half of Frank
Steunenberg went quickly to crimson crumbs. At the town hotel,
there was a man name of Tom Hogan, who claimed to be in the
region to buy some likely wethers, but when they poked around his
room, they found a few snickets that didn't quite go with sheep.
There was a matching piece of fish-line in his piss-pot, and a satchel
was good for a set of burglar-tools and three or four disguises (of all
the many, which?).

Put away to soak, he soon came clean to the same Pinkerton that
peached on the Molly Maguires. His story took three days to tell, a
spill that spread across 135 pages of Pitman jottings. He wasn't Tom
Hogan, he said; he was Harry Orchard. In fact, he owned, he wasn't
even Harry Orchard; he was Albert Horsley, a Canadian from On-
tario. Off and on, he'd been a miner in the Coeur d'Alene country,
but of late, he told the shorthand clerk, his main line of work had
been killing for pay.

His current employer, he said, was a Labor union, the Western
Federation of Miners—or, to be more exact, one Bill Haywood, its
secretary. For various sums of money, coming in all to four thousand
dollars, he affirmed that he'd assassinated nineteen men to Hay-
wood's order: two supervisors at the Vindicator mine in Cripple

Creek, a detective hired by the mine-owners, fourteen scabs in a batch at the Independence depot, a bystander in a try for someone else, and, finally, Frank Steunenberg. All these had been done in with bombs except the dick, who'd been shot to death in a Denver Street.

All this time, Haywood was just where he'd been when Steunenberg opened that garden gate—in Colorado—but that didn't stop certain parties in Idaho. They kidnapped him, and behind a special engine that'd kept up steam all night, they sped him across state lines to Boise. When the Supreme Court looked the other way, he had to stand trial for murder along with Harry Orchard, or Hogan, or Horsley, or whatever he chose to call himself for the occasion.

It so fell that eight members of the jury were farmers, and the rest had been farmers once, a cramped kind, all twelve, and it was to such that Orchard told his tale from the box. It's said that he was quiet, cold, and plausible, giving dates, names, and reasons freely, and stating method, deed, and outcome with ease, and it's said too that you could see Haywood die a line at a time, and toward the end by the word. They sat there taking it all in, those farmers and formers, and at the close of the case, the smell of rope seemed to fill the air.

There was just one trouble, though: the jury believed Orchard only as to himself. He'd sworn to the killing of nineteen men, and they took his word for them all—but as to Haywood, they held he'd lied. Orchard, or Hogan, or Horsley spent the next forty-seven years in a cell, and Christ only knows where they buried the son-of-a-bitch when his time came, under the crappers, maybe. Haywood sleeps in the Kremlin wall.

FREDERIC REMINGTON   *1909*

A PARSIFAL OF THE PLAINS

Oh hell! Here comes a damned woman!
                                        —Frederic Remington

He turned up when the day of the bold stroke seemed to be ending. There were only two poles to put a flag on, only so many peaks to crest and deeps to fathom, and all the wars had been fought and won. The last tusks were being mounted and the last leopards worn, and in his quest for other Grails, this knight stumbled over rails and rights-of-way and ran afoul of wire. The deeds were all done, he cried, and those who did them dying! He never found the all-space that was lying under his hat, the place where heights grew higher even as heroes climbed them. He never thought, and he never found it. Instead, in three thousand pictures, he composed an epitaph for chivalry.

It was his own epitaph too. *He Knew The Horse*, he wanted his stone to say, and all through those scenes of his, they run in the sun-burnt sand and stand on picket in the snow and rain, and bison gore them, and arrows grow from their eyes and ears, and they go the way the wind blows them, and they balk at snakes and switch at flies, they wheel guns, they drag travois, they bear men toward and away from death, they do (they're always doing!), and they die. *He Knew The Horse!*

No skirts bloom in those illuminations, no hair unfurls and flows: men ride and fire, and they kill or fall, and they come back dead or living, but never to a woman's bed. They wear other men's garters, these chevaliers, they champion other men.

JOHN MARIN   *1909*

A WATER-COLOR

My dear Stieglitz. . . .

—John Marin

My dear Stieglitz, he wrote, and so began an exchange of letters that would span the thirty-five years his patron would stay alive. He'd die at eighty-and-some, Stieglitz would, and he'd still be possessed of every scrap with a Marin scrawl, paper napkins, menus, the margins of magazines. He'd treasure those effusions, God knows why, he'd prize those tries in another medium. Maybe he'd marvel that one who spoke so well in aquarelle should hone to speak in words: what was there in language, he'd wonder, that color failed to say?

All his life he'd save those flashes from Marin's mind, glints like lures, flies flicked or spinners grazing reeds, and at times he'd turn them in his hand, surprised to learn that they contained no words at all, only failed pictures, pale washes for the eye. He'd keep them as long as he lived, and he'd never know that not a line of his own would be found when the painter died. His letters, his scraps of paper, all would have been thrown away, as if he'd never replied, never written *My dear Marin*. . . .

DOWN EAST   *1909*

THE STATE OF MAINE

It is change that is so hard to bear.

—Sarah Orne Jewett

I paint it exactly as it appears.

—Winslow Homer

They lived and died a carriage-ride apart. It was only a day's journey from Prout's Neck to the Piscataqua, forty miles direct, fifty along the shore, but either way, among the rocks or through the firs, it would've been a hard Maine road before she came to his place or ever he came to hers. So the chances are, they didn't try the forty miles of woods or the fifty stone, and it may well be that neither had known the other's name. And yet they seem to have met, those two, that twain, they seem to go hand in hand, those locket halves of one. More than their Maine was going, more than that point of land he painted, more than the pointed trees she wrote; all was going, but for their own going moment, they held it a moment back.

VINSLOW HOMER   *1910*

TO THE PASSENGER-PIGEON

You will see, I will live by my water-colors.

—Winslow Homer

When he died, salmon still swam in the Saguenay, and hills beyond blue hills receded to the sky. Pines still made pavilions there, and eyes still pried from the shade, and live lures milled, coachmen, silver doctors, and trout still broke in bits of flash. Men are rare in those pictures of the woods, a pair at most, a part of the ramage, trees themselves, witnesses to near and far events, a mink at work, teal in tandem, shredding mist. *I will live by my water-colors*, he said—and a dead world too.

CHRISTIAN SCIENCE   *1910*

FAITH IN THINGS UNSEEN

All is God, hence All is Good.

—Mary Baker Eddy

It was hard to tell whether her sentences were coming or going—they read equally well from the front and ass-end-to—but despite what she wrote about God, He wasn't quite as all-good as she claimed: the first half of her ninety-year life was an all-bad dream. Born frail, she wasn't expected to have a second half, not with those fits she had, those spells when she fell to the floor, screaming through a sponge of spit and voiding in her drawers. Sound was pain to her, or so she said, and they had to deaden the road that ran past her room, and there was something wrong with her spine (it was a cross, and she was on it! she contained her own crucifixion!), and almost as late as her wedding-day, she had to be rocked to sleep in a cradle or cribbed in her father's arms. There were seizures when voices cried her name, and she required mesmerists, morphine, a hired man to keep her down— ah, she couldn't live long, poor thing, those throes would undo her,

she'd swoon some day and never wake, death would come and take
her off.

She was on the small side, all say, meagerly made but with a grace-
ful way of going, and her eyes at times would change size, it seemed,
and color, and she wore her hair in spirals around a rouged and pow-
dered face. She struck poses chosen from picture-books (piety, pity,
disdain), and though neither bright nor pretty, she used her middling
mind and looks to win three husbands and the odd and suety swain:
there was always a whiff of lard about her, there was always an
Ebenezer, an Asa, a Calvin flipping up her clothes. Still alive at five-
and-forty, she'd grown to be a scold, drier, thinner, a chiller of desire,
a slow- or no-pay boarder, a guest but seldom and snotty then, high-
and-mighty with her host, a slob about the house, and purposely late
for meals. A fighty kind of squatter, she was, and one night, the bag
and her baggage, she was kicked out in the rain.

What made her live through those dreary, deadbeat, threadbare
years, unwell and unwelcome, pinched for the price of staying and
the cost of going away? Why go on, when where she knocked, there
was no answer? Why with those fits and fears she had, that bad back
of hers, that passion she suffered on a hidden cross, why did she
stand there outside the door, why did she bear the pain, what did she
hope to gain from a future like the present and the past? Who can
say, when she herself may not have known?

That was the first half of her life, and it ended as though half was
all she'd get. She'd taken a spill (the fall in Lynn, they call it now),
and no knife could reach the hurt, no medicine still it, and there was
no one to deaden the sound outside or hold her in his arms—she'd
never walk again, it was said, never leave her bed except for a colder
grave. And then in her strait, there came to her a name, *Phineas,
Phineas*, and softly she uttered it, remembering a layer-on of hands
in the state of Maine, *Phineas, Phineas*, and she seemed to hear him
speak, saying that health was truth and sickness error, that the body
was all in the mind, and the mind through faith could expel what
ailed it—*Phineas, Phineas*. Mouth of brass, she knew it meant, and
from it she drew another five-and-forty years of life. *Mirabile dictu*,
she was healed at last!

Or so she swore—which was enough to give her a start in the
paramedical art of curing the rest of the world. If she was as good as
her word, she worked many marvels: she made a felon disappear, and

a clubfoot unkinked when she touched it with her hand; fevers abated for her, dropsies drained, and a prolapsed uterus returned to place; the halt ran, the deaf heard, and a case of endometritis was unseated by her eye, and consumptions likewise, diphtheric throats, cancers of the breast and neck, one of the latter so far progressed that the jugular was exposed; she banned the pain of childbirth merely by her presence, and carious bone stopped stinking, and though she lost her own, she grew teeth for others, uppers, lowers, and once a whole new set of thirty-two; and while far from his pillow in Long Branch, she treated Garfield's wound by force of will until magnetic malice killed him. . . .

No more days now of making ends meet, of lacking friends, a home, a spare pair of gloves, a greeting in the street, love, a reason for sleeping and another for waking up. All her needs were filled, or all but one: the immortality she promised her followers she couldn't find herself, and saying *There is no death* to the end, she died at four score and ten. Of the three or more millions she left behind, she gave nothing to the poor: poverty, like sickness, was an error of the mind.

THE TRIANGLE FACTORY FIRE   *1911*

TWELVE DOZEN GIRLS

One of them shall not fall on the ground without your Father.
                                        —Matthew 10.29

Girls they were, but birds they seemed to be, perched there on the window-ledges ten stories up from the street. Below them stones, behind them flames, above them your Father making a needless sun, making one more star. And then they flew or tried to fly, those jenny wrens, those jew and dago Gibson girls, they filled the air, they turned and tumbled, streaming hair, and their plumage burned, their down of voile and bombazine, and end over end they went, those sprawling wop and sheeny girls, those flambant birds, those falling lives. It was ten flights to the deadlights in the pavement, and the bodies broke them, broke the street itself when they struck it, and the fires went out, went up in smoke.

Under oath one day, there'd be those who'd say that doors were locked or hung to open inward, against the flow of panic, and they'd swear, some, to blocked aisles and cluttered floors, to dark and narrow stairs, and the Court would hear of hoses unused or useless, of drafts that forced the blaze, and depositions would be read, attestations would be made—but it would come to nothing in the end, that apodixis of guilt, and the two on trial would walk away free. The blame for the twelve dozen dead would be on the dead themselves (they'd jumped) or on God, who'd let them fall.

Twelve dozen, a gross of girls, to them as they lay in the gutter with their purses, their shocked-off shoes, their spare parts, their singed and sodden hair, to them it no longer mattered who or what had killed them: they were dead now, torn, soiled, burst open, charred. Six of them, unknown, would go unclaimed, like worthless parcels, and they'd be buried as numbers (one would be 50, one 103); the rest would reach hell or heaven with their kike and ginny names. Your Father wouldn't even know they were there. He'd be working on another firmament or possibly another fire.

U. S. S. *MAINE*   *1912*

THE SHIP THAT SANK TWICE

All that showed above the surface was the mainmast and a squat island of convoluted steel; the rest of the wreck, some six thousand tons of it, was out of sight except at low water, when another foot of island hove and another foot of mast. For fourteen years, these things had reposed there and were daily seen from passing decks and high points on the shore: studded with shells and verdigreen, they were the scrap and scoria of the *Maine*.

It would've been better to let her stay where she was. It would've been better to give her to the crabs and the kelp, better if flake by flake she joined the bay, rising when it rose, falling when it fell, and forgotten. She had no further word for the world. But the longer she remained on view, the less could we leave her alone. Spain had blown her up, we'd said, but who else had been quite so sure, who'd known we were right but ourselves? It wasn't enough that we were pure in the wilderness; we had to be pure in the street: it was the old worm at work, and it wouldn't stop, it wouldn't die.

We spent seven hundred and eighty-five thousand dollars to build a cofferdam around the hull. Thirty-four hundred piles were driven, eighty-one thousand cubic yards of clay were dredged up to fill the twenty cylinders, and when the pool was pumped away, the bones of sixty-seven crewmen were screened from the silt, along with certain pickled trinkets—buttons, coins, keys, shaving mugs, and rosaries. None of these odds and ends spoke, though; none sent a message to the Pharisees.

All forward of Frame 41 was cut free with the torch, and all aft was calked and bulkheaded, and when the dam was flooded again, the hulk floated, the cripple walked. Now the piles were drawn, and the tug *Osceola* towed her stern foremost out to sea, where, three miles off Morro Castle, her gates were opened. Flying her colors from a jury pole, she sank in forty-one minutes. All the way down, six hundred and twenty fathoms, she had nothing to say. Deckplates, boilers, turrets and magazines, bunkers, pistons, none made a sound, not even Sigsbee's bathtub, ringed with mud and left as found.

But who sank her the first time?

Note: A salvaged bucket of coal was dried and tested. After fourteen years under water, it burned.

I. W. W.   *1914*

NO ASHES FOR UTAH

It is only a hundred miles from here to Wyoming. Could you arrange to have my body hauled to the state line to be buried. I don't want to be found dead in Utah.

—Joe Hill to Bill Haywood

In January of that year, up to around half past nine of a certain cold night, a man name of John Morrison ran a grocery store in Salt Lake. From then on, his widow ran it, for he was on the floor, shot to hell by a pair of gunmen. A cop, he'd been once, and none so well loved, because twice before he died there in his bacon, spice, and dried pic-ayunes, other gunmen had taken aim and missed him. The state of Utah said Joe Hill was one of those that put him down to stay.

Whether you believe that or not depends on this alone: how much do you own, a little or a lot? Withhold the sage and serious face, the frown, the rapt stare at blank space, the search for The Way on a wall; spare closed minds your pretense of candor, and stand or fall on your dollars and cents. How much do you own, mister, a little or a lot?

If you're rich, then you know Joe Hill was only a minstrel on the side. For his main holt, he was a stickup-man, a Wobbly stickup-man, and on that winter's night, he was one of the two that came to the store. And you know the rest, how he wore a mask, and how he prestoed out that .38, and how Morrison fell and where, and how his son shot the shooter and was shot to death himself, and, lastly, how two hours later and five miles away, a doctor treated Joe for a hole in the lung. You as good as saw it all happen—if you're rich.

If you're a different kind of stiff, though, if you're one of the hands, say (not a man, mind you, or even a worker, a toiler), if you break your ass for three a day and hide your card inside your shoe, then you know Joe Hill was no more in that store than you were. Those that swore they saw him lied, and no gun was seen in his clothes, and he threw no gun away, so God damn Doc Bird, and Doc McHugh the same. Joe was hit that night, and he never denied it, but when he said it was over a skirt, you took him at his word—if you were one of the hands, that is.

In Utah, mighty few others did, and when he refused to name the woman, he was headed for the door that opens once. As he went, he wrote more tunes for his sort to sing, and he sent Bill a second wire, saying *Don't mourn me—organize*, and then he drew a will in which he spoke a wish to become cinders and blown on the wind as food for flowers. And then a paper heart was pinned over a heart still full of blood, and when four shots drilled both, he was through the door and dead.

His friends came and carried him away, thirty thousand came, and he was burned in the fire he'd yearned for, and he was put in little packets, a pinch of him in each, and forty-seven states were made the richer by his dust. He was never found dead, though, in Utah.

TO DIE FOR ONE'S COUNTRY

I cannot get it off my heart. It had to be done. It was right.
Nothing else was possible. But I cannot forget that it was I who
had to order those young men to their deaths.
                                        —Woodrow Wilson

They came home in the colors, his nineteen dead, and through those
red-white-and-blues, they may have heard him say it was seemly to
die in Vera Cruz. It was an honor to meet their Maker in a spiggoty
street, he said, a privilege to stop lead with a lung and bite the dust
of dogs. Unsung before, he said, now their nineteen names were
known; they were shrined, those shot marines, they were seated in
the mind.

It was right to kill them, he said, it had to be done, nothing else
was possible—and he faintly heard some words he knew he'd not yet
spoken, *those dear ghosts, those dear ghosts*, and he seemed to stum-
ble on some trifle, or on nothing at all, and he well-nigh fell before
his time to fall.

A LAND TO LOVE

It was a desolate land, without trees. You expected minarets.
                                        —John Reed

He saw it for the first time from the roof of an adobe on the Texas
side of the river. A mile or so away, across sand, scrub, and a russet
stream, it began in the town of Ojinaga. By day, vines of smoke
climbed the air, and the sun broke on gun-metal, and pigmy figures
crawled, men in white cotton, women in black, and dogs, and when
the last light bloodied the sky, toy sentries rode in toward the fires.

A land to love, he called it, and it drew him as the pickets were drawn to warmth. Its colors stunned him like a disembowelment— the yellow water and the tangerine clouds, the red and lilac mountains, the stove-blue membrane all around and overhead. The heat stunned him too: a fanatical sun seemed more to rear than rise, and from ninety-three million miles off, it so enraged the earth that it shook, as if about to explode.

A land to love, it was, and he went there, and in its squares he found strewn straw, and in its streets women wended with water-jars among the droppings of burro, dog, and man. The stink of piss made a new element, thick in the sun and lank in the shade, and saddles stank of sweat top and bottom, and somewhere a game was seen, one that was played with a ball, and somewhere else a nameless grief was sung, and from under vast sombreros, small lives spat at death.

It was a land to love, but the minarets would be in another part of the world, and he would go there too, and die, and lie at last at their feet.

THE LEO FRANK CASE   *1915*

HOW DOTH THE GABERDINE IN GEORGIA?

Little Mary Phagan
She left her home one day;
She went to the pencil factory
To see the big parade.

Leo Frank he met her
With a brutish heart, we know;
He smiled, and said, "Little Mary,
You won't go home no more."

—F. B. Snyder: *Ballad*

Little Mary didn't go home no more. When a watchman found her in the basement the next morning, she was simply something thirteen years old, soiled, outflung rather like discarded clothing, dead, and already cold. She'd been strangled with a jute cord and a rag torn from her drawers, and there was a dent in her skull that might've been made with an iron rod, a wrench, a ball-bat, or the peen of a hammer. Both eyes were black-and-blued, the cheeks were slashed, and dislocated fingers had stiffened out of joint. Face, throat, hands, thighs, all visible skin was so begrimed, so dredged with blood and cedar shavings, that the color of the corpse was only guesswork until a stocking was taken off.

The factory manager, Leo Frank, was thought to have been the last person to see Mary Phagan alive, and under questioning by the police, he was deemed to have shown a certain uneasiness, an agitation that seemed consistent with evildoing. This assumption, added to the fact that Frank was a Jew from the North, led to his arrest, indictment, and trial for murder. To reach a verdict of guilty, it was essential that the jury be made to accept *in toto* the testimony of one Jim Conley, a Negro sweeper in the factory's employ; all the rest of the evidence, even if undisputed, would not have supported a conviction.

Conley deposed that on Saturday morning, the time of the murder, Frank had posted him as a lookout while he took Mary Phagan to his office to seduce her—in an unnatural way, he supposed, since Frank had told him once *I ain't built like other men.* He heard a scream, Conley swore, but he did nothing about it and dozed off, and after a time he was awakened by Frank, who *looked funny out of his eyes.* The girl had refused him, he was reported to have said, and he had hit her and killed her, and now he wanted Conley to take the body to the furnace in the cellar and burn it. For this service, Conley was given $200 on the spot, but he said *Mr. Frank, you are a white man and you done it, and I am not going down there.* Thereupon, Frank took the cash back, Conley testified, and announced that he was going home to dinner. At that point, the two men parted.

The jury believed Conley's account, including the portion about Frank's recess for food (*I ain't built like other men*). There was no room for doubt, reasonable or otherwise. A Jew from Brooklyn, twenty-nine years of age, holder of a B. Mech. E. from Cornell, married to a family flowing milk and honey, and president of Atlanta's fraternal order, the B'nai B'rith—that was just the sort to adjourn for a meal after a ritual murder (*I ain't built like other men*).

Those twelve good men, they weren't taken in: it was just a bit too clever, the dumbness shown by Frank. It was dumb, telling a black and drunken petty thief that he'd killed a white girl; it was dumb, trying to buy help, and dumber to take the money back. But the jury wasn't fooled for a minute, not those twelve men true: dumb is how Frank had wanted it to look, too damn dumb for a Jew with a Cornell degree, a mechanical engineer.

After a month-long trial, they were out four hours—the teller, the broker, the bookkeeper, the manufacturer, the contractor, the optician, the claims agent, the mail clerk, the salesmen (two), and the two mechanics. They were out just long enough to piss, to chew a chaw, to tell a few jokes, to dwell on that muff-diving stuff, to piss again, and to cast twelves stones against the Jew. By their reckoning, though, it had been quite a fair proceeding. Before it began, only a couple of them had sworn to hang the defendant, and none had been aware of the mob of five thousand in the streets.

He swang, finally, Frank did, but not exactly as the law laid down, with a gallows in the jailyard, a trapdoor to stand on, a right reverend Rabbi, and a chapter from the Book. His gibbet was an oak tree, his scaffold a table (kitchen? dining? dressing? drop-leaf?), and his hangman a collect of Baptists, anti-pope, anti-coon, anti-ikey, and sometimes (shoot, He was half-and-half, wasn't He?) sometimes anti-Christ.

Many and many came to view the new wind-gauge, the anemometric Jew. Some tore pieces from his nightshirt or snipped a fiber from the rope. Some took pictures. Some stood and rubbernecked at the rubbernecked crowbait, some called out to it (*We've got you! We've got you now!*), and some merely bawled at the wind. A few, not more than a handful, glanced and turned away.

ANTHONY COMSTOCK   *1915*

VICE AND VERSA

Comstock is the one who is lewd.

—Gutzon Borglum

Many said the same, because it was the easy thing to say—evil's in the mind of those who find it—but if right about themselves, they were wrong about Anthony Comstock. No man on earth and none under it ever caught him in an impure act, and it was only the unthinking who guessed at an impure thought. For all the French circuses he raided in his lifelong dirt-hunt, for all the undraped window-dummies he seized and stored away, all the Chinese ticklers, all the gutta-percha phalli, for all the priapic editions of Rabelais, all the tons of philters, pictures, abortifacients—a Comstock Lode of bawdry!—for all that pitch, he died quite as he'd lived, undefiled.

His enemy was sin, and he found it in all directions from anywhere he stood. It was in the home that allowed light reading, it was in papers sold on the street, it was in idle hands, barrel-houses, and horse-pool rooms, and it beckoned from doorways decked in red. It was in the human form, all of it, from head to foot and halfway back, it was in self-love and lack of prayer, it was in smoke, drink, and any color worn but black. Sin, the stifling weed, the tare—he would not suffer it to thrive.

He claimed it would've taken a sixty-car train to carry all those he'd harried to jail. That didn't include the fifteen who'd killed themselves while awaiting trial, among them the Fifth Avenue abortionist, Mme. Restell. When told that she'd cut her throat in a bathtub, Comstock didn't split or turn a hair: *A bloody ending to a bloody life*, he said, and he kept on sorting confiscated rubber-goods, the condoms and pessaries of some drugstore dragonnade.

He had his eye on Heaven, and nothing blurred his gaze. No bribe could tempt him, no plea dissuade or threat dismay, and he paid for his one-way will with beatings, stabbings, and falls down flights of stairs. He was always limping, always bandaged, always green and blue, and splints seemed part of his garb, like the bandage around his broken crown. He didn't die of those things, though, nor of a whore's hatpin, and it wasn't the gonococcus of Neisser that took him off, or the lues, or a liver that had changed to stone: it was simply pneumonia. He went to bed with it a few days after nailing a boy for mailing a dirty book. He never got up.

HENRY JAMES   *1916*

A *CONVERSAZIONE* AT HENRY'S

His guests dwelt in some element of their own, less than water and
more than air, a mist, it might've been, a gas that slowed the pulse
and softened sound, and in it life idled, like steam in a bath. They
spoke in parts of speech, rarely with a predicate, as if all their verbs
were intransitive—a sort of exhalation, their talk was, a sighing in
words, birds of thought too weak to walk or fly. It was a place where
language wasn't quite *used*, at any rate not in the sense that money
spent was gone; rather it was *tried*, tried *on*, even, like a hat, a boot,
a set of furs, and therefore nothing said seemed final.

Beyond the walls lay that which they knew as *out there*, a surround
where calls might be made, but only by patrons (no card, of course)
to bid on an *objet d'art* or to endure some secret service on the hair.
For the rest, it was a hell of appetites, of new and impingent horrors.
Within was the better world, the one where the desires, the horrors,
were all in the past, and of these those who'd been invited there
drifted about and spoke. It was high-class gas, with tone colors and
clang tints, with innuendoes, half-questions, hints and hinted replies,
with leads and lures, their hooks hidden as in feathered flies, with
italic glints among the roman lines. Ah, what delicacies they
achieved, what pinnacles of meaning they built!—all in denial of *all
that* outside.

HETTY GREEN   *1916*

WITCH OF WALL STREET

*When I see a good thing going cheap, I buy a lot of it and tuck
it away.*

                                                    —Hetty Green

All her life she ran from death—and death was any stranger she en-
countered in the street. There was a poisoner in every passerby, a rip-
per, a doer-in, and the police were doom in blue disguise. A bandage

hid a gun, and so did bundle, so did muff and dinnerpail, every
drayman was a burker, every clerk a crank, and where a hand was in
a pocket, it held a ticking bomb. At night, she'd cower in a Bowery
bed, a furnished room, a dim hotel, and she'd switch at a whim,
telling no one where she came from and none where she went. For
some reason, the deuce alone knows what, death pitied her and let
her live for eighty years, by which time she had two hundred million
in her poke, and only then did the stranger touch her, the dreaded
passerby, and down she fell and died.

They say she went around in deep-dark clothes weatherworn to
opalescence, and they say she tricked out in torn veils, men's draw-
ers, and furs gone bald, and sat on public floors while she ate from
paper bags. And the tale is told of how she sold a chamberpot and
then made a sale of the lid. And she skimped on soap and stank, they
say, and tellers at her bank swear to the carriage she kept in the
vault, the rubbers, the dresses, the railroad or two, and the pan she
made mush in on the cashier's stove. It goes the rounds that she
trussed her own hernia sooner than fee a surgeon, and that she vetted
others too, her son for one, the time he broke his knee. She wrapped
it in tobacco leaves, the story has it, and she baked it in hot sand, and
she rubbed it with oil of squills, whatever that might've been, but the
leg turned greener than the rest of Mr. Green, and he lost it, along
with half a thigh. Schemers were after her money, she thought, and
she sued without mercy and was sued without end, and it's said that
she never learned to spell, never forgot a loss, never forgave a slight,
and she'd sort out rags, they say, and get a penny a pound more for
the white. . . .

Yet who were they that looked down their nose? Were they beau
ideals, those that sneezed at her, were they gems, salt, faultless fel-
lows all? Or were they one with the one they blackened, were they
black themselves, tradesmen, scrapers of flint, flagrant in their crime
of trying to grow a dollar from every God damn dime?

MARKET, CORNER OF STEUART

You got him off this time, but we have got a red shirt on the son-of-a-bitch now, and we are going to put something good on him some day.

—J. J. Barrett, PG&E attorney

The Ferry Exchange, they called it, and it was rather like a bazaar for the two-way trade that crossed the Bay. You could get a haircut there, and you could buy cigars, picture postals, and Frisco souvenirs, and fruit and flowers were sold in season, and there were stacks and jars of gum and candy, and from racks beside the shoeshine stand, you could choose your penny's news. On the border of an awning, these avails rippled in a printed strip, and few were those who had never strayed off the pavement and into the flavored shade.

At six minutes past two on the afternoon of July 22nd, while a parade was passing by, a bomb exploded on the Steuart Street front, and nine died, none in one piece and some with pieces a block away. The living picked the dead from their faces, hot meat still, and a blown-off foot was found standing, as if about to cut and run. There were screamers of blood on the cream-colored brick and stained-glass bits at the base of the wall, and the torn awning offered tattered wares. Some of the bodies were bare, their clothes gone as in some change too quick for the eye, and crowds without shame came to stare.

The name of the son-of-a-bitch in the red shirt was Tom Mooney.

The Ferry Exchange—how many times had he bought a nickel cheroot there, a box of raisins, a sack of macadamias, or simply slowed down to inhale? Did he know the bootblack's name (the last, that is; the first, of course, was Mose)? Did he ever meet a friend in the place, did he ever talk to a stranger or the bull on the beat, did he ever stop outside in the sun, at the curb, or along the line of the building, or below the barber's sign, the one with the pointing hand —and did he ever, in a dream, see the hand point at him?

The state found some who'd say, and swear to it, that he planted the bomb that day (*we are going to put something good on him*), and they'd reel off his height and hat-size, the way he walked, and the color of his eyes, they'd know to the tick the time of day, they'd tell the kind of car that brought him and the one that took him away— and those things too they'd swear to God were true. God would know better, but it'd be twenty-three years before He let a played-out old man come back to the Ferry Exchange.

He'd be sick, beggared, soft, half bald and the rest grayed, ruined in a human zoo, but still able to lead his own parade. A host, most of them in black, a black mass would march behind him, and only the banner of his union would be flown. No flags would be borne, and none would be shown at windows or tied to trolley-poles. There'd be no bands, no honor-guards, no reviewing-stands, no silk and sacheted gash—all such would be saved for the asses that the asinine licked. Nor would the state and its witnesses be there—the buyer of liars and the liars bought. The D. A. would be somewhere else that day, and as for the syphilitic snitch and the coked-up whore, they'd be praying, maybe, for another paying case.

Coming up Market (four-tracked now), there'd just be a black-dressed throng led by a sick old man, and when he passed the corner of Steuart, he'd show his fist to the ghosts of the Ferry Exchange—to stooping Mose, to Cinco-smoke, to witch hazel and bay rum, to those nine strange names and twenty-three unspent years.

WOODROW WILSON   *1917*

PROFESSOR OF HISTORY

I advise that the Congress declare the recent course of the Imperial German Government to be in fact nothing less than war. . . .

—Woodrow Wilson

His life began in a smother of Cloth—his father was a preacher, and the father of his mother was the same—and through that swaddle of blackcoats, he felt the chill of faith. An angel came to him, or God Himself, or a wind seemed to blow in a windowless room, and thereafter he read each day from the Book, and each night he knelt and prayed.

Thus sustained, he fell but once, and though the fall was long, from Heaven to hell, only thirty-two minutes were spent on the way. To the House, the Senate, the high court, and fat galleries, he spoke for thirty-two minutes, and when the applause began to soar, he sank. He sank to the bottom of his heart, and from that deep he never rose.

He would end with a mind that sidled, an arm that hung like an empty sleeve, a mouth on one hinge, and eyes that cried at their own sweet will; his left leg would drag, and the good hand would shake at solitaire, and spit would flow for the funny turns of the vaudeville show. But when the box at Keith's was dark, when pip and court cards blurred, when the crowd in his head broke up and went home, would he put the Word away, or, in that last hour, would he pray for the power to pray?

ALBERT PINKHAM RYDER   *1917*

METAPHORS IN OIL

He lived on Olympus; he slept in New York.

—F. N. Price

How rare day is in his pictures, how common night or night coming on! Dim figures tend to merge with dimmer places, and faces are merely threadbare gloom; clouds impend like powers of the air, moons are ever at the full, and boats ascend the sea that has no shore; in his pictures, beasts engage the eye, as if about to speak, and there are dream encounters in russet glades, and trees stream in a painted breeze.

Those who knew him have left their page or two of recall. They tell the same few stories, all of them, they attest his queer ways of seeing and saying, and none fails to find that his windows faced the south. He was shy, they write, he was simple, absent, fitful, a random man in a linear age, and though his sight was poor, he liked to walk the city in the dark. He gave away nothing but money, they say, saved empty tins, deadwood, odd ends, cloth and paper sundries, legless chairs, stale bread, impairs of shoes, keys to locks forgotten, and there were trails, they claim, through the trash that filled his rooms. He painted butchers, newsboys, strangers he met in the street, he wore rags, he borrowed once to buy a pot of beans—but these things are parts that make no parcel, a broken set of bones, and it's from pictures now cracking to pieces that the lost must be supposed.

In those pictures, heavy women dance and bathe, death rides the wrong way of the track, and there are drownings, pursuits, treacheries, fauns, and resurrections; in those pictures, the earth is the pit, the lower world, and the skies are lit by its fires, soiled by its smoke. . . .

THE BISBEE DEPORTATIONS   *1917*

IT DON'T APPLY IN ARIZONA

Consatution! What the hell's the Consatution got to do with the price of copper? Every sheeny organizer that sticks his nose in Bisbee hollers Consatution, and the louder he hollers, the sooner he goes. Out here, nobody runs off about Consatution, only sheenies and Wobblies. Give you an example.

We're in the war a couple-three months, and there's work enough around for a thirty-hour day—and that's the time them unions pick to ship in their sheeny troublemakers. First thing you know, they whip up a strike over in the Warren District mines. Sheriff of Cochise County—Wheeler, his name was, Harry Wheeler—he rings up Governor Campbell, saying all hell's tore loose, and he needs the soldiers, but knowing full well, just like everybody else, that there ain't no how-do-you-do in Bisbee that us deputies can't handle with a tin whistle. Some colonel gets named to come on over and have a look, which he does twiced, and the only thing he can report is a greaser got throwed out of a whoor-house.

The upshot is, we don't get the troops, and the strike goes better than ever. In fact, it looks so good in Warren that the bohunks begin to get the itch in Jiggerville, Upper Lowell, and the Winwood Addition, and if they *all* go out, Phelps-Dodge ain't going to mine no more copper to kill the Huns with. They're patriotic, the Company— give away all that copper for nothing. Which is how come the mine-managers fix up a meet with Harry Wheeler, and in the middle of the night, they dope out a plan. Talk about your Consatution!

The plan went like this. That same night, Harry deputizes every white man that owns a .45, near about two thousand of us, and we pull off a raid on the most peaceable bunch of strikers that ever struck. We split up in crews, and having lists from the Company showing where all these spics and polacks live, they're as easy to bag as laundry. We nail 'em doing practicly everything harmless—sleeping, eating, playing cards, taking a leak, and having a piece of nooky —and there's scared ones and sore ones and boiling-mad ones and here and there an asshole showing fight. We roust 'em out one and all, though, and by sun-up there's twelve hundred strikers locked in box-cars on the Espee. Meanwhile we sewn up the operators at Bell Phone and Western Union, and up to the time we hook an engine onto that freight and haul it towards New Mexico, there still ain't been a peep to the outside world.

A bunch of us deputies ride along—on the roofs—and it's a two-day picnic to the state line, bug-juice and all. Town of Columbus, though, they don't let us dump our load, so we back out over the desert again to a switch called Hermanas, and there we open the doors and let the strikers fall out. One of 'em has to be helped out account of he's been dead since last night, and the rest is as good as dead with thirst—and stink, mister, they stunk till hell wouldn't have it! Peeyoo!

There ain't much strike left in the bastards, but we still don't want 'em in Bisbee, so we leave 'em there in the mesquite and ride back on top of the empties—inside would've stank a dog off a gut-wagon —and I'm here to tell you it's hot up there, hotter than the Devil's crotch.

Talk about your Consatution!

V. I. LENIN   *1917*

OLD NICK ON NEVSKY PROSPEKT

We shall now proceed to construct the Socialist order!
                                        —Lenin at Smolny

All other devils were dreamland fear and fancy, ciphers of smoke and steam; this one was the real thing. Long foretokened and finally here, this one was the prince of the world, snare-setter, sire of lies, sower of tares in the grainfield, tempter, murderer from the first beginning— this was he of the many names, germ of all known evil and carrier of whatever remained to be found.

This was no fool's fire, no shape or vapor at a window of the mind —this was a fact as actual as rain. Of no avail against him the oils of anointing, calamus and cassia and sweet cinnamon, nor the willow-wand or the twig of olive waved, nor would a bath in *gomez* serve, which is to say in urine saved of the sacred cow, nor would spitting do, or blowing the nose, or the sting of ants, or asperging in water that had laved a cross. Nay, nothing would make this devil go but killing.

This was the Enemy, not the serpent in the garden, not the dragon with seven heads and seven crowns, nor even was it the great beast which rose up from the sea, he having crowns that numbered ten. This was the Enemy, that little baldpate from Simbirsk, town of fruit tree and lilac, this the chess-player with gastric tb., brother of a gallows-bird, conspirator in codes and milk-made ink, snipe-shooter out of Turgenev, writer of ten million words in thirty years, thread-bare emigré, in debate a vivisectionist, master and servant of himself, tireless, cocksure, venomous, a will on a one-way track that ran straight-smack to violent revolution—he and none but he was the devil.

He came as the mighty fought for the supreme bone, the prime rib —the earth—and when they saw him from Broad and Wall, they marveled, for he was hard to tell from a man. No red satin domino set him apart, no deformity, no sulphurous smell, nothing but a Jew-blood tinge on his mother's side. That kind had overthrown their tables once before. That kind you had to kill, and they tried.

THE BLACK AND THE BLUES

How then shall Pharaoh hear me, who am of uncircumcized lips?

—Exodus 6.12

They were stolen from the Portuguese, these people, or, if bought from some Bight of Benin chief, they were paid for in doorknobs worn as ornaments and pisspots used for hats, but, sold or crimped or simply sued from the beach, they were corded in a hold and sent to where that evening sun went down. They took nothing but themselves along, a skinful of black meat, not more than that, for no white weighed their sense of song. Some, though, it stayed through forty days in their own bilge, and one in every two lived to land. That was the beginning: ahead were three hundred years of the *Hat in Hand Blues* and the *Yessuh and Yessum Blues* and the *Beggarly Game Blues* and the *Blues for a Nigger on a Rope.*

And then came the Freedom War, and off went the Misters and the Masters to fight for their right to be pale snakes in dark grass, and fanfares played them down the one-way road. When found in some ditch or fished from a stream, they still had their Dixie cash, their Daguerreotypes, and their keys and knives and locks of hair, but, strange to say, no drum was ever seen, no wind-machine of wood or brass. Split, bent, and verdigreen, they were somewhere else and hidden, more highly prized than eyes, and soft on the air thereafter were the *Missy Screws for Vittles Blues* and the *Blues for Kike, Coon, and Pope* and the *Blues for the Blues* and that same old *Blues for a Nigger on a Rope.*

And now the courtly ones were gone, the better sort, the kind that wept when they let a nigger go: they were dead, without doubt, of the *Eeny Meeny Blues.* Back-door whites used the front door now, lesser lights than the nigger had been, counter-jumpers and mortgagees, would-be gents and one-gutted all—these took the place of the cream of the cream, and another three centuries began, another coon's age, another blue moon to bend the knee. In cellars and similar caves, reeds quavered, drums were mauled, and the wind was wound with horns, and the sound was called the *Free When Hell*

Freezes Blues and the *Never the Twain Blues* and the *Like it or Lump it Blues* and, as usual, those *Blues for a Nigger on a Rope.*

And now for street carnival they played, and for *carne vale* at the grave (O flesh, farewell!), and where the whores made hay, in Storyville, but they still weren't free, and it all went down the drain, down the brown river, it all flowed away with the New World trots—the *Blue Ointment Blues* and the *Blues for Junk and Booze* and the *Blues for that Created-equal Bunk* and of course the one about the nigger and the rope.

And then one day they wondered where that great spate came from, and someone said from Timbuktu, and someone said from the Dead Sea, and someone said from the God damn whites, and someone said let's go find out, and so they steamed a thousand miles and then a thousand more, and all they saw was the northern part of the south and a store of that rope, and they stopped looking for whatever it was they'd been after (who remembered any more?), and when someone sighed out *Hope Deferred and Heartsick*, someone else said *Blues.*

RANDOLPH BOURNE   *1918*

ENCOUNTER ON 8th STREET

The war or American promises: one must choose.
                                                        —Randolph Bourne

He walked a good deal, much further than his curved spine would've seemed to allow, and if you'd seen him coming toward you, his cape filled a little by him and a lot by the wind, you might've marveled that he got the distance, those nighttime miles through street and mews. Five feet high was all he stood, and he was as pale as veal, and pinched in, and he had a wounded way of going, like an animal hit and healed, and his head, too large by a size or more, looked to be a spare one he wore when the weather lowered. The singular blue of his eyes, the hands (they say) that blossomed from his arms, such fine things you'd've missed. Instead, you'd've caught the grotesque that his friends were blind to, the galley-west shape, the scarred face, the nearly torn-off ear.

His cape wallowing, he'd've appeared to be something blown along the pavement, a plane figure, a great commotion of goods, and as you passed, a wonder would've stirred in your mind: would you trade him pack for pack, your twist for his twist, your fear for his back? would you swap your lack of bravery for his exemption? to avoid death in your body, would you settle for life in his, misconstructed, stunted, wrung—and safe? And you'd've said *Yes! Yes! Yes, I would!*

It was all a suppose, of course: you never passed him on 8th Street or any other street, never saw or spoke to him, never chose between the war and promises. You imagined, therefore, that *he* wouldn't've made the exchange, that he'd've stayed as he was, physical junk and secure. You didn't dream that he *wanted* to be called, and that when called he'd refuse to serve. He prayed for the chance to choose against killing, but with that jackknifed back of his, he was never asked the question, and in the end, that's what killed him. He died as the war did, far from the front and not reckoned among those lost in battle. He was simply the animal as before, and when somehow hit a second time, the wound failed to heal.

WOODROW WILSON   *1919*

THOSE DEAR GHOSTS

> *I was responsible for sending our soldiers to Europe.*
>   —Woodrow Wilson
> *We are verily guilty concerning our brother.*
>   —Genesis 42.21

I must go and speak to the people, he said, and he went ten thousand miles in a blue Pullman called the *Mayflower*, and at many a point in those many miles, the people swarmed, and he spoke to them. He spoke in halls and ballrooms, and at an Indiana fairgrounds, he spoke in the open air. He spoke at K. C. and St. Joe, and he spoke from the back end of that private car—a slack mouth, it seemed to be, and he on the lower jaw—and at Omaha too he spoke to Caesar, and at Sioux Falls and Billings, and he still had a long way to go.

He spoke under the big top at Coeur d'Alene, and in a Spokane park, he spoke to a sward of straw hats, and in the Pasco yards, faces shook in the jellied heat. Into way-stop winds he spoke, into the stink of lathered horses and the punk of sweating feet, into dust and rain and smoke and noise he spoke, and after the train had gone through fire, he spoke to more heads and more shoulders, to skin, hair, collars, cigars, lockets, and pairs of suns in spectacled eyes, and he still had far to go.

He was due at Tacoma and then at a city with a hippodrome, and somewhere else a race-track waited, and beyond that a stadium, and a tabernacle, and a Greek theatre coiled in the Contra Costa hills, and people stood at crossings and on viaducts and where tunnels began and tunnels ended, and he spoke to waving windows and fluttering streets, and even to some vags who tried to ride his rods he spoke, and still he wasn't there.

He spoke from a stage in Reno, a stage in Cheyenne, a stage in Denver, and always the crowd looked like a mass of pink dishes held up to him for words. Words, he may have thought, and they seemed to come of their own accord, flights, migrations, and then there was another stage or stand or dais in another park, another square, another peopled place—and all at once he was there, with no more miles to go!

He may have known that if not now, then never would he sow his heart and watch it grow, wherefore he dwelt on the graves he'd seen, on the stones that were strung in strands, on *those dear ghosts that still deploy upon the fields of France.* He told of women who had wept on his hands, of heads bared for him, of benisons and signs of the cross, of the flowers that were thrown at his feet, so many that it was rare when he touched the ground. They gave him a hero's laurels, he said, they sang him a savior's praise, and he marveled that he should be so graced for his fifty thousand dead. He was guilty, he cried, and he felt the guilt inside him as he would have felt a solid, and it seemed to expand, to wring and rend him. *Those dear ghosts, those dear ghosts,* and in the blue car that night, his mind broke and joined them.

THE PALMER RAIDS

UNDESIRABLE ALIENS

This lowest of all types.
                                        —Atty. Gen. Mitchell Palmer

They had wry and skywest faces, he said, sloping brows and mon-
strous heads, and in their sly and knowing eyes, cupidity could be
read, cruelty, crime, madness. He dragged seven thousand such from
their beds or their benches in the park, from crappers, jobs, turn-
vereins, hash-houses, pushcart routes (*I cash! I cash clothes!*)—the
young and old he bagged, the silent, the bewildered, the sick and
sore, one and all he collared them, one and all he jailed, and then he
cried *I've saved the world!*

Tom Watson, senator from Georgia, called him a 100% idiot, but
the old Populist was wrong: Mitch Palmer wasn't a 100% anything.
He was a made-up man, a gig of parts that poorly fit, a jigamaree of
odd sizes that somehow or other ran. He'd been born a Friend, but
the faith went only a little way in, and you could read it through his
skin, like a tattoo. Lacking a creed, he fought no fight for a cause: he
was a knight without a garter, and the steed he rode was a hack. He
always chimed in late with that silver mouth of his, or silver plate—
by the time he spoke, the new was showing age, the perilous growing
safe. He was smoke from a small fire, Mitch. He leaned toward labor,
that is, when he wasn't leaning back, and, quack Quaker, he only
hated war till it came.

All around him there were skewgeed and catty-corner faces, Ga-
litzes, Dutchmen, Danes and Finns, Sinn Feins and Fenians, but
mainly there were black-hair peepuls, Jews, no-coppishes, gypsies
without shoes, off-white peepuls with slantwise jaws and catawam-
pous eyes, with two left sides and no right, the lowest of the low. He
caught several thousand of that kind, and he caught them in the act.
It made no never-mind that it was only the act of living: they were
foreigners.

ALEXANDER BERKMAN

THE ANARCHIST

Well, anyhow, he left the country before I did.
—Alexander Berkman

He meant H. C. Frick, whom he'd plugged and stabbed in Pittsburgh twenty-seven years before. It hardly seemed that far back, the Great Day when he'd barged into Frick's office at Carnegie Steel and drawn that pistol and the stiletto he'd ground from a file. He could still hear the three shots, he thought, he could still feel the way the sticker slid through clothes and Frick, he could still see blood and, though he couldn't quite smell it, the look on Frick of fear. The Great Day, had it gone so soon such a long road off?

And now, this very afternoon, they were going to deport him from the U. S. A., and as he waited in some hall, some cell, some room that opened off another room, he dwelt on his fifteen years in a Penn State pen, wasted all, for Frick hadn't died there in the coke-oven smoke over the Golden Triangle. He'd died that very morning in a Fifth Avenue *palazzo*, when his heart stopped as he slept among his Goyas and Constables. He'd died just that morning, twenty-seven years after those poor potshots, those useless punctures. It was true, therefore, that he left the country first: his hundred and fifty millions couldn't buy him the day he needed to see Berkman off and wave him down the Bay.

Seventeen years later—in Cannes, was it, or was Nice the place?—somewhere along the Riviera, Berkman fired his final round. His aim was better now, and he blew out his own pancreas, dying as he'd lived, without a pot to piss in. You wonder why he killed himself—or why he went without some Frick to beguile the journey. Why in going, you wonder, did he let the enemy stay? Did he forget, or didn't he care any more, that while the rich can take nothing, the poor can take the rich?

EUGENE DEBS

CHAMPAGNE FOR OUR REAL FRIENDS

As I left the prison for the homeward journey, the last inmate I clasped hands with was a Negro serving a life sentence. I felt as if I was deserting my friends.

—Eugene Debs

We simply desired that he float an opinion,
A five-word asseveration to be taken as true—
This country needs a war—no more than that,
A posture he might've gotten from Theodore,
Nothing that left a taste or defaced the mind,
A clause, but one we measured in army corps.
We'd've put him on pennies and on penny-stamps,
On ships and camps, on new elements, new stars,
We'd've named a day for him, a national park,
All for one small speech from his jumbo mouth.

He had that, Debs did, a big wide-open mouth,
But you couldn't point and pull out your poke
As though choosing from a showcase in a store,
Wherefore when he climbed up on a bandstand
Or a flatcar or a wagon-tail, anything handy,
He spoke some not-for-sale language, to wit:
The master-class has always declared the wars;
The subject-class has always fought the battles.
We didn't like that, *en bloc* or by the inch:
It was the crime of the black heart, treason,
And it cost the traitor ten penitentiary years
And lost him the memory of coins for his face.

He was a sick old soul when sent to Atlanta,
And he grew no better there nor grew he younger
While his appeal wormed its way to Mr. Wilson,
A stuck-up, got by a D.D. on a D.D.'s daughter
And therefore closely inbred to God, who said:
They will say I am cold-blooded and indifferent,
But it will make no impression on me, none at all.
This man was a traitor to his flag and country,

And he will not be pardoned in my administration.
Mr. Wilson kept his promise *verbatim et literatim:*
He was a tried Christian and a true Princeton man.

A time came when nine hundred thousand people
(Subject-class, other traitors, etc.) named Gene
For the chair that Mr. Wilson sat hemiplegic in,
But the show of hands cut no Presbyterian ice,
And, good side and bad, he twitched out his term.
It took a more distant kinsman of the Lord
To remit the sins of Convict Nine-Six-Five-Three,
It took a man with spots on his vest (yes, oil),
A man with a sprig of nigra on his family-tree
(*We understand each other perfectly,* Gene said),
A brandy-soak, a poker-player, and a womanizer,
A smoke-filled zero from a smoke-filled room,
But even so a candidate for the Marble Halls—
And when he was Godsped through the Gate,
Mr. Wilson raised hell and picketed Heaven.

Debs never even thought of getting in.
He wanted to stay where he belonged,
With the subject-class,
With other traitors,
Etc.,
Meaning the people.

EUGENE O'NEILL   *1919*

SUPERMAN WITH QUALMS

There is always the monotone of the surf on the bar—a back-
ground for silence—and you know that you are alone—so alone
that you wouldn't be ashamed to do a good action.
                            —Eugene O'Neill at Peaked Hill

He'd swim in any weather, they say, and at any stage of the tide,
high, low, or in the rip of change; he'd swim deep water or shoal,
water worked up by the wind or stilled by a fall of snow or rain; he'd

go in drunk at times, whored-out, recreant, and on certain days suicidal, and he'd head for the horizon though shadows showed on x-rays of his lungs. The sea didn't feaze him: he was a sea of sorts himself, variable and wandering, opposed to all, with black trenches, with monsters seldom seen and never caught. It was odd for such a one to be afraid of lightning, but he thought they were meant for him, those electric accusations (fornicator! bibber! apostate!), and he seemed to shrink when he saw them, as though they'd find him out if he stood up straight.

THE BLACK PERIL   *1919*

THOSE ABE LINCOLN BLUES

Seen many buddies back from war. Can't be satisfied. Some mighty bitter. Say country don't treat 'em right.°

That was a big man what he come free the slaves,
Six-four in sock-feet, they say, but sinful thin,
Sunk-chested, like he taken the gallopin' grief,
And sad, graveyard-sad, less he makin' a smile,
And then, Great Law, he Christ in the blue!—
A big tall heist-up man, a long-chalk buckra
From who laid the chuck, and he change things.

Overseer man with taws for eyes, he gone now,
And the sombitchin' preacher what he preach us
Work hard and you go to the kitchen of Heaven,
He gone too, and so's ole Marse, ole top-hoss,
Spit dreen down the stroke-side of his mouth,
Side he smoke on when they still was a South—
That homemade drawed-out man, he change things,
That skinny high-up man, he done some changing.

But they shoot a gun and kill him to death,
And what he fix to change with the freedom-war,

°A black soldier in the A.E.F., from *Wings On My Feet*, by Howard W. Odum.

They half-change it back with that K-K-Klux.
We don't show passes to come and go no more,
And we don't look slippy for no blast on a horn
(None but the last), and we get to book-read some,
Which they like to wore you out for that oncet,
And they don't make us fight, buck agin buck,
Or breed us like dawgs or feed us in a troth,
And they pays us with cash, not Sundays off,
And we own more dirt than we need for a grave.

But in the end, half-free come to all-slave,
And they's a sign that says it wherever we look,
On their fadedy eyes and their ruddled necks,
On courthouse, schoolhouse, shithouse, trains,
On the dirt we eat and the tools we use,
On ever damn church and ever damn jail,
On the God damn pork-pale white-meat sluts,
On blacks hangin' twitchety from tupelo trees.

If you follow them signs and stay in your place,
If you stand downwind and grin like a chimp,
If you roll your eyes and wear pokey-dot ties,
If you go back on your soul to keep your balls,
They calls you a good nigra, a shiny example,
Meaning raggin' off shoes and privity-seats —
The trash under sheets, they change what counts.

We waitin' long now on a brother of that Abe,
Big or small, short or tall, sad or otherwise,
But it look like that kind don't come in pairs,
Else he dead too, shot in the head and forgot
(Them good ones sure suck up a lot of lead),
But the bad can die from the self-same sick,
White skin bein' no harder to stick than black,
And hot blue blood ain't so blue when it cold.

Three hundred years is too much bowin' down!

THE FLIVVER   *1920*

MOTHER AND CHILDREN

*The way to make automobiles is to make one automobile like
another automobile.*

                                  —Henry Ford

His essence, his intrinsic being, was female, and he was a creature,
further, that once fertilized, never stopped producing young. Supine
and outflung, he issued them one a minute from his groin, alive, in-
dependent, and ready to run, and he had no other principle, no other
property or aim. His single truth was more of what he was doing, at a
greater rate, if possible, a pour instead of a flow, but ever and only
more, more, more of the same.

    The new Messiah, he became, as if the old were out of date, and
he was sung as Prince and Savior, Heaven-sent and meant to serve
the world. If he ever did, he served it right: he ended it. Tinker,
mender of clocks, mechanic, tender of pistons and epicyclic trains,
teeming old matrix of machines, he ended the world! Those little
black high-assed bugbears of his, that nonstop litter of full-grown
freaks, throbbing, fidgeting, farting fire and livid smoke, they spilled
from between his thighs, from his abundant inguen, and doomed the
world to death on wheels.

THE WALL STREET EXPLOSION   *1920*

THE SEPTEMBER HORSE

Equus October—a horse sacrificed to Mars at a feast.

                                 —Webster's International

They never did find out where it came from, that September horse.
They tried every livery stable on the Atlantic seaboard—five thou-
sand, there were—but no one had ever seen or heard of a mare or
gelding to match the sample shown, a swatch of hide with dark bay
hair. In the end, for all that was known, it might've come up from
the waters or down from the air, sent by some God to be destroyed in
his name.

It was first seen, they say, late in the morning of September 16th, and it was said to be pulling a wagon westward along Wall Street, a small sort of rig, slat-sided and covered with canvas. The driver, someone noted, was a man—not an old one, though, or a young one, not short or tall or medium, not black or white or in between, and neither lackluster nor a sport—a man minus all adjectives, an unqualified man. He stopped the wagon in front of the Assay office, climbed down from the seat, and disappeared. In a moment or two, it'd be straight-up noon.

The horse stood in the sun, or what sun there was—it was a pale sort of day—and it dozed. It paid no mind to J. P. Morgan's on the far side of the way, or to G. Washington, grown to thirteen feet of bronze, on a nearby flight of stairs, and it was blind to people passing and deaf to the time a clock was telling from a belfry up the street. It twitched a flank, it cocked a hoof, it sighed softly in the Indian summer haze, and, half asleep, it died.

At the twelfth clapper-stroke in the Trinity spire, the wagon blew up. Glass broke for a mile roundabout, and a snow of shivers began. Crystals spun and flashed and slowly fell, and when they struck the ground, they made a music seldom before heard on earth. Chimes without number, they were, chimes played by the wind, and no two tones seemed the same. In that downpour of sound, thirty bodies lay, and three hundred bled. Of the horse, all they found was that patch of hide with a few bay hairs, but to what God it had been offered, no one seemed to know.

THE UNKNOWN SOLDIER   *1921*

MUTE INGLORIOUS RICHARD ROE

Under a flag in the rotunda of the Capitol lay a coffin brought from France on the cruiser *Olympia*. Three years in the ground near Châlons, it had been stained by the chemicals in the surrounding soil, by wood-rot and rain, and, from within, by the blood, urine, pus, bile salts, and spittle of a dead soldier. Little now remained of him but a crumbling uniform, a set of tarnished buttons, a pair of mildewed boots, and, if the body had been complete when found, a kit of two hundred bones. Out of these sundries, a piece of metal might have been mined, a splayed bullet, say, or a bayonet-tip, or a curlicue from a hand-grenade. Reposing on the flag, and not quite as white as star and stripe, a bunch of Marne River roses had grown dry and died.

Two days hence, at Arlington, the coffin would be inhumed with prayer and gunfire, and from *Taps* to the time another trumpet played, it would wear its honors in the grave: the Congressional Medal, the Victoria Cross, the Croix de Guerre, the Médaille Militaire, the Virtuti Militari, a war-bonnet of eagle feathers, and a bunch of roses two days deader than before. Mighty men would attend the rites, and many would come from afar. Admirals would bend to the reverend ash, and in plume and sash a prince of Japan, and peers of the realm, equals who equaled each other, and fez and turban would be there, and Chief Plenty Coups would stare at scalps and make some crawl. Lesser souls too would rally at the hallowed hole, soldiers old and new, and Gold Star Mothers, and black coachmen, and chaplains of all the faiths, each with his whack of the jigsaw God.

All the bigwigs would be seen, but not quite all the best: Dr. Wilson would be left off the list of guests, along with the rest of the dead. A belated card would give him the right to ride in the procession from the Capitol to the White House, and in a carriage drawn by a matched pair of black-and-tans, he would begin the redolent mile and a half. Along those seventeen blocks from the Hill, the crowds would keep still for the slow-step columns: the dirges, the massed and blending regiments, the colors and the pipe-clay, the gray heads of great men, the gun-carriage itself, all would pass through a hall of quiet.

But then someone would spy the President—Wilson, not that other who whored on the floor of a Mansion closet—and a roar would arise as when all France cried him to the skies, and the sound would spread and flood the avenue, and for a mile and a half, the people would hail him instead of the man he had killed. Once or twice he would remove his hat, but not for the living thousands. He would uncover for the thousands boxed like the one ahead, and in his mind, in the part of his mind that worked, he would try to find a name for a name-plate, a blank of polished brass.

THE SACCO-VANZETTI CASE   *1921*

THE DISTRICT ATTORNEY

I am innocent, and no perjuring harlots, no crooks, criminals, venals, deficients, no black-guards, no thief, no Katzmann, no sadism of jurors, no verdict of guiltiness, no death sentence, no Webster Thayer, no Massachusetts, not even all of this can change an innocent man in a guilty one.

—Bartolomeo Vanzetti

Frederick Gunn Katzmann, he called himself, relying on the middle name—it was Scotch, and it came from his mother—to make him safe from being taken for a Jew. In and around Boston, that would've helped him the way Christ was helped by the vinegared sponge, so he wore the caste mark to his last day kicking, a vermilion signal that glowed between his eyes. It didn't quite noon the night, but it shone enough to be seen.

Meant to run for seventy-eight years, he'd seem at the end to have spent them stranded, a sawyer in a stream: he'd've lived himself out in the space of a mile. There'd been no auguries of his birth, no eclipse, comet, quake, no clock going backward, no uncommon flight of birds, and nothing much would happen when he died. A long low-slung life, it'd turn out to be, and he'd've endured it a little stooped, as if the ceiling had been built too close to the floor.

There was never a time when he didn't know that the two Italians were the Braintree murderers: doubt never stirred, never sighed in his private mind. The fatal bullets (why even bother to fit them? he thought) were fired by the only .32 Colt automatic pistol in existence, Sacco's, and the 5-shot Harrington found on Vanzetti was the one that he'd pinched from the body of the guard: these were certainties. The cap had been torn (he'd've sworn to it) by one special nail in one special wall, the shotgun shell (why, you could almost smell it) stank of eels, or saffron, or whatever else a wop would stink of, and when a witness spoke of men who ran like foreigners, who could they be but the pair in the cage?

What made the D. A. so sure? Was it second sight, a sixth sense, a funny feeling, or was it fear of his father's name that gave him such knowing bones? Did the word *Jew* spook him in a dream, did the dagoes become what he knew he was not, did he kill them to quash his dread, did he need them dead to stay alive—or did God in perfect English urge him on to the deed?

A BLACK SCHOOLBOY   *1922*

A VOICE FROM HARLEM

WHAT I WANT TO BE WHEN I GROW UP

a paper by Julian Pollard, Class of 1922, P. S. 604 Manhattan, to be read at Graduation Exercises

Honored mother, teachers, friends, and my father that got killed in France, I am going to write down in this paper the thing I would most want to be when I grow up. I would want to be a lawyer. When you are a lawyer, you can go in the court and argue for justice. There is a lot of people that want justice, and when you are a lawyer, you can help the people get it. Poor people want justice all the time, but they have not got the money to pay for it, and somebody else gets the justice. So when I was a lawyer, I would try to get the poor people justice free of charge.

I do not think I could be a more honorable thing than a lawyer if I was a honest lawyer, and that is what I would always try very hard, to be honest. It is not easy. Some people think it is, but that is because they are not poor. They have all kinds of things that they want, and so they do not have to be unhonest to get them, although they sometimes are. But if you are poor, then you are like to get in trouble. I feel sorry for the poor people that live in poverish without justice, so that is why I want to be a lawyer when I grow up.

That is what I *want* to be, but it is not what I am *going* to be.

I am a poor people myself, so I am going to be something else, and I think I should write that down in this paper too. I am going to rack up balls in a pool-parlor, and I am going to shine shoes under a elevator-station on Eighth Avenue, and I am going to be a janitor, and a waiter, and a Red Cap, and a Pullman porter that has to sleep sitting up. I am not going to be a lawyer getting justice for poor people in the court. Somebody is going to have to get it for me, because

I will be having my hands full being a dishwasher, and a window-cleaner, and a price-fighter, and a garbage-collector. Also, I will keep on being black.

Yes, those are the kind of thing I am going to be, and I am not going to like it. I am not going to laugh about wanting to be something with honor and only get told *A lawyer! What's a matter with your head, boy? You crazy?* I am not going say *Yessuh* and grin like Aunt Jemima. I am going to be mad. I am going to get in trouble. There is a sign in our classroom that says all men are created equal. It don't say anything about only being equal if you are white, so I am going to try and be equal whenever I get a chance, and they are not going to let me be equal, and I am going to get in trouble about that, and I know it.

That is all I have to write in this paper.

SINCLAIR LEWIS   *1922*

THE MAN WHO WROTE BLANK PROSE

Oh God, no man has ever been so miserable!

—Sinclair Lewis

What with those starveling eyes of his and that pocked and pustuled face, he looked like one of God's ill-used. His hair was a red confusion and his head a skull in skin, nor had the hand of God been cordial to his ways, given him the will or the power to still the din he made with his brays of laughter. It hadn't buffed away his roughness or put him at ease, and he never found a haven here, never felt at home. He was a lout, graceless and loud, and shunned down the road toward death in Rome.

Small wonder, then, that his writing matched him. It heehawed, as he did, it scratched itself, it snotted through its fingers and wiped them on its sleeve. It had an arrhythmic mode of going, uncadenced and accidental, it suffered from the shakes, the fits, it lunged, it strove, and its trail was littered with crumpled phrases and greasy parts of speech—a lifelong strew of language, and not a glitter among the trash. Unseemly scrivener, he offended even with his punctuation.

It took that kind, though, raw, half-smart, and cock-a-hoop, to grasp that his country was the same. No one less coarse could've done it, no one using prose more chaste, no stickler or stuck-up, no man of taste: it took a shitepoke, it took brass to savvy the brazen. They're in his books, the small-town boosters, the Vere de Veres of the barbershop, the pool-hall sloganeers; he's got them pegged there, the joiners, the persecutors, the enemies of the strange; they're in print now, the prim profane, the tellers of salty stories, the spiders in their stores—they're known, and they wear his name.

WARREN HARDING   *1923*

THE PRIVATE CAR *SUPERB*

I can take care of my enemies all right. But my God damn friends. . . !

—Warren Harding

The story goes that his friends killed him, or that his wife did (the Duchess, he called her) to preserve his name. But whether he died from the outside-in or the inside-out, he went to hell or higher water from the city of San Francisco. Full of formaldehyde for the four-day ride back to the Mansion, he was put on view in a cutaway and a touch of rouge, and callers allowed that he looked alive—he seemed to be asleep, they said, and if so, he slept well, slept long. His train, streaming black and purple crape, ran all the way east to the Capital, and he all the while slumbered on.

At trackside, there were millions from near, far, and further. They stood in ones and twos and strings and crowds, they covered every stack of ties, every gantry, they scared the crows from every cornfield, and in the last car some saw a casket pass, and some, with the sun behind them, saw only speeding panes of sky. A second or so, the blink of an eye, and the hot-shot hearse was there and gone. Not many missed the six gold letters of the word *Superb*, and those who were close told of the ghost of sour-mash whisky and, mixed with engine-smoke, the smoke of a Vuelta cigar, and though a nose or two caught a whiff of oil, it was thought to have come from the piston-rods.

As yet, the door of that White House coat-closet was shut, and it still held its stew of smells—rubbers, umbrellas, chew-tobacco, an old man's sperm, and his dearie's perfume. But soon now, someone would try the knob, a guard, a guest, maybe even the new tenant.

PANCHO VILLA   *1923*

A GRINGO: *DO YOU SPEAK ENGLISH?*

Si. American Smelting y son-of-a-bitch.

—Pancho Villa

His blood ran hot, just this side of steam, and he'd kill sometimes to cool it off, to suit, as they say, his trigger-finger, and tales are told of prisoners shot in enfilade to save lead, of a woman made to pick her husband's brains from pocks in a wall, and *corridos* are sung of his blown-up trains, of his rapes and ravaging, of the Chinks he hung by the hair, of how he'd fall asleep after love, after eating, after burning an old sweetheart alive, just close his eyes and doze, a child worn out by a game. . . . But such things were very long ago, and he's dead himself now of sixteen bullets he stopped in an ambush, four through the head, though he didn't die, the songs will tell you, till he'd said, "What I do wrong, Johnny? What I do wrong. . . ?"

In the land of brown hills and too much sand, the *peones* sing of him still, and you will learn if you listen that it thundered the night he was born, that bright stars, quite suns in size, faltered in their courses, changed their color, dimmed, and so he was called Doroteo, meaning *gift of God*, for clear it was, the part God played in his coming here. The other half of him was Indian, and at sixteen (dark number!), he shot his *hacendado* dead for breaking his sister's cherry, after which he fled a world that Castilian gentlemen owned but never made, where piss-poor lives were short and the shit-rich had it sweet.

He fell in with bad company, one song goes, but in those days there was nothing good on the road, and when he met the bandit Parra, he took a dead bandit's name and became a bandit too. He never denied it: there was only one other thing to be in that day and age, a puller of weeds for some *gachupin* landlord. Death to that! he said, and he began to please his trigger-finger—fingers, for he had two, one on his gun-hand and one between his thighs. They sing, the poor, of those digits yet. They fly their little verses, less songs than sighs, soft, unrhymed, and mourning, and the air seems filled with love and murder.

He was a bandit. To those who'd eaten today and knew they'd eat tomorrow, he was a bandit, and he was a bandit to a thousand generals and a million priests. To jailers and moneylenders, men with many keys, to savers, owners, counters of things, to buyers and sellers, to legatees, to the careful, the overweening, and the clean, to all who said to the hungry *God will provide*—verily to these he was a bandit. But to the shoeless, the landless, the simples who had no use for pockets—to them he was not a bandit, he was the Giver, the Defender.

He crossed the Rio Grande once, and by the time he crossed back again, we needed seventeen boxes to bury our dead in. We sent twelve thousand soldiers down there to bring him in—alive if possible, a corpse if not—and we were a year trying to flush him from the brown hills and the sand, with the Mexes all the while giving us false leads and laughing in the shade. We never did catch him: it simply wasn't in the cards, it wasn't in those stars he was born under in zags of fire and claps of thunder, and before we came home, we had to call for more boxes, and when we got them, they were a little out of true—that no-good Chihuahua wood! Down that way, they still sing about such things, softly, sadly, and at the end they spit.

In the songs, they tell of a seller of pumpkin seeds (beware of those that buy and sell!), and they say that one day when Doroteo drove past him at the roadside, he rose from his tray and cried, "Viva! Viva Villa!"—and at once, as if *Live!* meant *Die!*, the shots came. Sixteen found his body, four of that number his head. "What I do wrong, Johnny. . . ?" he said.

To the poor, he still lives, and at night in many windows, candles are burned to light his way.

CALVIN COOLIDGE   *1924*

A VERMONT SAP-BUCKET

She'll find I'm human.

—Calvin Coolidge

The picture was taken on the grass near the steps of the kitchen porch. A cornerpost can be seen, and a pair of shutters, dark and doubtless green, and a white run of shiplap siding, bright in the sun. Between the glare and the camera, six people are seated in an arc of straight-backed chairs. The President holds an old sap-bucket on his knees, and he is waiting to present it to a man named Henry Ford, a collector for a museum. Ford at the moment is facing away, gazing, it would appear, past Thomas Edison (kinetoscope, incandescent lamp, phonograph) at the First Lady, whose sight, it seems, is turned within (wasn't there something between her and a Secret Service man?). From the right-hand edge of the picture, the President's father is quite clearly intent on a tangible outside the frame, a dog, perhaps, or a tree, or simply the left-hand edge of the world. Only Harvey Firestone (rubber) has kept his eyes where they belong: he is watching the President pick at a splinter on the rim of the bucket.

All life and then the dead earth will have to end before that sliver is detached from the dry and friable stave. Harvey Firestone will have a long stay of it in his relentless chair, and long will the elder Coolidge stare at nothing ever to become known, and long too will Henry Ford fix his face on a rumored fall, the fall of Grace. Longer still will the woman wait, but her day will arrive with the death of days: her odd stick of a man will show her a maple-flavored shivareen, and he will say *I have thought of you all the time.*

LOUIS SULLIVAN, MASTER BUILDER   *1924*

A LOYAL LITTLE HENNA-HAIRED MILLINER

A democracy should not let its dreamers perish.

—Louis Sullivan

Not much is known about the woman: the few who knew her drew the shade, and what remains of her is hardly more than those three of Frank Lloyd Wright's adjectives and a noun that ticks off her trade. Loyal, little, and henna-haired was the way he described her, and in some loft in the Loop, she made toques of satin and picture-hats with plumes. When free, she'd come to stay with Sullivan, and she'd sit out the day in his stale suite at the Warner, or she'd steady his frailty as they traipsed the street. They'd do no harm to his aneurysm, she supposed, those strolls to the corner on Cottage Grove or across Thirty-third to the beach—how could they, when he merely inched his way and stopped each yard for breath?

Enlargement of the heart would be his death, the doctor said, but some die without dissolution, and Sullivan was already dead. He'd died at the Fair of '93, and what killed him there was all those Parthenons for belly-dancers, all the dollar-billed shrines. The Midway had been athrong with plaster temples, Doric and democratic, and when the dreamer stood among them, though his ticker kept on running, he no longer cared about time.

So they slowpoked around, he and the little milliner, or they sat and spoke, or she poured him a drink, or she received his gray desire, but often they moved not at all except in the mind, she to some parade of fashion, he to the prairie city lined up at the foot of the sky. In fancy once, he may have seen his Getty tomb (a requiem, Wright had called it), and once the tower he'd built on Congress, the corbeled and machicolated tower, and with it may have come his partner's peculiar name—*Dankmar*, he may have thought on one of those days. *Bitter thanks*, it meant, and he may have said it to his loyal little henna-haired milliner—*Dankmar*—just before he closed his eyes.

THE FORD PLANT   *1925*

ASSEMBLY LINE

*A Ford employee at River Rouge was discharged when caught
in the act of smiling.*°

At what?

At a joke he heard or one he told, or was it something on the air, a
word, say, or a wordless sound, or was it the hardware he held in his
hand, the nut, the screw, the shim, the bin of such behind him, the
slew of the same outside?

The five-a-day they paid him for an inch or so of his life, was that
what made him grin, the price they put on the priceless thing, or was
it the tin wagon he had to fix every sixty ticks of the clock?

Or, if it took more than that to crack his face, was it the black place
in the white Master's head, the one-horse brain that hated unions,
coons, and Jews?

Or did hard lines amuse him, the thorn in a shopmate's side—the
torn-off arm, the shoeful of jellied foot, the chronic cough—or this,
the four-hour rule about taking a piss?

Or did his glee derive from the years ahead, when his speed would
slacken or stay the same on a sped-up line—was that what seemed so
funny, the day his age would do him in?

Or, if none of these had grown the smile, had he smiled at all, had
he merely twitched? Had he suddenly seen what he'd helped to
cause, a canned and bottled land, numbered, named, each foot of it
found? Had he been shown its pure and plain beginning and its ruin
in the reign of the Wheel?

EUGENE DEBS   *1926*

ON THE BANKS OF THE WABASH

They had Johnny Appleseed just east of us, where the road comes
from, and they had old Abe just west, where it goes, but that don't
mean we're only a blank space between the last place and the next.
We're as good as the best: we had Gene Debs.

°*The Legend of Henry Ford*, by Keith Sward.

We're not too long on scenery, having mighty little timber that isn't laid crosswise for crossties, and with hills about as high as wrinkles in a rug, we naturally save our logging lies for the Liar's Bench. We aren't old, and we aren't new, coming later than the Original Thirteen but sooner than your come-lately states. We aren't rich, and we aren't pore, and having treated the Indians neither better nor worse (Tecumseh might put it otherwise), we aren't proud, but we're a long damn sight from meek. We could be smarter, and also we could be dumber, and our weather leaves a lot to be desired, being hot in summer and cold in winter, but if it was the other way round, come to think of it, it'd sure be tough on crops. We've got two sides of the track here, one for the early bird and one for the worm—but we don't have a third, where the Sambos live. We were Whiggish once, but we're still a far cry from being Tory, and so, holding our nose at hell-fire and thumbing it at Popery, we worship higher than the kneeling and not quite so erect as the Elect.

By and large, we're ordinary sweet-and-sour Americans—psalm-singing but sinful, easy-going but tight-assed, bull-headed but right-minded, sore but serene, and mean often but seldom all day long. We aren't perfect, but God was good to us here in Indiana: we had Gene Debs.

ISADORA DUNCAN   *1927*

DIE ERSTE BARFUSS TANZERIN

I have only danced my life.

—Isadora Duncan

She didn't dance all of it with music, and she didn't always dance it on the stage. In the beds of rustic inns, *barfuss* she danced and bareass too, in *cabinets particuliers*, in empty rooms, in *wagons-lits* and *ateliers*, there as well, and on her back while drifting past Khartoum. She danced for Pim and his eighteen trunks of clothes, for someone she called The Ugly Pianist, for teutonic pedants, gallic pederasts, and the Duke of S. at Lake Leman, and she danced for Halle the Chelsea *délicat* and for the burning man of medicine at the *plage*, and she danced, as the years sped by and favor fled her, for companions of the hour, fellow-passengers, pickups, a few who happened to rap on her door, and toward the end, fat, drunk, all jazzed out, and broke, she danced for heavy women and a bevy of two-way boys.

Her art, she claimed, took its rise in the soul, an organ or attribute sited in her abdomen in front of the aorta and the crura of the diaphragm: it was from there, she said, and not from the head or heart, that the body's motion welled and ran. Long had she sought that font, long through days and lonely nights, still hours passed with her hands held so, crossed upon her brisket, and at last something stirred in the coeliac axis at the root of the mesenteric artery, some force began to vibrate, some *geist* began to yearn—and she danced.

Her art, she harped on, but there's nothing left of that, not even a reel of film, grained as if shot in the rain, over- or underexposed, and cranked at several speeds—nothing that moves after forty-nine years of motion that stemmed from the soul. And she dwelt on her body, that *lovely youthful naiad form*, those *lithe hands and nimble feet*, the *skin of satin*, and of such things only stills remain in the minds of bohunk Hamlets, titled triflers, and L. a maker of sewing-machines. She came and went, the *barfuss Tanzerin*, she danced her life, spent it, blew it in, threw it at the wind.

In Nice, a car-wheel caught and reeled her shawl, and by the time they cut her loose, she was dead, but she'd died here and there before, and her naiad body, not now young, would flow no springs. Her breasts, hard and small once, hung like pockets turned inside-out, her feet were veined and splayed, and her sodden soul exuded beer. As for the art that was stilled when she strangled, it too had been killed by the inch, and pieces lay on many floors, on sand and sheets, on grass and the roads of Greece, on the cindered seats of third-class trains. Already gone, Isadora, when death came for her— but all the same, in that ill-written book of hers, in that vain and silly screed, she seems to unfurl and flutter yet. Language streams back from her, a scarf of words, fringed and rippling, red, even, like the real one, gay, cosmetic, free, and none need cry *Isadora! Ton châle! Ton châle!*, for no spokes will ever twist it tight and choke her, not till the book becomes dust and dances away.

Her art was her forty-nine years, and she got nearly all of it into print—her sins and innocence, her gall and greenness, her pride and her lack of pride, her easy-come and easier-go, and her vainglory (the horses unhitched by votaries! the coaches they drew through the streets!), and there are lovers on facing pages, The Archangel, one was, and another Craig, and there were shy voyeurs in the moonlight and a fongoo as bold as an alp, and she names her footnote geniuses (who is Beaunier? who in hell Carrière?), and that pilgrimage of clowns is there, the Duncans gone to Hellas—see the staves they carry, the tunics they wear, the fillets that bind their hair. . . !

Foolish, the book, foolish, sad, appealing, rending, really, and pulsing with disarray, like the life it keeps alive.

SACCO AND VANZETTI, I   1927

BLUES FOR TWO GREENHORNS

Their faces were just faces, and if you saw them in the street, you'd forget them as soon as they passed. But if they happened to be talking, those sinful ginnies, then as long as you lived, you'd think they'd played you a score. It wasn't English they spoke, or even broken English: it was the kind of language the dumb might mumble and the deaf might hear, the kind a saint might use with animals and animals understand. But whatever it was, nothing so eloquent had been heard around Boston since the witches reigned, and when those wops opened their mouths, they worked such wonders that words, like birds, grew wings and flew. *We no want fight by the gun*, they said (to the pure, that was pure diablerie), and for refusing to fight for Who's Who and the Board, they were burned alive a mile or so from Bunker Hill. Not their words, though—the words turned out to be fireproof. . . .

SACCO AND VANZETTI, II   *1927*

BLUES FOR TWO DEAD ITALIANS

Brothers, he cried out in the dream, *brothers you will not fire on your own brothers just because they tell you to fire, no brothers.*°

But they fired all the same, those brothers of his, and they killed him once to sweeten his sleep and a second time and sweeter when he woke. *Brothers,* he said, but where were his brothers when he went up in smoke in the Chair? *Brothers,* he called them, but shit they were his brothers, because they were other things first. They were troops, they were company-cops, they were night-riders, they were lily-white sports with telescopic sights. They were bush-whackers, vigilantes, armed guards, and crack shots, sitting, standing, and prone. They were firing-parties, they were Kike-Koon-and-Katholic killers, they were Pinkertons and picaroons. Triggermen all —and if they were ever his brothers, they were his brothers last. . . !

CHARLES LINDBERGH   *1927*

THE MECHANIC

33 hrs., 29 mins., 30 secs.   —New York to Paris

He had the touch. He could throw away a handful of parts, they say, and will them to land a machine, as if he had plotted their curve from the start, designed their end at the beginning. He had the sort of mind that lined up a day before he lived it: it was all there on the bench in tooled hours that, when assembled, would fit flush and run as planned. He had the touch, they say, he had a feel for such things as the wheel and time. To those who knew him, therefore, it was no surprise that he stayed in the air all the way to the Old World; they'd've opened their eyes only if he'd fallen short. The winds were always right for him, they say, or he made right ones out of wrong. He could outfly the Angel of Death, they say.

°Nicola Sacco

They bowed to that talent of his, to those powers over the pull of *g*: at a prize-fight, forty thousand rose and prayed to the god of birds, and, lo, in thirty-odd hours, the Bright and Morning Star returned to earth! But He wasn't quite the same as Him that came from the Cross. A savor seemed to have been lost, or age had cost Him some of His glow, some of His pink, and for all His height, He stood lower than one would think a Savior should. He spoke little and that gravely, He claimed nothing as His own, nothing as the first-born Son, and He wore worn clothes well, yet those that yearned for more found none: the engine of this Christ burned gasoline.

THE DEPRESSION   *1931*

THOUGHTS ON A BREADLINE

When in the Course of human Events, they wrote, and then there was something about the laws of nature and the consent of the governed, and they followed that with seventeen paragraphs of abuses and usurpations—*he has plundered our Seas, ravaged our Coasts.* . . .

But it was all for the record and meant to fool the Simple Simons due to fall between frozen stools at Princeton. The enemy was never the Crown. It was us, that great beast the people, and though we bled vintage years into the Brandywine, it was us, not George, they feared—and it was still us in the piss- and pus-yellow slush at the Forge. We were to win the fights while the elite won the loot, this sweet land of liberty for all but four races and more than half of the whites.

The king is gone now, and in his place we have kings home-grown, lower-case, of course, and lower caste, but kings all the same, and as they lord it where the Lobsters did before, they know that their enemy in peace is the one they knew in war. *All Men are created equal*, they told us, and they tell it yet, and we still pursue that little pea from shell to shell and still let our gaze be guiled.

But God save the kings when the Simons grow less simple and see them as not so simon-pure. . . .

LETTER FROM THE GRAVE   *1932*

FROM WASHINGTON ON HIS 200th BIRTHDAY

Sirs:

I take my penn in Hand to correct some Misapprehentions which came into Being at my Death, & which have persisted untill the present Time. I am not concernd with these erronious beliefs insofar as they touch upon Events, for Events, under the forme of Govt known as a Republick, are susceptible of as many Interpretations as there are men to make them. But I begg leave to say that I am most deeply concernd with such Beliefs where they relate to Character. My owne Character, Sirs, has been most grieviously misunderstood.

Whether willfully or otherwise, this Misunderstanding has been fosterd by some of the very best people, to such an extent that I now find some of the very worst speaking my name in the same connexion as Thos Paine, Andw Jackson, & A. Lincoln, Esqs, to cite but three Instances of the tortious Mingling which I have reference to. It cannot fail to be noted that I do not include the Honble Thos Jefferson, nor can my reason for the Omission be obscure: Mr Jefferson was at least a Gentleman. The others, whatever their Accomplishments may have been, & however great their Contributions to the power and independency of the United States, were members of the Mobility.

To put the matter flatly, Sirs, I deplord the notion of Equality all my Life, even such a fictitious Equality as the Constitution guarantees, & similarly, all my Death—espetially since being joind here by Mr Hamilton—I have deplord the constant encroachment of that fiction upon the reality. If this trend should continue without Lett or Hindrance, I make free to say that the evil day cannot be far removd when the Tresspass will have been compleated, & the Squatter become the Soveraigne.

Sirs, this must not come to pass. It was toward no such dismal End that I spent my 67 yrs on earth. It was not for this that I accompanied that Lobster, Genl Braddock, among the Savvages in the wilderness of Penn's Sylvania, that I servd 6 yrs without remuneration as Commdr in chf of the Continental army, or that I accepted the office of the Presidency to the Negleckt of my Affairs & family. It is humiliating in the extream to find it necessary to point to a Career which one might suppose would speak for itself. That I deign to call attention to it should prove the Depths of my Anxiety. I do strongly believe, Sirs, that if what was fought for & won in my time should be lost without a fight in yours, it were far better for our Interests that we should still be under the dominion of the Crowne.

This correspondence, I venture to remind you, is for your Private perusal only, & once read and assimilated, it were prudent to Destroy it. Trusting to your Discretion, then, I should like to animadvert upon what I feel is the cardinal Sinn of the nineteenth and twentieth centuries: the Spirrit of Doubt. Persons of Substance & quality have sufferd their minds to become poysond with the fear that, after all's said, they do hold their Havings by the will of the Mob, & that the course of wisdom is to placate, to trimm and truckle, in the hope that the Mob, pacifyd by such outward Deference, will live & lett live. Nothing, Sirs, could be further from the Truth. Indeed, the reverse is true, for the only limit to the demands of Inferiors is the sum-total possessd by their Betters, their Bloode included. Who, Sirs, can deny that Shays' Rebellyon might well have ended as the French revolution began—with the Knife?

It was with no such intention that our owne War of Independency was fomented: we who had a tangible Stake in the Collonys did not propose to break the shackles of King George only to bend the knee to King Tom, Dick, or Harry. It is no secret among ourselves that *we* purposd to rule the new World. In order to achieve that aime, Sirs, it was indispensable to assure that while our battels would be fought by the Many, the profitts would inure to the Few. In the raising of slogans to rally support from an apathetick Yeomanry & a hostile Artizan-class, great risks had to be runn in the respeckt that words seeming at the time to promiss Everything might later be constrewd to yield Nothing, nor were we invariably successful in this due to the Rantings of such plebeians as Paine, Benj Franklin, S. Adams, & others. But that which was possible to us, we did do. Item: we officerd the army with Gentlemen. Item: we establishd a Continental Congress of Gentlemen. Item: a Gentleman wrote the Declaration, & 56 Gentlemen signd it, but not one Artizan nor one Farmer that workd with his hands. Item: through the genius of Mr Hamilton, we funded all certificates of Debt issyued to soldiers during the War, & despite Mr Madison's unreasonable opposition, we managd to conceal that Gentlemen bought up those certificates from needy Veterans at 5 cents on the dollar and cashd them at Par. And lastly, item: we shewd the proper hostility to a certain Event in France, the excesses of which bore too close a relation to our owne Popular temper.

It was but natural, therefore, that the Constitution would emboddy the Principles for which we had sufferd so much Irritation, & sacrificd so much Money & time. That Document, I rejoise to say, has a noble ring to it even now, & none of the Amendments—aye, not even the 13th—injures the Tone given it by the Signers, all of whom, here beside me as I write, are satisfyd with their work. Structurally, the Country is much as it was when we confided it to your Care, & from a legalistick point-of-view, notwithstanding an Extention here & an Elaboration there, what you have is on the Whole what we fashiond for you, to wit: a Nation with a strong and unrepresentative central Govt; a spate of Tradition & Language rendered harmless by judicial misconstruction; & a two-party System of succession & self-perpetuation immutable enough to assure the ascendancy of Property; to say naught of a People now long tutord to condemn Revolt as unAmerican.

With so much in your favor, Sirs, nevertheless you have wrought so poorly as to fill us with Apprehention & Dismaye. You are haunted (to change a figure of Speech coind in the middle of the last Century) by the Spectre of Democracy—and well you may be. But the way in which to lay that Ghoast is not to temporize with it, but to oppose it by Force, to put it down with cold Steele and hott Ledd, as Genl Wayne did with his mutineers. But mark you, Sirs, if you wait for the Ghoast with hatt in hand, good God and God damn, you will find yourself with Alms in it! With Mr Hamilton and the rest, Sirs, I say put this Brute the People down!

Be assurd that I am, Sirs, with most unfeignd Regard, your ever obedt servt.

HART CRANE   1932

VOYAGES, VII

> *hold—*
> *Atlantis,—hold thy floating singer late!*
> *—Hart Crane*

They put the ship about and crisscrossed the wake, but all they found was what they'd tossed him, a life-buoy broaching a block-letter name: S. S. *Orizaba*. All morning, she'd been steaming north in the Straits of Florida, her speed the better for the four-knot Stream, the running road that ran her way. On the wind, her smoke went too, towing her, and birds, their screaming thinned, and in the noonday sun, like small change strewn, schools of mullet broke and flashed. It was then, they say, that he'd come on deck, gone to the taffrail, and jumped into the champagne scum simmering from the stern. They made the turn and searched for an hour, they gave him two bells of their time.

Did he go in slow motion down to where some cankered anchor lay, some molluscan ewer, a pair of old-world earrings in newer-world lees? Or did he straightway join the past, was he shredded then and there, a great barbless bait, ingested even to the rags he wore, to his own and his buttons' bone, his cut-glass brain, and the deposits of time accrued in his blood? Or did he never, as he'd prayed, submerge at all?

They beat up their wake, seeking him where they'd been before, but why, in that hour, could he not have been borne four knots onward by the Stream? Why must he have sunk, shunned, voided, spewn, why could he not have ridden the flume psalming the Cold Wall and the warm weed, the *Monitor* as he cruised above it, the bluefins in between? Hold! he'd cried, whereat why would the Stream not stay him from the sea's black fractures while he phrased for squids, arrow-worms, anemones, eels, lilies growing in submarine groves, for pelagic snails and tidal reeds? Why would he not spin forever on the gyre, and why, once each round, would he not play upon a mile-wide lyre strung across a harbor sky?

JUDGE WEBSTER THAYER   *1933*

DOOMSDAY FOR A DEEMSTER

I only and alone can see him a self-conceit nerroved mind little tyrent.

—Bartolomeo Vanzetti

He suffered a stroke at the University Cl ɪb in Boston and couldn't be taken home. From some vascular blowout, some broken inner tube, blood effused and flooded the motor region of his brain, in particular the angular gyrus and Broca's convolution, whereafter he could move no more, nor speak, nor follow the spoken or written word. He could only stare at a square of ceiling that seemed to be a continuation of his mind, a white opacity, but to an undefined fraction of his left cerebral hemisphere, it had ceased to be featureless plaster: it was Paradise, and hidden behind the glare of its hundred-watt sun was the seat where sat the Lord.

For a time, if time still ran for him, if clocks ticked and sand poured, nothing but the chandelier could be seen in the space above him, but then as through a screen—steam, it might've been—the lineaments of a face appeared, dim and wreathing, as if they were vapor too. It was a face at first unfamiliar, but he came so soon to know it that he could well have been wrong about its strangeness: it was the face of God, and he might've known it all along.

He was a Deity who did not warm the world: His mouth was an incision open and a stigma closed; His cowled eyes were those of a lesser animal peering from a lair, and they shone with the low brilliance of a protective color; and His voice was cast in the head register, thin-toned and short-term, and now and again spleen wound it up to a whine. A spiteful Almighty, obdurate, crass, seventh-Heavened by the sight of pain, and in a way that bypassed the process of comprehension, the paralytic knew that he was on trial for his life before that indurated Solomon, and he knew too that the case was going against him.

God was his judge, and the stricken man was afraid. That meager mouth, he thought with the remnant few cells of his mind, those small-game eyes, those raptorial hands—he knew them all so well, especially the hands. It was as if they'd bathed him, fed him, picked his nose, gratified his flaccid desires. His own hands, they might've been—and his own hands they *were*! Why, God damn it, he was God, and he was judging himself—and in that red and pounding instant, he knew that his plea to go on living was about to be denied. *Did you see what I did to those anarchistic bastards?* he thought, and a final wisp of recognition brushed him (was it the smell of fish, eels in seaweed?), and he died.

THE DEPRESSION   *1933*

APPLES OF SODOM

When plucked, they turn to smoke and ash.

—according to Josephus

Near a bench in Madison Square, a crate of fruit lay on the gray macadam walk, and a man who stood beside it steamed—a kettle come to a boil, he seemed, until you saw the rime, the frozen rheum, that hung from the hairs of his nose. His eyes watered as he stared out at the cold from the cold inside, and rocking slightly on his feet, he beat himself with his hands while a passerby chose a Northern Spy, a Pearmain blue, a yellow pippin. . . .

There were other crates on other paths in the park, and there were other steaming men, but each was aware of no more than his own breath freezing in the sun, as if each terrain were bounded by nothing, each the only world. People came from nowhere and to nowhere went, and now and then one bought a Northern Spy, a Pearmain blue, a yellow pippin. . . .

A stray dog crossed one of the swards, following some telltale trace or trail in the threadbare grass. After many a sashay, it reached one of the crates on the pavement—and there rumor grew and bloomed. The dog cocked a leg and pissed on a Northern Spy, a Pearmain blue. . . .

HUEY LONG   *1935*

EVERY MAN A KING

I wonder why he shot me.

—Huey Long

He promised them five thousand dollars each, debt-free, and if they
needed a car to fetch home the loot, or a home when they reached
where home ought to be, they'd get one or the other or both to boot.
They didn't have a pot to piss in, the trash that listened, and it rang
true (shit, a pound of grits would've sounded fine!), and it grew all
the truer when they found out who'd be supplying the cash—the
tick-full rich, he'd stick the sinful sonabitchen rich!

Even if never kept, promises like those would take the maker far,
and Huey's took him to Baton Rouge and after that to the Hill,
which was only a mile or so from where he meant, please God, to go
—the White House—and he might've made it if somebody hadn't
shot him. A Doc Price, it was, or maybe Weiss, an eye-and-ear man,
they say, and his slug went through three festoons of intestine and
blew off one end of a kidney, and Huey bled to death. His murderer
was buried first, but without any eyes and ears and with damn little
nose and throat: there were seventy holes in him.

The rich weren't rich enough to foot Huey's bill. He'd've had to
levy for it right on down to the poor, and even then he'd've come up
shy. The poor didn't know that, though. Only this Price did, or
Weiss. *I wonder why he shot me*, said the Kingfish, and he was still
wondering when he ran out of blood.

BILLY SUNDAY   *1935*

YOU'RE OUT! THE UMPIRE CRIED

I have no interest in a God who does not smite.

—Billy Sunday

Billy was a ballplayer once, but all that was long behind him, and
now when he took the field, he strove in a nobler game. Not for runs
and stolen bases did he strain these days, nay, and not for stops and

throws and sports-page praise: his strife was for the life and soul of man. He was an evangelist, Billy, and his adversary was Satan, who wore the red Number 1 of Hell on his back and on his black heart its red monogram.

Billy had just played nine hard innings against him, and he was tired. A thousand sinners had hit the trail at the end—a thousand had been kept from the pit!—but he was tired, Billy, and he slept. In his sleep, he dreamed that he was on a platform in a vast and teeming place, a tabernacle, he took it to be, but one with walls at the curves of the earth and a roof nearly lost in space; it was a tabernacle built for the Last Campaign, he thought, not to save Sioux City, but to redeem the entire world. From the benches below him, row behind row to a vanishing point, a multitude of transgressors gazed at his face—the vile host, descended from the Garden embrace, fruit of the fall.

He gathered, Billy did, that he'd come upon himself midway through a sermon. He knew nothing of what had gone before it, though—had a hymn been sung by his chorister? had there been a collect? had he told any stories designed to thaw the crowd?—nor, since the text seemed strange to him, did he know what lay ahead. It was as if his mind had caught the sermon on the fly. That was bad enough, but there was worse, he found: he had no say about what he said; he was bound to speak the words that came.

I have no interest in a God who does not smite, he heard himself say, but gone for once were his customary game, the boozers, the spooners, the users of the weed, gone the dirty-joke tellers, the swearers, the sellers of spirits and wine, gone the pool-shooters, the fox-trotters, the Onans and other aliens, the coons, the Jesuits, and the Jews. Gone those, and for one time these, whose ring he wore in his nose, became the goats: the pretty-penny, always-partridge, King's-ransom rich.

He was dismayed, the old base-runner, by the spate that gushed from his mouth in hyphenated compounds, diamond metaphors, and slang transliterations of the Writ, but the dream streamed on and bore him with it, and now, still more appalled, he began to list the Who's-who names. They were all present, those respectables, they were on the dais and among the choir and in the choice seats at Billy's feet, and one by one he arraigned them, the John Ds and the JPs and the Teddy Rs and the butchers from Chi and the picklemakers from Pitt.

Remember the camel! he heard himself cry, *Remember the needle's eye!* and he besought them to be saved, the obdurate rich, the 5-and-10, the A-and-P, the flivver-and-400 rich. *Decide!* he implored them, *Decide for Christ!* But no one stirred, and when he heard a humming as from some tumult coming toward him, Billy grew afraid and ran. *Slide, Billy!* he thought, *Hit the dirt!* The tumult on the way was Death, though, and as Billy slid, he died.

ANTI-FASCIST MEETING   *1937*

THE SPANISH-unAMERICAN WAR

Spain was a shape on a map, yellow, irregular, dense with words, numerals, fine and winding lines, these for places and altitudes, for all-year and intermittent flows. It was populated by files of tinted pins, blues confronting greens across a thicket of printed names and numbers and the tangled string of streams. Black dots, towns once, had been punctured out of existence, black dots had become black holes, but no one had died in the change, because there were no people, only pins, in that yellow shape Spain. . . .

". . . The Badajoz thing of the bull-ring, is no espression of the mouth that will espress the cruelness of esecuting four thousand of peoples, eSpanish peoples, for the crime of—what, *what*? They wish a form of governament, and they vote for that governament, and they win the vote, and for this nothing is come that *maricon* Franco with Moros and shoot like dogs. Is no espression for such thing, not even in the tongue of a peoples that have much suffering in history. The eSpanish peoples are poor like the poorest—work and die, work and die, that is España—and they go like that for a hundreds of years, and then at last they stand up one time and chase away the sick and unspeakable disgrace on the country, that Alfonso with his dirty blood, and they make the Republica, and after so long of misery, they are a little happy. But the sickness of the rich and the landlords and the bad peoples of the Church, these sick things the Republica tolerate to remain, because the governament is not a Red governament, as many falsely say. A Red governament would not chase away Alfonso; it would have shoot him to death. It would not have leave the rich bishops and the rich to remain and work behind the back; it would have espose them and put the hand on the riches. I am a Catholic, and yet I say is wrong, a sin, for my Church to be fat and rich; a good Church will be the most thinnest, and it will not have gold possessions while hungry children give money for candles. But these sickness remain in the Republica, and soon come the Moros with that *novia* general, and you have the affair of the bull-ring in the name of God and Jesus Christ. And then is clear that not only the bulls have been bred to die in the dust, but the peoples of the country much more, for all eSpanish life have been one great bull-fight always. The matadors have been everywhere, the cities, the villages of which the ground would not grow the smallest thread of grass, but they have not until now been reconize, for they have wear on the back not the gold-lace embroiderings of Belmonte, but the black of the Church. And the picadors come riding over the peoples not on blind old horses, but on the silver stallions of their Isottas, and the peoples are crazed by the banderillas of impoverty, and they die on the sword of work in their own dung and the dirt, like the dumb bulls. All my country is one bull-ring, one Badajoz, and many more of my peoples will die as dumb bulls before is change this condition —but it *will* be change! Bulls too kill some time, and they will yet make a great *cornada* in those that come murdering them, crying, *Viva El Cristo Rey! . . . .*"

It was a shape on a map, yellow, irregular.

WILLA CATHER   *1939*

ON THE ENCHANTED BLUFF

There seems to be no future at all for people of my generation.
                                        —diary of Willa Cather

It was still eight years off, the page that bore her particular date, the line she'd leave at some comma, some phrase, at some word she'd just begun or one that remained in her mind—and ahead would lie a ruled void, a future that belonged to someone else. And then it would be said of her that she never had to look for things to see: they seemed to come unsought, drawn by her stillnes and unafraid, and they stayed while she wrote of them quietly, keeping her voice mild, her motion slow, and they'd show her their colors as they went about their ways. There was no future, she said, but she put a stop to time, she warmed old suns and made clouds drop anchor, and birds forever applauded on the wing.

EMMA GOLDMAN   *1940*

CASTLE-BUILDER IN UNION SQUARE

*The waving of their outstretched hands was like the wings of
white birds fluttering.*

—Emma Goldman

At the end, the crowds were only apparitions, the smoke remainder of a stroke at seventy, shades of the furniture in a burned-out brain. And yet, how like they were to the crowds at the start, waiting for her in the Kovno air, there at parturition—the reaching hands, the beating wings! They must've governed her, those auguries, drawn her toward the Square. Mystery codes her: there's no way to construe her choice of roads.

Can we say it was due to her being plain, a five-foot Jew with light brown hair and *pince-nez* worn on a chain? Or that it was because she had tb. at times, sugar in her urine, an inverted womb, and a tendency to fall? Would such things ravel out a taste for pain, would they gloss her lifelong suicide? Would we know her if we knew of the varicose veins, the broken arches, the throe she had every twenty-eight days? Would it sink in then why nothing swayed her, nothing changed her mind or ways, neither the fines she paid nor her days in jail, not spite and exile, not the poison penned her, the spew from the pulpit, the dead cats we threw—would light be shed and she become clear? Or would she stay a cipher, a disarray of symbols, a lock that lacks a key?

When no one would rent her a room (free lover! anarchist! antichrist! suffragette!), she slept in whorehouses and other public places—streetcars, doorways, toilets in the park—and when horseshit hit her soapbox, she kept on talking and spoke it away. For those she prized—the poor, the put-upon, the ill-used—she went to the stake and lit her own fire. She gave up family, easy money, and the right to come and go, she gave up fashion, honors, nationality, even, and finally the quiet and crayon hours of old age. There's no unriddling that, there's no seeing around the corners of such a heart.

A fat little woman, she grew to be. Her glasses were thicker than before, and she wore them with temples instead of a chain, and she was shorter by an inch or more, and her lungs were scarred, and there was still a trace of sugar in her water, and her legs seemed stuffed with worms. A big-tittied little dame in a dime bandana and a hand-me-down, a sick old soul, and, damn us all, only yesterday she was stumping for Man out there in the cold! We'll not know why. We'll not know why.

We let her come back to God's country when she died of that punctured artery. We opened the door a crack, about wide enough for a fat little coffin, and she came from the outside world to lie at Waldheim, near those Hunkies we hanged for the Haymarket. We'd rented her a room at last.

F. SCOTT FITZGERALD   *1940*

SEVEN BUCKS FOUND IN A TOILET

All night the saxophones wailed the hopeless comment of the Beale Street Blues *while a hundred pairs of golden and silver slippers shuffled the shining dust.*
                    —F. Scott Fitzgerald: *The Great Gatsby*

He came out as you went in, and it took your mind a moment to see in the slush downfall of his face the one that once was snow, and by then the door to the hall had stuttered and closed. On the floor near the urinal lay a crush of green paper, two ones and a five: it was his money, you supposed, and picking it up, you wondered how he'd come to drop it where he did. Had he been counting it while he took a leak, reading the print on the Great Seal, staring at the peak of the Pyramid, at God's Eternal Eye? You looked him up on the directory outside, and with the five and the ones in your hand, you went down the hall to his room. He frowned when you entered, first at you, then at the bills, and then at you again, but afterward you couldn't recall what he'd said or whether he'd spoken at all.

They were about the rich, every page of those books of his, those tales of the age, and he wasn't quite at home there, he didn't seem to belong. He hadn't been invited, you might say, he'd been left out of his own parties, and when he couldn't crash the gate, he hung around in the dark that was made by the light within, somewhere in the shrubbery, behind some tree or car, in the shadows he wrote for the lawn, and if he heard tunes and talk and laughter, it was due to doors he described as open and to sound he allowed outside. He ran after a world he'd built of words, a better one, he fancied, and peopled with the better sort—he honed for it till the day he died.

The next time you saw him, he was dead, laid out in an open coffin at some out-of-the-way funeral parlor. A dim place, it was, and quiet except for the carpet's asper underfoot. In death, his face was snow again, and he might've been back in Louisville, with those silver slippers and golden horns. And who knows? He might've had a card for once, he might've been inside.

THE FUNNY PAPERS   *1940*

TRAGIC STRIP

The Bayeux Tapestry is a band of embroidered linen seventy-seven yards long, on which, in scene and legend, the tale is told of the Norman conquest of England.

Here Edward Rex, nearing the end without issue, is seen to send Harold earl of Wessex to pledge the sceptre to William (*Willelmi*) duke of Normandy.

And here his knights and Harold cross the sea (*hic Harold mare navigavit*) from Bosham to the land of Guy, where, after besting count Conan, the duke confers on Harold arms, and he, by taking, becomes the giver's man.

And here, on relic bone, Harold swears away the throne of England (*Harold sacramentum fecit*), and, honor bound, he sails for home.

And here Edward is dying, and here found dead (*et hic defunctus est*), and here Harold, false in one and false in all, fits his head to Edward's crown.

And here a comet, a fardel of fire, is shown in the sky, and ghostly ships ply the winds from France.

And here evil token turns to fact, and in actual oak William floats his men across, seven thousand, of which (*hic exeunt caballi*) two thousand horse.

And here the landing at Pevensey, and here the march to Hastings, and here the fall day the comet had foretold, the long day of flights and pursuits, of stripped slain, arrows in the eye, and crushed grain in Sussex fields—and here Harold dies for his broken word. . . .

We tell the same story in four panels of black and white (and red and green on Sunday). We tell of the same traps set, the same perjuries, the same blood let, and our faithless Harolds and euchred dukes are an orphan with O's for eyes, the Hallroom Boys, the Yellow Kid, wise guys, spies, yids, mutts, chinless wonders, men from Mars, cats, clowns, and Claude Eclair, a leprechaun, the Hooligan clan with tin-can hats, Buster Brown, and Ignatz Mouse, but instead of saying *Here fell the English king*, we say *Pow!* and *Plang!* and *Zowie!*

MOUNT RUSHMORE   *1941*

HEADSTONE

A biotite-muscovite granite interlaced with pegmatitic veins containing tourmaline and beryl.

—souvenir brochure

The Shrine of Democracy, it says on the sign, and eyes climb to four faces cameoed in stone and stare at the twenty-foot nose of Washington, at Jefferson's effeminate hair. The Soul of America, the guides recite, and they point out Teddy's chin and all of grieving Abe. A memorial good for half a million years, they claim, another hundred ages of the Book. Think of it—another hundred Exodi, another hundred Crucifixions, a hundred more Judeo-Christian eras for the earth to pirouette, and still there'll be asperities to show where the nose once was, the hair, the chin, and Abe!

Below the four faces lies a pour of brash, the blown-off stone, the trash we made in making our mark, and it's as much our monument as the mountain, as much our soul and shrine. It too will last five hundred thousand years.

PEARL HARBOR   *1941*

EAST WIND RAIN

Higashi no kazeame.

—Japan Winds Code

This time, the air was stiff with sound, and if God had chosen to speak, He'd've found no room for His radiant waves among the waves already there. *Adore and be still!* He might've said, but only other planets would've heard. The earth was listening to recipes, to longing sung and played, to the scores made in games; it was also listening to the traffic of ciphered signals to and from Japan, but that was merely noise behind eulogies of oleo, spiels for gasoline. There was wind in the east, and coming on the wind was rain, but no sign of these could be seen as yet—the sky was still clear, and it might stay fine all day. . . .

The Navy buried drowned sailors for a month, and now and then it buried a collection of their parts that seemed to have fallen from a height—heads, arms, shoes containing feet. Nine hundred and sixty men were listed as missing: if they sank, they never surfaced; if blown up, they never came down.

STATUE OF LIBERTY 1945

BIG DUMB BROAD

Heel to top of head: 111' 1"
Length of hand: 16' 5"
Width of mouth: 3'
Thickness of waist: 35'
Head, thickness from ear to ear: 10'

F. D. ROOSEVELT, I 1945

THE SUGAR-TIT MAN

They are unanimous in their hate for me.

—F. D. Roosevelt

The rich were always in the dark about him. All that wind he blew, all that dust he raised over all those years and miles—he was hard to see for the murk he made, hard to hear for his noise. They never knew that the more he spoke the less he said, and that all he moved were those quick and clever hands. A bad time for the people, that one was, a black day: there were queues along the curbs, the soupless many, but when he asked the few for a tithe, a penny in the dime, a bone to save their meat, they gave him their hatred and cursed him as a cripple getting even for their feet.

Snake in the grass, they called him, and they called him Jew, Judas, New- and double-dealer, and traitor to his class, but the sum of his betrayal was their small and copper change. He never meant to disendow their world, not the Groton boy, the boy-patroon: it was his world too, and he prized its hereditaments, the manors, the Guernsey herds, the regattas, the coaching clothes, and, pearl and precious, his distant kinsman's conjure name. Quite to the end, though, they'd fail to understand: he was a leveller, they'd think, one who took from the hill to give to the dale, a bulldozer, a maker of plains.

He was pleasant, capacious airy, and unoccupied, spaces bright with the light outside. There was nothing else in all those cheerful divisions, none of the furniture of principle, none of the drapery of belief, and it was so he stood for sixty-three years, murmurous with extramural voices, lit by passing lamps, but empty to the end.

F. D. ROOSEVELT, II   *1945*

OLD FLAME AT WARM SPRINGS

I have a terrible headache.

—F. D. Roosevelt

They sat in facing chairs with much of the room between them, and though others were there—someone crocheting and someone at an easel—they were hardly aware they were not alone, and had they spoken, they might not have known they were overheard. They made no sound, though, the man being drawn and the woman watching him, no more than the chalk did or the hook weaving wool, but even so the quiet seemed full of their words.

He wondered whether she saw how his hands shook, ever so little, as if their joints were rubber bands, and he wondered whether she took note of his grayness, his flagging face, and the way his eyes showed surprise at unsurprising things. He wondered whether she knew that his blood now flowed through straiter mains in a stricter stream, whether she guessed at his vital numbers, at the weaker signals his heart was sending. He wondered whether she remembered when there were no contractions and expansions to scan, no levels and counts to compare with par, when his shaking hands, his agitans, took rise in her.

She wondered whether he found her eyes a paler blue these days, hazier skies, and did her voice sound the same to him, she wondered, or had it grown thin with time and shrill, did he still enjoy her design, did he still dwell on her skin and bearing, did he savor her taste in his mind? Did he know, she wondered, did he sense that her blood was going wrong, and her spleen, and her bone-marrow, that in her too there were fatal quanta now—or was he thinking a long way back, to how he looked down at her and she looked up at him?

He'd be dead in three more hours, she in three more years.

F. D. ROOSEVELT, III   *1945*

AMONG THE ROSES

. . . a plain white marble monument, no carving or decoration,
no device or inscription, except on the south side. . . .

                                                        —F. D. Roosevelt

It reclines in the rosary, a straight-cut stone, 8 x 4 x 3, setting off a
grave, and all day long, people come to see it, some from far away.
All day, from ten in the morning till five in the afternoon, they stand
and stare across the hemlock hedge, and in their minds, they hew the
shrine to suit themselves. On its three blank faces, they carve other
dates and other names, and scenes stir in the marble, four-mile falls
in flames, and the dead die a second time in the Tuscarora Deep and
while asleep beneath a tree. They stare, those pilgrims, and in their
minds, the block of Danby comes alive with flags, with screams and
speeches, with something running from something red, it comes alive
with death. And then, each evening after five, it's a stone again
beside a grave.

ELEANOR ROOSEVELT   *1945*

AMONG THE ROSES, cont'd.

It is my hope that my dear wife will on her death be buried
there also.

                                                        —F. D. Roosevelt

When they quarried and cut the stone, she thought, it would be
brought here to head the grave, and on its south face, as the will
provided, someone would chase their names, his with the dates of
birth and death, hers as yet with one. She tried to read ahead to the
missing year, to see herself dead, an occupant of the room next door,
but tomorrow was cast in a haze of remembered things, and it was
the past she saw, not the days to come.

In her mind, pages turned back to a photo of a child in a white
dress and a wide black sash, a bucktoothed and chinless child clutch-
ing a toy dog hung with two tin bells that still thinly seemed to ring.

And there were other pictures, some with her impassive mother and her randandy father, both soon gone, and there were pets, picnics, boats, classmates on a lawn, and then came a sped-up series of weddings, hackneys, brownstone fronts, hats like aeries, fifth cousins once removed, and a pose, taken in a gondola, that showed her holding her husband's boater—and they were all beginning to blur when one of them stopped the machine. It was a beach-scene, and in it a young woman in a white dress and a wide black sash waded through the train of a wave; the figure faced away, and hiked skirts bared comely legs to the knees, and she stared, as Franklin may have done that day, and she wondered when she'd ceased to please him.

She rummaged for a reason. What phrase had offended, what silence when she should have spoken, what gown had been wrong, what color off, what error of taste had she made, what truth told, what dispassion shown when heat was called for, what had she given or refused, what done or not done, what duties had she enjoyed too much and what pleasures had left her cold, what had cooled him, what awkward gesture had he caught, what light had revealed her plainness and hidden her sightly eyes?

And now a mutoscope of pictures, stills wheeled by memory, and she saw streets and styles change by the moment, she saw people age and die, and armies and armadas passed, and birds flew in strange formation, and she heard guns in the distance and the tin bells on a toy dog, but nothing at all from the adjoining room.

HIROSHIMA   *1945*

THE THOUSAND-MILE STARE

It was an indescribable emptiness. I felt as if I were thrown into white air.
                                                          —Yoko Ota
Ever since the blast, the screws of our hearts had been loose.
                                                          —Dr. M. Hachiya

If you meet them on the way to where the way ends, if you pass them on the downhill street or the winding stair, if you find them before you are found by the broken step, the missing stone, what face will you put on the face you own, and will you speak or merely listen to a mice of words that race across your mind?

Scarecrows, they were, but from their broomstick bones no torn clothes hung. They were barer than bare, for all they wore was melted skin.

Will you bow to them, will you try to shake some keloid hand, will you make a gift, endow a bed, a ward, a wing, will you found a fund in their name, will you raise them a shaft, and where will it rise, in your white-cloud skies or in theirs of the black and epicentral rain?

They puked shit, and sixty times a day they stooled slimes of pus. They bled inside, and dead before they died, they bred maggots that grew into fogs of flies. They were garbage-cans in swarms of sound.

Will you bend the knee, will you rend your coat and tell your beads, will you plead some reason for pissing on the world from the Cross?

When they burned the bodies, some said a blue fume was seen in the usual flame, a blue billow like crepe-de-chine—it was the spirit of the dead, that blue-gas ghost, and it wished to leave the earth.

Will you go through fire for them, they that went for you? Will you, for your sin, become the ram, the bullock, the suckling lamb, will you offer to die for the sun you dropped from the *Enola Gay*?

They told of one who sat by a roadside, holding an eye in the palm of his hand. With the other, he stared at something or nothing a great way off.

What will you say? God Almighty, what will you say?

H. S. TRUMAN   *1945*

JEHOVAH

*I regarded the bomb as a military weapon and never had any
doubt that it should be used.*

—H. S. Truman

I never lost any sleep over my decision.

—H. S. Truman

He gave an order that mass be converted to energy half a mile above
Japan, and on a certain day, taking off from Tinian, the *Enola Gay*
turned time ahead toward the end. He had no doubt, he said, and he
slept the sleep of the just and dead. He was all serene about the dust
he'd raised, quite undismayed. A little of this had become a lot of
that; it was a trade, really, a matter of numbers, nothing to quicken
the pulse or deepen the breath, nothing to suggest the death of the
past. Quiet, his mind remained, and the blind hung still, as if there
were no wind outside, no hurry.

CHARLIE CHAPLIN   *1945*

THE REVELATION

*In Albuquerque, 120 miles away, a blind girl said, "What was
that?"*

—the press

What happened when they told him about the White Sands flash?
Did he feel for once the need of words, or did some reel unroll in his
mind, did old shadows speed on the silent screen of his mind? Did he
try to state his views, or did he rely on his slapstick shoes to speak, on
his cane and spastic smile? When they described the sight and swore
to light that seared the eye, that made the sun seem the one spot of
shade in the sky, did he find his voice at last or simply tip his dented
derby from behind? And the colors, was his tongue untied by the col-
ors, gray, blue, topaz, mauve, and wine, or by the blister of fire, or by

the sound, as of the earth falling down, or by smoke that grew and kept on growing, a fungus going wild—did he overcome his dumbness then, or, still mute, did he shoot his frayed and shirtless cuffs, did he look shy or sad, did he walk away scratching and let himself be sealed off, irised from the field of vision? Or did he do nothing, having done it all before?

What was that? said a blind girl, and he might've answered, the little knight without luck, he might've set her right about that brilliance in her head. *What was that?* a blind girl said when they touched off matter, and he knew enough to tell her, the little celluloid soldier who'd fought so many wars. War was all he'd ever known, and numberless his enemies: the rich and their eight-foot butlers, the poor and their unchristian dogs, the mercenaries of custard, machines imbued with hate, inhuman children, and anti-human things, things that lay in wait, a whole world mined with things. And to a blind girl's *What was that?*, he might've said it was more of the same, the last stuffed club, the last splash of mud, the last stumble, the saunter toward the final fall.

EZRA POUND   *1945*

IN SHORT THE USUAL SUBJECTS

of conversation between intelligent men.
                                                        —Ezra Pound, Canto XI

They were foreign to us, his queer creed and cranky ways. We didn't hold with his baiting of the Jews, we said, with his aiding of our enemies and the views he aired on Money; we were aggrieved, we declared, by his averted face, by the cold shoulder he gave his place of birth; it was odious that he dressed as he did (those cape-worn coats, those two-toned shoes), and it wouldn't go down, or wouldn't stay, that he owned little and saved nothing, as though not for him the reckoning, never the rainy day. *Il piccolo trovatore!* Who was he to mock our documents and our sovereign power, abuse our causes, our systems, and our age, and in his railings at the sheenies of Wailing Wall Street, did he not excite domestic Insurrection amongst us, destroy the Lives of our People, ravage our Coasts? The popinjay, the billy-goateed scold—with that lore he set such store by, his dead and dying *linguae*, the trash he talked of metrics, even so what did he betoken but some stiff little chair at Hamilton, say, or maybe at Wabash. . . ?

Lies, all! We know better why we hate him, but it's a lash we enjoy in privacy: he makes us small. The wind of Acts informs him. He has the gift and gabs, reducing us with archival bombast and mint phrases, old and new coin, with cadences and intonations, with slang and chink and jokebook hebe—the rage *loquendi*, he has, and another to match it in ink. The silk scrolls, the vellum-bound libers, the fly- and rat-beshitten screeds of prothonotaries, God knows where he found them, in what vault, what scriptorium, what corner six centuries forgot, and God knows too why he chose to use them, or *reuse*, because he seems to have lived before, been himself a bought sword, Ghibelline or Guelph, a *condottiere*, a brawler with the blueballs, a *quattrocento* dicer with the clap. Tongues!, he has, his own and those he was given, and in whatever comes to mind, guttersnipe, *provencal*, japonee, in that four-a-day twang *du pays* of his, he rotten-eggs us and, worse, ravishes us with such lyrics as seraphs and birds bandy on the wing. They're pentecostal, those voices he got from the Holy Ghost, and with them he lifts his lays of early times and nowadays, flies his recitations of love and murder, letters, fine steel, and prodigies, *in short the usual subjects*, and in them the wine-sea surges, and the dawn breaks rose, and there are rains, ambuscades, ideograms, and spiteful gods, and doom caroms along blind arcades, *lussurioso incestuoso, assassino, sodomitico*. . . . Dear Jesus, what does he not embrace in words!

Forty years gone from us, he's been, and they've told, the lines between the eyes, the gray, the skin, and now we bring him home, an old man we mean to try for treason. But if we hang him, we know it won't be for the bees in his bonnet about Money and Jews or for what he said in Rome. It'll be for this—that we fear he'll be remembered, and we'll be merely dead.

U. S. A.

PRAYER FOR A DEAD MOTHER

Yisgaddal v'yiskaddash sh'meh rabbo

—Mourner's Kaddish

The *schul* had been on the second floor of the building, only a door or two from Bergman's pool-room, where Lefty Louie and Dago Frank once played. Long gone, that time was, but you could still hear ten old men in shawls intone, still hear the tick of cues, the click of kissing bones. You could still hear a pour of hallelujahs, a mumbled falls, and through it came the sound of ivory on ivory balls, of ivory beads that told the score—until the hosannas seemed part of the game and the game a part of the praise.

b'olmo di'vro kir'useh v'yamlich malchuseh

You climbed a flight of steps to a hall grown small with age. No light shone down on green baize now, and there was no smoke these days on the air. Bergman's was gone, and with it Dago, Lefty, Gyp the Blood, and the *schul* too where ten old men had prayed, and the boy (you) who, half-asleep among them, half-dreamt of his mother's grave.

b'chayechon uv'yomechon uv'chayeh d'chol

You remembered the funeral. Black cars and the new perfume called gasoline, streets that seemed Sunday still, Sunday vacant, a bridge that led to other streets, all of them dim, drained, as though the sun had begun to fail, and then you stood beside a hole in the ground, and you looked at flim-flam grass on a mound of fill. You remembered (you now, as the boy then) the chime of spades, and when you tried to help, your father cried and held you back, and dirt fell, dirt fell, and from under veils a wailing came, and you remembered the evergreen word *Adonai*.

bes yisroel baagolo uvisman koriv v'imru Omen

The hall wore strange names now, and it had strange and nameless smells, a bad breath, but through it somehow you drew the fragrance of talcum from a pool-room, of saffron from a *schul*. You heard shots called and balls collide, you saw ten shawls against the Ark and the altar in the blue-gray winter dark, you felt a hand touch you (whose?), and you rose, an only son, to say a prayer for the dead. . . .

You stood there in the hall, knowing that in a moment you'd go down the stairs and walk from one part of your past to another, from your own mother to the mother of a headlong race, and as you went, toward the Brandywine, the Wind River Range, and the Gate, you'd say goodbye to Chai Esther, dead at thirty-three, and dwell on malign rains, on white air, on the screws of the heart and the thousand-mile stare, and you'd say in your mind *How shall I pray for this dead mother? How shall I pray, Lord? How shall I pray. . . ?*